Warriors and Politicians

With hist
in Iraq, t
masters –
of warfig

By ex
the arme
relations
shows hc
resist pre
Congress
Revoluti
radical ir
Donald I
rooted ir
US histor

Illustr
studies, t
the Revc
Bush/Do
terrorist-

This k
politics,

Charles
relations
professor at the National War College. He also served as a member of the
Secretary of State's Policy Planning Staff specializing in political–military and
civil–military issues. He is now a Professorial Lecturer in American Foreign
Policy at the Nitze School of Advanced International Studies.

Cass Military Studies

Warriors and Politicians

US civil–military relations under stress

Charles A. Stevenson

Routledge
Taylor & Francis Group

LONDON AND NEW YORK

First published 2006
by Routledge
2 Park Square, Milton Park, Abingdon, Oxon OX14 4RN

Simultaneously published in the USA and Canada
by Routledge
270 Madison Ave, New York, NY 10016

Routledge is an imprint of the Taylor & Francis Group, an informa business

© 2006 Charles A. Stevenson

Typeset in Sabon by
HWA Text and Data Management, Tunbridge Wells
Printed and bound in Great Britain by
Antony Rowe Ltd, Chippenham, Wiltshire

British Library Cataloguing in Publication Data
A catalogue record for this book is available from the British Library

Library of Congress Cataloging-in-Publication Data
A catalog record for this book has been requested

ISBN10: 0-415-77007-6 (hbk)
ISBN10: 0-415-77008-4 (pbk)

ISBN13: 978-0-415-77007-1 (hbk)
ISBN13: 978-0-415-77008-8 (pbk)

To Sue

Contents

Figures

Preface

Most writers on civil–military relations focus on the balance of power between the government leadership and the armed forces and define civilian control in terms of the integrity of the chain of command. They ask top-down questions of command and control. Is the military truly subordinate to civil authority? How great is the danger of a military coup? When the president or prime minister gives an order, do the armed forces comply faithfully?

This book has a somewhat different focus. It is about the United States, not other countries, both because I know America best and because the United States has some historically unique features which give it a more unusual system of civil–military relations. The US Constitution was framed by men distrustful of standing armies and any concentrated power. They established a government with separated institutions sharing power. In particular, they created a dual system of civilian control – direct command from the President within the Executive Branch but also control by the Legislative Branch by means of laws and money. Other countries may have strong presidents or strong prime ministers based in powerful parliaments, but few come close to America's system of truly separate and roughly co-equal branches of power.

I came to appreciate this dual system during more than two decades' service on the staff of four US Senators. I observed and frequently participated in legislative efforts to recommend, direct, fund, and control the activities of the US armed forces and even the President. I witnessed and heard military complaints, outside the chain of command, about policies and actions of senior civilian leaders, often with entreaties to take countermanding measures. I became convinced that the US military is a very loyal and subordinate institution, but it is often cross-pressured by its two masters and it often feels compelled to turn to one for relief from the other.

Later, as a professor at the National War College, I developed a course on civil–military relations organized around the dilemmas faced by senior officers and their civilian leaders. When and how can one dissent from official policy? What are the proper roles of civilians and military leaders in planning and executing combat missions? How should military officers relate to the Congress? Should officers avoid or engage in partisan politics? I teamed with a military faculty colleague in order to counteract my own biases on these issues. We drew upon historical examples from American experience with these and other questions.

This book is an effort to expand the examples available for study. It seeks to show how US civilian and military leaders coped with periods of extraordinary stress and controversy – fighting wars, rearming to meet emerging threats, and radically changing the structure and missions of the armed forces. It is not a comprehensive history of US civil–military relations. It does not cover instances, such as the conduct of the First and Second World Wars, when the president or Congress was relatively quiescent or inactive in applying their levers of civilian control. Instead, I have picked significant and illustrative episodes and have tried to tell the story of how the triangular relationships worked in practice. I have discovered patterns, more continuities than change, which make me believe that this is a useful focus on the issues of civil–military relations.

I am especially grateful to my colleagues over the years – in the Senate and at the National War College. They helped me to understand and appreciate the quite different perspectives which senior leaders bring to their responsibilities. My contribution in return, and in this book, is to explain and defend the political factors which often influence policy. Civil–military relations in America is not necessarily a struggle, but it is certainly a contest of differing views, perspectives, and professionalisms.

Charles A. Stevenson
August 2005

1 Introduction
The peculiar nature of US civil–military relations

A Standing Army, however necessary it may be at some times, is always dangerous to the Liberties of the People. ... Such a Power should be watched with a jealous Eye.

Samuel Adams, 1776[1]

The Union itself, which [the Constitution] cements and secures, destroys every pretext for a military establishment which could be dangerous.

James Madison, Federalist, 41

Of all the cares or concerns of government, the direction of war most peculiarly demands those qualities which distinguish the exercise of power by a single hand.

Alexander Hamilton, Federalist, 74

United States armed forces take an oath to support and defend a piece of paper – the Constitution. The British military take an oath of allegiance to the monarch. German forces swear to defend the law and liberty of the people. The Japanese vow to maintain the nation's independence and peace. Russians swear loyalty to the Fatherland. Perhaps not surprisingly, the French armed forces, after five republics, two empires, numerous monarchies and several attempted military coups, take no oath.

The oath to the Constitution means that US military personnel must protect not only the structure of the Federal Government but also its processes. It means that they must even accept outcomes that are contrary to the wishes and interests of those in uniform. The dirty secret about democracy is that its test is fairness and faithful observance of the rules, not the wisdom or justice of the outcomes. To be a voter in a democracy one does not need to be informed, or smart, or consistent – only registered. Similarly, the top leaders and lawmakers in a democracy do not need to be wise or moral or logical – only elected.

The US government is unusual, too, because of the strength and independence of its branches of government. In parliamentary democracies, the legislature is supreme. In presidential systems, even when the parliament is nominally important, the president is usually dominant, especially with regard to control of the military. Warriors prefer hierarchical systems because they value the unity of command – the clear line of authority so important in the stress of battle. In the United States, however, the commander-in-chief, the President, controls only the immediate chain of command for the issuance of orders. The Congress controls the system of issuing orders, the organization of the forces, and, most importantly, the funds for their equipping and use. Responding to these dual sources of civilian control gives US military personnel special challenges and opportunities. This will be illustrated throughout this book.

Since the Constitution is the basis for civil–military relations in the United States, we must turn to the substance of that document and the history of its application to the armed forces. How the process works in wartime is particularly important and difficult. But it is also valuable and informative to consider how civil–military relations work in other challenging circumstances – in periods of rearmament and preparations for war, and in periods when the civilian leaders try to transform the military to deal with new threats and new technologies. From over 230 years of history, this book has selected a handful of significant episodes to illustrate the major patterns of US civil–military relations. These case studies were chosen both because they seem interesting and significant and because most prior studies have neglected or minimized the role of Congress in these events. This book seeks to redress those omissions with fresh analysis.

Legacy of distrust of power

The founders of the American republic were familiar with ancient history. They recognized the role military forces and commanders had in the making and unmaking of governments in Athens and Rome. And they were acutely aware of recent British history, especially the ouster and execution of King Charles I, the Civil War, and the dictatorship of Oliver Cromwell. Samuel Adams was only one of countless American patriots who believed that standing armies were a threat to representative government. As he wrote in 1776,

> A Standing Army, however necessary it may be at some times, is always dangerous to the Liberties of the People. Soldiers are apt to consider themselves as a Body distinct from the rest of the Citizens. They have their Arms always in their hands. Their Rules and their Discipline is severe. They soon become attached to their officers and disposed to yield implicit obedience to their Commands. Such a Power should be watched with a jealous Eye.[2]

Americans in 1776 revolted not only against British taxation without representation, but also against military domination. The Declaration of

Independence complained that King George III had kept standing armies "among us, in Times of Peace" without local consent and that he "has affected to render the Military independent of, and superior to the Civil Power." As will be seen in Chapter 2, the American revolutionaries fought their war of independence with unusual procedures precisely in order to forestall a military dictatorship.

The first system of government devised by the Americans, while the war for independence still raged, imposed tight restraints on the creation and use of military forces. The Articles of Confederation gave the central government "sole and exclusive right and power of determining on peace and war" as well as authority to pay for "the common defence" out of a "common treasury." There was no separate executive, only a congress which could act, with each state having one vote, by supermajorities of nine. The congress also had the powers of: "appointing all officers of the land forces, in the service of the united states, excepting regimental officers – appointing all the officers of the naval forces, and commissioning all officers whatever in the service of the united states – making rules for the government and regulation of the said land and naval forces, and directing their operations." The states were forbidden to maintain land or naval forces in peacetime above the number congress might deem "requisite." These powers were undercut, however, by the fundamental weakness of the central government. It could not tax directly, but had to ask the states to raise funds proportionate to land values. It had no standing forces of its own in peacetime. Moreover, the Articles declared that "every state shall always keep up a well-regulated and disciplined militia" with sufficient weapons and equipment and with all officers of colonel or below appointed by the state legislatures.[3]

The government under the Articles could not even decide whether to create a peacetime military establishment to staff western forts and otherwise guard against Indians. And it was so inept at paying troops that it required an emotional appeal from George Washington to prevent a mutiny at Newburgh, NY in 1783.[4]

When the delegates gathered in Philadelphia in the steamy summer of 1787, they were determined to create a stronger government, better able to deal with threats at home and from abroad. While most historians credit the internal security concerns demonstrated by the tax revolt in Massachusetts called Shay's Rebellion as the strongest impetus for the Constitutional Convention, Richard Kohn argues persuasively that the United States faced several other security threats – from the British in Canada to the Spanish in Florida and Louisiana as well as from the Indians along the frontier. Kohn also notes that of 18 explicit provisions of the Constitution listing Congress' powers, 11 related to security.[5]

The Framers had a theory of government, derived from Montesquieu and Locke, which called for divided government and safeguards against the concentration of power. What they created was a framework of separated institutions sharing power, in which action was possible only with the concurrence of at least two of the three components of the government. It is misleading to call the Constitutional system a "separation of powers" because the actual powers are shared: no expenditures by the executive without appropriations by the Congress; no enactment of laws without the concurrence of the President; no enforcement of the laws without support of the judiciary. Each branch of government had some checks and balances on the other two.

The Framers had a theory of national strategy that permitted isolation from and neutrality with regard to the wars in Europe. The Atlantic Ocean was a huge defensive barrier to the east; thus the only major threat was from the European empires and their potential Indian allies on the frontier. To deal with those threats, the political and military leaders planned to rely on the local militias, with the possibility of federal command in acute circumstances.

Over half the delegates to the Constitutional Convention – 30 of the 55 – had served in uniform during the Revolutionary War. At least 15 had seen serious action.[6] They were wary of a standing army but recognized the ultimate necessity of military capability. As William Paterson of New Jersey said when he presented the plan favored by the small states, "[N]o government could be energetic on paper only, which was no more than straw; there must be a small standing force to give every government weight." Many of the delegates also had had enough experience with ragtag militia units to want a more professional army. They knew, Gouverneur Morris of Pennsylvania noted, "that to rely on militia was to lean on a broken reed."[7] George Washington felt the same way: "They come in you cannot tell how, go you cannot tell when, and act you cannot tell where, consume your provisions, exhaust your stores, and leave you at last at a critical moment."[8] Despite these doubts about its effectiveness, the delegates saw the militia as a counterweight to the small standing army and voted to allow the states to choose militia officers.

Elbridge Gerry of Massachusetts, later famous as Vice President under James Madison and designer of a state legislative district that looked like a salamander and gave rise to the term "Gerrymander", was the most vocal opponent of a standing army at the convention. He was joined by George Mason of Virginia, another foe of a strong central government. When the delegates debated the military provisions in the draft document in August 1787, Gerry argued vigorously that "There was no check here against standing armies in time of peace." He proposed limiting the force to two or three thousand men. George Washington is said to have uttered a loud whisper that the document should also limit invading forces to the same number.[9] The numerical limitation never gained much support, but the delegates did approve a two year limit on the availability of funds for the army.

The delegates also changed the draft text from the Committee of Detail, which had given Congress the power to "make" war. After some delegates questioned the legislature's ability to meet and act in a crisis, Madison and

Figure 1.1 Signing of the US Constitution, 1787 (National Archives)

Gerry proposed changing the wording to "declare" war. Madison argued that the new language would allow "the executive the power to repel sudden attacks." And Roger Sherman of Connecticut agreed, saying "the executive should be able to repel and not commence war."[10]

Ultimately, Gerry refused to sign the Constitution, as did George Mason. And one of the strongest criticisms raised by the Antifederalists during the ratification debates was the issue of the standing army. Patrick Henry, for example, argued that the Constitution provided "a government of force, and the genius of despotism expressly." Other opponents used similar inflammatory arguments, calling the standing army "the nursery of vice", "engines of despotism", the "bane of freedom."[11]

One proof of the power of these arguments is that nearly every state's ratifying convention urged further amendments to the Constitution, such as limits on Congress' power to raise forces and a ban on quartering of troops in private homes. Several states also urged restrictions on federalizing the militia. To respond to these concerns, early in the First Congress, Madison included provisions on weapon ownership and troop quartering as the second and third amendments in his Bill of Rights.[12]

Constitutional safeguards

The Framers wrote a Constitution filled with what now may seem quaint details regarding military forces. But at the time they were considered necessary safeguards against a large standing army that could repress the rights of citizens. By design, the army and navy were intended to be creatures of the Congress. In enumerating the powers of the legislative branch, the Constitution specifically provides that the Congress could "raise and support Armies" and "provide and maintain a Navy." But it was also specifically empowered "To make Rules for the Government and Regulation of the land and naval forces" and "To provide for calling forth the Militia to execute the Laws of the union, suppress Insurrections and repel Invasions." Those were the threats the Framers feared and for which they were willing to create armed forces. But the militia – the citizen-soldiers living at home – was the primary force envisioned for local defense. To give some coherence to such forces, however, the Constitution also specifically authorized Congress "To provide for organizing, arming, and disciplining the Militia" – so that the troops might easily be melded into a federal force. They remembered the difficulty Washington and General von Steuben had training the Continental army.[13]

The Framers gave Congress three additional powers to control the military. Most important was the power "To declare War", words carefully chosen to give the legislature the right to authorize combat, while letting the executive branch control its conduct. The Philadelphia convention revised the original wording – "to make war" – to recognize this distinction. Second was the power given to the Senate to advise and consent to nominations for military officers as well as civilian officials of the government. While this was probably intended as a check on the appointment of unqualified or corrupt people, it became over time an important source of congressional leverage on the executive branch.

The third power, the power of the purse, applied to all of the executive branch, not just the military: "No Money shall be drawn from the Treasury, but in Consequence of Appropriations made by Law."[14] Over the years since 1787, Congress has authorized some deviations from a strict reading of this language, such as permitting later reimbursement for "food and forage" for troops in remote areas and allowing some secret accounts that do not need to be publicly reported, though Congress must be informed. But this basic requirement makes the military beholden to the legislature for pay and weapons and peacetime bases – and subject to the limitations on expenditures the lawmakers frequently have wanted to impose.

As evidence of the particular concern over standing armies, the Framers specifically provided that "no Appropriation of Money [for the army] shall be for a longer Term than two years." In theory, each new Congress must re-establish the army, or it would be forced to demobilize. In practice, the law now allows money for weapons procurement and research and development – though not for pay or operations – to be spent over a longer period of years.

Congress has claimed for itself another power, fully accepted by the other two branches of government: the power to oversee and investigate the military. As one might expect, this has been used – ever since Washington's administration – to look into military disasters, such as failed campaigns against the Indians, and to expose mismanagement of government contracts. While the authority for oversight is linked in theory to the development of new laws, in practice it is another instrument to use for political purposes, especially the embarrassment of those being investigated.

The President also has important powers over the military, ones more direct and practical than those of the Congress. The Constitution designates the President as "Commander in Chief of the Army and Navy of the United States, and of the Militia of the several States, when called into the actual Service of the United States." He also has the power to make nominations – to pick the senior officers for various units – subject of course to the advice and consent of the Senate. Once confirmed, however, officers may be removed from their positions only by the President. The Constitution gives Congress the power to impeach and remove from office only "civil officers" of the government, including the judiciary, not "military officers."[15]

The Framers were not very detailed in listing the powers of the president, for they anticipated that Washington would be the first to hold the office and they recognized his good judgment and leadership qualities. They were not worried about limiting the power of the executive branch because they thought that the Constitution imposed sufficient limits.

The Supreme Court filled a logical vacuum in the power balance by asserting its right to declare laws unconstitutional, thus checking even a united legislature and executive. On questions of war fighting and civilian control of the military, however, the court has historically been quite deferential to the other two branches. Presidents have been given wide berth in their conduct during major wars, and the court has avoided deciding what it considers "political questions," such as the constitutionality of the war powers act. Yet it remains as a potential player in disputes between warriors and politicians if compelling circumstances arise.

The framework established by the Constitution was given flesh and motion in the early years of the Republic. This book pays special attention to these periods because America's initial political and military leaders set precedents which influenced later history. George Washington tried to consult with the Senate on treaties and military operations, but was rebuffed. The Congress investigated and criticized a disastrous operation against the Indians. Adams used partisan criteria in picking military officers. Congress maintained tight control over the expenditure of funds for the army and navy, and directed contracts to favored localities. Peace and war decisions, which arguably should have been made with regard to a common national interest, in fact became embroiled in domestic politics and partisan disputes. Not all of these early precedents have survived to the present day – but only because of conscious decisions to act differently in response to other developments in the course of US history. This book cannot cover all of these twists and turns, but it does try to illustrate some key patterns.

Three challenges

In peacetime, civil–military relations fall into a comfortable pattern, accommodating the interests and concerns of the various institutions of government. Short, limited deployments – such as the numerous operations of the 1980s and 1990s in places like Lebanon, Somalia, and the Balkans – may provoke controversy and friction, as indeed they did, but those effects subside.[16]

This book deals with the much more stressful challenges of wartime, rearmament, and transformation – situations which last longer and are viewed by the participants as much more consequential. If a political system can handle these cases, then civil–military relations can be judged in balance.

Wartime is the greatest challenge. Lives are at stake. Costs are high. The risks are substantial but not always knowable. War forces agonizing decisions on civilian leaders, not the least of which is how much trust and discretion to give to military leaders. Combatant commanders face obverse problems – how to obtain needed guidance and resources from their superiors without compromising their professional standards and judgment. The longer the conflict, the more elusive the desired victory, the more friction builds up between warriors and politicians.

For this book, I have chosen to describe US civil–military relations in three lengthy and difficult wars of the distant past, plus the still-unfolding story of the wars and military transformation of George W. Bush and Donald Rumsfeld. The Revolutionary War discussed in Chapter 2 is significant not only because it was America's first war as a nation but also because the civilian and military leaders learned key lessons which they applied to the design of the Constitution and its republic – in particular the need for a well-resourced central government and a military under singular, hierarchical control. The Civil War was America's most deadly, the only one that truly threatened its existence, and the one that raised for its warriors and politicians the most profound political as well as military questions and choices. While thousands of books describe Lincoln and his generals, few explain, as I do in Chapter 3, the significant impact that Congress had on events. The Vietnam War was America's longest conflict, its least successful, the only one to bridge two presidencies, and second only to the Civil War in its divisive consequences for American politics. Thus the story in Chapter 4 describes deft political calculations, angry military leaders, and profound Constitutional battles.

There are other episodes that could be examined, given enough time and space. Thomas Jefferson fought an undeclared war against the Barbary pirates, setting precedents for after-the-fact involvement of Congress. James Madison, briefly and ingloriously, took field command of US forces in the War of 1812, a conflict spurred by one region and strongly opposed by another. James K. Polk engineered a war which he wanted to fight with Mexico and left his political opponents sputtering and helpless. The stories of the Spanish–American War and the two world wars have been ably and extensively told in other books, which the curious reader should seek out.[17]

Rearmament stresses civil–military relations in different ways. It requires a strategic judgment that conflict is approaching and then strong leadership to persuade the people and their representatives to shift resources from peacetime pursuits to military requirements. The military, too, must be responsive to the new situation and willing to undertake different ways of dealing with the expected threat. In Chapter 5 I describe the first real rearmament undertaken by the US government, to deal with the growing threat from the French in the 1790s. This was the time when the United States finally created a navy and a standing army, and it occasioned vicious political disputes between the emerging political parties. This case also demonstrates that even the staunchest American patriots, men who had fought the revolutionary war together, were unwilling to suspend their political disagreements to confront a foreign foe. Quite the contrary: the question of whether America's national interests were best served by closer ties to Britain or France was the basis for the development of the first two political parties.

Chapter 6 tells the story of Franklin Roosevelt's deft maneuvers to prepare America for what became the Second World War. The issue was deeper than military preparedness, which all politicians favored. Roosevelt challenged the long American tradition of neutrality and isolation. He succeeded both through his own skill and through bipartisan political support. He was also fortunate in having and choosing military leaders who were knowledgeable and willing to share the political burdens with him.

Chapter 7 covers Harry Truman's slow acceptance of military rearmament, despite his prompt willingness to use political and economic instruments to contain Communism. It also shows how Truman accepted and asserted leadership in an unexpected war in Korea, including how he dealt with an insubordinate but popular commander.

Other rearmament episodes could have been studied, and perhaps also the disarmament and demobilization that occurred under Jefferson, Andrew Johnson, and Woodrow Wilson – for postwar adjustments are often as stressful for politicians and warriors as the buildup to conflict. America did rearm in anticipation of the First World War, and the military greatly expanded after the first Soviet sputnik in 1957 and in the 1980s.[18] The cases studied here, however, involved profound strategic decisions and reorientations, not simply a muscling up to deal with a recognized threat.

Military modernization and transformation pose different problems, concentrating more on the armed forces themselves than on strategic judgments by politicians. Yet history has shown that military institutions tend to make radical changes only in response to defeats, and that successful militaries are slow to change what they believe provided past victory. When outsiders try to impose their own vision of a modern military, they tend to confront tough resistance from the officer corps – unless they make strategic alliances with those mavericks who advocate major innovation.

Modernization stories here tell of wrenching change imposed by two strong personalities who sustained political support until their efforts took root. Chapter 8 recounts Theodore Roosevelt's bullying efforts to turn the US military into a force worthy of a world power and capable to police a growing empire. Chapter 9 describes Robert McNamara's centralization of power in the office of the Secretary of Defense and his imposition of a new language – systems analysis – for thinking about budgets and strategy. How he subdued the generals and admirals, and kept support in Congress, is an amazing tale – all the more tragic because of his subsequent failure in Vietnam. Chapter 10 gives a different example of transformation imposed from outside – the case of the Goldwater-Nichols legislation that forced the US military to set aside their longstanding service parochialism and think and act more jointly. This case shows that Congress, too, can be an instrument of valuable innovation, even against a reluctant Pentagon.

There is a large body of literature on US military innovation, with many tales of heroes and villains and exciting stories of success against long odds, like the brave efforts to develop aviation in the period between the two world wars. There are also examples of failed innovation, when the politicians and warriors did not embrace the new concepts and technologies we now see as vital. It is depressing to consider how long the US navy resisted steam power and ironclad ships, how slow that navy was to appreciate aircraft carriers, or how many obstacles it placed in the way of Hyman Rickover's efforts to build nuclear-powered submarines. It is instructive, but not surprising, to study how long the US air force smothered the development of unmanned aerial vehicles so that pilots could remain the lords of the sky. It is only mildly reassuring to examine how the US Army eventually accepted helicopters, special forces, and lighter, more rapidly deployable combat units.[19]

At the strategic level, the most important military transformation not included here was Dwight Eisenhower's "new look," his effort to reduce conventional forces and thereby the defense budget while relying on nuclear weapons for deterrence and possible war fighting. The army's efforts to resist the president's strategy were an important part of the politico–strategic debate in America in the crisis period launched by the first sputnik and continuing through John F. Kennedy's election.[20]

All three challenges – warfighting, rearmament and transformation – came together under George W. Bush and Donald Rumsfeld. The top civilian leaders entered office determined to reshape the US military in radical ways; they then got involved in two geographic wars and a global fight against terrorists which required a different type of rearmament. Initial military resistance to the transformation efforts in 2001 was replaced by a surge of patriotism and political support following the September 11 attacks. And congressional actions during the wars in Afghanistan and Iraq followed a different pattern from many earlier conflicts.

These case study chapters are simple narratives. In the concluding chapter, I try to point out some patterns and draw some lessons about civil–military relations in the United States. But this is not a book about theory. Many other scholars have done interesting work in that area,[21] but they fall short, in my judgment, because they give insufficient attention to the role of Congress and the triangular relationship, the dual sources of civilian control, that is a key feature of the American system. The final chapter offers thoughts on how to view and understand these unique aspects of US civil–military relations.

Part I

The challenge of warfighting

2 Revolutionary war by committee

[The Congress] think it but to say Presto begone, and everything is done.
George Washington, 1777[1]

We don't choose to trust you Generals, with too much Power, for too Long Time.
John Adams to General Horatio Gates[2]

George Washington was torn by the Continental Congress' offer to lead the army assembled outside of Boston in June, 1775. Like other eighteenth century gentlemen, he welcomed the chance to demonstrate his military prowess and win fame and glory. But he knew the risks were great and his family and estate might suffer. As he wrote to his wife Martha on June 18, enclosing his hastily drafted will, "life is always uncertain, and common prudence dictates to every man the necessity of settling his temporal concerns while it is in his power ...." He also proclaimed, "I shall rely, therefore, confidently on that Providence which has heretofore preserved and been bountiful to me, not doubting but that I shall return safe to you in the fall."[3] In fact, Washington was to be on duty and away from home for the next seven years, except for 10 days just before the climactic battle at Yorktown in 1781. Besides enemy forces and the privations of eighteenth century military encampments, Washington also had to contend with the Continental Congress, a body ill-suited to manage a life-or-death conflict. The Congress was a part-time group of lawyers, merchants, and farmers gathered from the 13 colonies to fashion a common response to British policies in North America. It had no power to raise money or armies, but was dependent on the voluntary responses of the various provincial legislatures to its requests. Prior to independence, foreign recognition, and the election of new state governments under new constitutions, it had questionable legitimacy. Twice it was forced to flee its home base of Philadelphia to escape capture by the British. Yet it wrote the rules and gave the guidance to Washington and his Continental army, and struggled to acquire the weapons and supplies that allowed it to survive and fight and ultimately win. In that long process of war and diplomacy, fund-raising and law-making, consideration of matters profound and mundane, the Continental Congress and Washington set precedents and practices which have endured into the twenty-first century. The civil–military relations during the Revolutionary War established the model, including tensions and flaws, for later conflicts.

Decisions for war

It was by no means inevitable in June 1775 that the 13 colonies would declare their independence or be successful in achieving it. The First Continental Congress, meeting in the fall of 1774, declared its fealty to King George III and blamed parliament for "unjust, cruel, and oppressive acts" against the people of Massachusetts. The delegates called for a boycott of British goods and passed Articles of Association to monitor its implementation through local committees of correspondence. They hoped that redress could be achieved peacefully. When sending copies of its resolutions to Benjamin Franklin in London, the Secretary of the Congress, Charles Thomson, wrote, "Even yet the wound may be healed & peace and love restored: But we are on the brink of a precipice."[4]

By the time the Second Continental Congress assembled on May 10, 1775, however, blood had been shed at Lexington and Concord and an army of perhaps 18,000 New Englanders had gathered near Boston to fight the British force. The delegates authorized several preparations for war even as they named a committee to draw up a petition to the king for peace. On June 3, the congress set up a committee to consider ways and means of borrowing £6000 to buy gunpowder. On June 14 it called 10 companies of expert riflemen be raised in Pennsylvania, Maryland and Virginia and sent to Boston. The same day it appointed a committee to "draft rules and regulations for the government of the army." On June 15 it voted to name George Washington "to command all the Continental forces." And on June 16 it adopted a plan of organization for the army and established a committee to prepare instructions.[5] The next day, redcoats and patriots clashed in what came to be called the battle of Bunker Hill.

Washington was chosen because the New Englanders recognized the value of having a Virginian in charge of what were then mostly local soldiers. John Adams made the nomination, and the assembly agreed unanimously. Connecticut delegate Eliphaler Dyer wrote that it was "absolutely Necessary in point of prudence" to pick someone from outside New England because "it removes all jealousies, more firmly Cements the Southern to the Northern, and takes away the fear of the former lest an Enterprising eastern New England Genll. Proving successful, might with his Victorious Army give law to the Southern or Western Gentry."[6] Congress' endorsement and Washington's leadership made Boston's fight America's fight.

Dyer's comment demonstrates that, even if fighting for their liberties, the colonial leaders were concerned about the threat from a standing army. They knew quite well what Oliver Cromwell had done barely a century earlier in Britain when he led his New Model Army first against the king and later against any who opposed his dictatorship. Samuel Adams warned,

> Soldiers are apt to consider themselves as a Body distinct from the rest of the Citizens. They have their Arms always in their hands. Their Rules and their Discipline is severe. They soon become attached to their officers and disposed to yield implicit obedience to their Commands. Such a Power should be watched with a jealous Eye.[7]

Even the Virginia Declaration of Rights, written by George Mason, explicitly said, "that standing armies in time of peace should be avoided as dangerous to liberty; and that in all cases the military should be under strict subordination to, and governed by, the civil power."[8]

While the Continental Congress sometimes gave near-dictatorial powers to Washington and other commanders for specific operations in particular regions, it remained on guard, and with tight purse strings, throughout the revolutionary struggle. And the Framers of the Constitution took special pains to guarantee civilian control in the new government by numerous provisions, including a reliance on a militia force rather than a standing army.

Washington's commission from the Congress told him "punctually to observe and follow such orders and directions, from time to time, as you shall receive from this, or a future Congress of these United Colonies, or committee of Congress."[9] His formal instructions listed as the first requirement to report back as soon as possible on the status of his own troops and their provisions. He was, however, given the power "to use your best circumspection and (advising with your council of war) to order and dispose of the said Army under command as may be most advantageous ...."[10] In deference to this provision, or perhaps from an excess of caution, Washington felt compelled at least until 1777 to consult his senior subordinates and obtain majority approval from that a council of war before undertaking major operations.[11]

A persuasive explanation for why Washington accepted Congress' nitpicking and micromanagement, and tolerated its frequent failures to provide adequate resources, comes from his definitive biographer, Douglas Southall Freeman:

> In dealing with Congressmen and in winning their support, Washington's experience as a member of the Virginia House of Burgesses was of value beyond calculation. Nothing he possessed, save integrity, helped him so much, from his very first day of command, as his sure and intimate knowledge of the workings of the legislative mind. In the discharge of every duty to Congress and in the presentation of every request, his approach could be accurate, informed, and deferential. ... Now that he had met and had conversed with some of the best men of every Colony, he was able to understand their problems and those of America.[12]

Congressional guidance reached a surprising level of detail in the general orders approved on June 30. These articles of war were a slightly revised version of the existing British provisions, running through 69 paragraphs. They included: a recommendation "diligently to attend Divine Service" – article II; a 4 shilling penalty for "profane cursing or swearing" – article III; demotion to private of any noncommissioned officer for neglect or waste of ammunition, arms, or provisions – article XV; immediate death penalty for anyone who "shamefully abandon[s] any post committed to his charge" – article XXV; a limitation on non-capital punishments to 39 lashes and fines of two months pay – article LI; a ban on selling liquor or entertainment "after nine at night …or upon Sundays, during divine service or sermon" – article LXIV.[13] By the end of 1776, however, in response to military setbacks, Congress increased the number of permitted lashes to 100 and also increased the number of crimes for which the death penalty could be imposed.[14]

Not content to pass resolutions and appoint committees, more than half the delegates journeyed to Cambridge after their August 1 adjournment in order to see the fledgling army firsthand.[15] They returned in September eager to continue the military buildup.

War aims

Prior to the Declaration of Independence, the Continental army had a limited objective: "for the defence of American liberty and for repelling every hostile invasion thereof," in the words of Congress' instructions to Washington. In passing the articles of war on June 30, Congress acknowledged that British reinforcements were headed toward Boston and declared that an American force "be raised sufficient to defeat such hostile designs, and preserve and defend the lives, liberties and immunities of the Colonists."[16]

In practice, these words meant removal of the British troops from Boston, repeal of the other sanctions imposed on Massachusetts, and a restoration of pre-1774 colonial liberties. Although Congress urged a direct attack on General Gage's troops in Boston, even offering a bonus of a month's pay in case of success, Washington instead maneuvered. In a nighttime surprise, his troops seized Dorchester Heights, thus allowing them to threaten British land and naval forces. The Redcoats' withdrawal on March 17, 1776 was part of a strategic decision by the new British commanding general to relocate his expanding forces to New York and try to sever the New England colonies from their brethren to the south.

By that time, sentiment throughout the colonies was turning in favor of independence. George III had proclaimed the colonies in a state of rebellion in August 1775 and ordered that "all our Officers, civil and military, are obliged to exert their utmost endeavours to suppress such rebellion, and to bring the traitors to justice."[17] Local assemblies began petitioning the Congress to declare independence, but many delegates, especially from the middle colonies, felt that the time was not yet ripe and held out hope that British peace commissioners might arrive with conciliatory proposals.

Although British troops had been withdrawn from Boston, the Crown was assembling a huge force of British and German troops, more than 32,000, to send against the rebels. Anticipating an attack, even the moderates supported measures to prepare for war. In the spring of 1776, Congress approved funds for presents and bribes for Indian leaders, to try to keep them neutral, and summoned Washington to Philadelphia for consultations at the end of May. Those conferences led to decisions to send 6,000 reinforcements to Canada, to raise a force of 13,000 for New York, and to establish what was called a 10,000-man "flying camp" of militia that could be deployed where needed.[18] A few months before, Congress had authorized privateering against British ships and building four armed ships for a new American navy.

On June 7, Richard Henry Lee offered the radicals' three-fold plan for dealing with the British threat. The first provision was the famous declaration "That these United Colonies are, and of right ought to be, free and independent States ...." But the second and third provisions were equally significant. They called for "the most effectual measures for forming foreign Alliances" and for "a plan of confederation."[19] The rebels recognized that independence required support from abroad and greater unity at home.

Throughout the long conflict, the congressional leaders never wavered from their insistence on full independence. Even when their major cities were captured by the British, when the army was nearly destitute at Valley Forge, when the currency collapsed, when soldiers turned mutinous over inadequate pay – the patriots held firm.

And they suffered for it. By the time the war ended, more than half the members of the Continental Congress had seen their property looted or destroyed. Many were imprisoned or driven into hiding. Of the 342 men elected at one time or another to the Congress, 134 served in the militia or the Continental army – and of them, one was killed in action, 12 were seriously wounded, and 23 were taken prisoner.[20] In these and other ways, they paid a price for their patriotism. Their pledge of their lives, their fortunes and their sacred honor was not mere rhetoric.

Strategy

From Congress' standpoint, the way to achieve independence was to persuade others of the justness of the American cause, to enlist foreign support, to raise a large local force to fight the British when they approached, and to capture Canada so that the British had no foothold in North America.

In support of this strategy, Congress took numerous actions in the month after voting to create a Continental army in June 1775. It approved a formal "Address to the Inhabitants of Great Britain" complaining that "our Petitions are treated with Indignity; our Prayers answered by insults." It also sent letters to the people of Ireland and Jamaica and the "oppressed inhabitants"

Figure 2.1   Washington and a Committee of Congress at Valley Forge (National Archives)

of Canada, expressing the hope "of your uniting with us in the defense of our common liberty."[21]

On July 6, 1775, Congress issued a declaration "setting forth the causes and necessity of their taking up arms." This document, a blend of drafts from moderate John Dickinson of Pennsylvania and the radical Thomas Jefferson of Virginia, summarized the history of "These devoted colonies" and their "peaceful and respectful behaviour" until the British government decided to change the established form of government and impose a new despotism. The declaration charged that British troops "have butchered our countrymen" and "spread destruction and devastation." It asserted that "Honour, justice, and humanity, forbid us tamely to surrender that freedom which we have received from our gallant ancestors." Yet it stopped short of independence. "We have not raised armies with ambitious designs of separating from Great-Britain, and establishing independent states." Instead, it pleaded for "reconciliation on reasonable terms."[22]

In addition to these rhetorical appeals, Congress took several concrete actions in the same period. On June 22, the delegates approved the issuance of $2 million in bills of credit to pay for the army. On June 27 it ordered preparations for talks with Indian tribes, to assure their neutrality in the conflict. The same day, it directed Major General Schuyler to seize St. Johns, Montreal, and any other parts of Canada "which may have a tendency to promote the peace and security of these Colonies." And on July 15, it voted an exemption from the boycott law for trade in gunpowder, saltpeter, sulphur, cannon, muskets and other munitions. On July 18 it recommended that each colony take steps to defend its harbors and seacoasts. And on July 21 it received for later consideration Benjamin Franklin's proposal for Articles of Confederation.[23] In December, Silas Deane of Connecticut would be sent to France to seek moral and material support.

These measures demonstrate Congress' approach prior to the Declaration of Independence – public appeals, military mobilization, search for allies, and political cooperation. The intended role of the army was to drive Gage from Boston and to capture Canada.

Washington saw the strategic problem differently. He thought that not to lose was to win, that the British would ultimately tire of a protracted conflict. He was at first dubious of obtaining sufficient foreign support and, as an infantryman, failed to appreciate the impact of the French navy in diverting and defeating the Royal Navy. He opposed excessive reliance on the militia, rather than the Continental army, because he repeatedly witnessed its shortcomings – poor training and command, brief enlistments, and a tendency to retreat from battle. "Are these the men with whom I am to defend America?" he cried at the battle of Kip's Bay in New York. Earlier, he had described the forces assembled at Cambridge as he took command as "an exceedingly dirty and nasty people." He was indifferent to the congressionally mandated invasion of Canada, which ultimately failed.[24]

The commander-in-chief adopted a defensive strategy, hoping to avoid a decisive battle which could result in a decisive defeat. As Russell Weigley wrote, "the strategy of the American armies in the Revolutionary War had to be a strategy founded upon weakness."[25] Washington said he could not divide his army without risking great losses. And he opposed making major attacks "since the Idea of forcing their lines or bringing on a General Engagement on their own Grounds, is Universally held incompatible with our Interest."[26] As a result, Washington avoided confrontation with main British army units whenever possible.[27]

Congress was ill-equipped to manage the war but felt responsible for its conduct. A legislative body, by its nature, cannot easily make timely decisions or regulate the implementation of its orders. It is better at retrospective oversight than day-to-day management. Yet there was no other entity to run the war effort. There was no other government that involved all of the colonies.

Starting in 1776, Congress felt obliged to be in session almost continuously until 1784, recessing only for a few days at a time. That reduced attendance, as members went home from time to time to take care of personal business, but it preserved some sort of government in being throughout the war. The demands were even heavier on those appointed to serve on committees, which dealt with particular issues. At first, the assembly created new committees for each subject and proposal, from drafting documents to handling relations with Indian tribes. By the end of 1775 it created standing committees to replace the ad hoc ones. A Secret Committee was set up to import munitions and other necessary supplies. It later became the Commerce Committee. A Committee of Secret Correspondence maintained communications with American agents and informants abroad. It later became the Committee on Foreign Affairs. One of the most important panels was the Board of War and Ordnance, which was concerned with supplying the army. It acted as the executive over the army until 1777, when Congress created a subordinate Board of War, consisting of full-time officials who were not delegates to the Congress. Only in 1781 did it create executive departments – for foreign affairs, war, and the navy.[28]

There was a voluminous correspondence between the Congress and the commander-in-chief. The general requested supplies and guidance and received a healthy dose of the latter. In addition, there were six special commissions sent to Washington's headquarters, at least one each year, mainly to investigate problems and report back to the Congress. As John Adams wrote, "This is the Way to have things go right: for Officers to correspond constantly with Congress and communicate their Sentiments freely."[29]

Washington sometimes resisted, as in this letter of March 14, 1777. "Could I accomplish the important objects so eagerly sought by Congress – 'confining the enemy within their present quarters, preventing their getting supplies from the country, and totally subduing them before they are reinforced' – I should be happy indeed, But what prospect or hope can there be of my effecting so desirable a work at this time? The enclosed return, to which I solicit the most respectful attention of Congress, comprehends the whole force I have in Jersey."[30]

In practice, Congress meddled more with the armies in the north and south than in the middle states, where Washington was usually headquartered. Although he was the overall commander, he acceded to those forces' greater autonomy from him and greater oversight by Congress in those regions.[31] War by committee proved unsatisfactory, leading to the creation of executive agents under the committees and eventual regular departments to manage particular activities. These experiences persuaded the revolutionary leaders, when they met to craft a new Constitution, to create institutions that vested power and authority in a strong executive – and in a strong central government. But those lessons came only after painful experiences.

Personnel

Just as Washington had been selected for geographical as well as military reasons, Congress named other general officers for the same reasons. Major general commissions went to Artemus Ward, head of the Massachusetts militia; two former British officers now Virginians, Charles Lee and Horatio Gates; and Israel Putnam of Connecticut and Philip Schuyler of New York. Brigadier commissions went mainly to New Englanders, since theirs was the only real force in being at the time. Regimental officers were supposed to be recommended by provincial assemblies, subject to Washington's approval.[32]

After two years of pleas and demands from would-be generals and their congressional patrons, Congress finally in February 1777 adopted what was called its Baltimore resolution on the subject: "In voting for general officers, a due regard shall be had to the line of succession, the merit of the persons proposed, and the quota of the troops raised, and to be raised, by each state."[33] In practice, both Washington and the Congress worked through the local governors in picking local commanders.[34]

As the war went on, Congress came under pressure to give high ranks to foreign officers recruited in Europe by Silas Deane. Some, like Steuben and Lafayette, proved enormously able. Others had inflated credentials and insufficient skill. American officers also used their political contacts to try to advance their promotions and careers – a pattern also followed in later decades. Congress insisted, during the revolution and as part of the Constitution, on having ultimate power over the selection of military officers.

Junior officers and enlisted personnel were recruited locally, though Congress requested particular force levels during the course of the war. Those in the militia typically served only a few months each year, and even the Continental army had trouble obtaining people for more than a year at a time. One reason for Washington's dramatic 1776 Christmastime attack across the Delaware against the German troops encamped at Trenton was to make use of his men before they returned home as their enlistments expired at the end of the year. He also desperately needed a morale-boosting victory after his defeats earlier that year around New York and while retreating across New Jersey.[35] Congress tried to boost enlistments with various bonuses and pension promises, but these proved less successful as the currency lost value.

During the course of the war, the Congress named 73 general officers. Fifty-two had previous military experience – 16 in an English or European army, and 36 in the colonial militia. Even some with no prior experience performed amazingly well, including Henry Knox, who organized the American artillery units, and Nathanael Greene, who learned so well and so quickly that he often commanded in Washington's absence and later organized an innovative guerrilla campaign in the south.[36] On the other hand, seven of the 29 major generals resigned, one died, one was discharged, and one committed treason.[37]

The Continental army never had more than about 17,000 under arms at one time, although over the course of the war as many as 232,000 men were formally enlisted. Perhaps one-fourth of the continental soldiers took unauthorized leave at some time. Militia forces were much larger throughout the war, but they served under short, irregular enlistments and were less well trained. The largest force in any one year, regular and militia, was estimated to be 47,000 men in 1776. Britain nearly doubled the size of its pre-war army, including hiring 30,000 German mercenaries – uniformly labeled Hessians, though they came from many Germany states. In 1776, it sent 50,000 troops to garrison Canada and fight the rebellious colonies. The armies directly confronting Washington ranged from 28,000 to 34,000 soldiers.[38]

The Continental navy was a much smaller force, and it faced the large and powerful Royal Navy. While some delegates such as John Adams saw the value of a fleet, other shrank from the high shipbuilding costs. Congress named a navy committee in October 1775. A few months later it purchased eight ships and ordered the building of 13 new frigates. In addition they sought to draw upon state naval forces, which never amounted to more than 40 boats overall. Consequently, the bulk of the commerce-raiding done by American ships was done by privateers. More than 2,000 got letters of marque authorizing them to attack and seize British ships. Interdiction by American and European ships was substantial – over half the 6,000 British ships involved in overseas trade fell into enemy hands at some point in the war.[39]

American shipbuilding, however, was far less successful. Only six American-built frigates ever got to sea, and only one survived the war. Only one larger ship-of-the-line was finished before the end of the war. In July 1777 Congress was so upset at the escalating costs of ships being built it gave permission to its committee to "put a stop" to construction because of the "extravagant prices now demanded for all kinds of materials used in ship-building, and the enormous wages required by tradesmen and laborers." Despite the cost problems, the committee felt the need was too great, so it approved continued payments.[40]

Supply

Congress also had the clear responsibility of obtaining the supplies for the army it had created and paying its people. These proved to be enormous challenges, poorly met. Three weeks before declaring independence, after repeated requests from Washington for the delegates to set up some system of management, Congress created a five-member Board of War and Ordnance under John Adams as chairman. It was to keep records of all personnel and equipment and was responsible for "the raising, fitting out, and dispatching all such land forces as may be ordered for the service of the United Colonies."[41] Later, in July 1777, a subordinate Board of War was created, with three full-time officials, not members of Congress. Only in 1781 did Congress create a regular war department.

The Board had an impossible set of tasks. There was little domestic production capability for key items – no gunpowder, saltpeter, iron and steel, or canvas for ship sails. Special committees were established to search, inquire, beg, and contract for needed items. The army in the field was often successful in capturing British supplies of needed items or in seizing them locally, often from British loyalists. Privateers also captured significant supplies at sea and turned them over to the army. Congress also let contracts to American suppliers for food and clothing and some other supplies, using early forms of advertising, bids, and proposals. When this system broke down in 1780, mainly because of the depreciation of the Continental currency used to pay for purchases, Congress turned the supply problem over to the individual states for the duration of the war.[42]

Even when supplies were available, logistical problems sometimes prevented goods from reaching the army. It has been estimated, for example, that there was enough food in the area to feed the forces starving at Valley Forge in the winter of 1777, but that there were not enough wagons available to transport it to Washington's camp.[43]

The contracting system showed many of the problems and dysfunctions that have plagued US military procurement over the centuries. Paperwork was burdensome; suppliers cheated; when complaints arose, Congress investigated. Nevertheless, a mere handful of overworked officials developed a system of contracting and delivery that equipped and fed a victorious army.

Congress tended to control even the smallest projects with its approval required for each payment. While it set specifications for army items, it used on-site supervision of shipbuilding. As Lucille Horgan notes, "No matter which organization or government official was given contracting authority, Congress usually reserved the right to approve or disapprove the terms of individual contracts, and especially of final approval for payment."[44]

Individual soldiers were usually required to supply their own firearms, blankets and knapsacks. Sometimes unit commanders were given authorization to provision themselves by foraging locally.[45]

To pay the troops and to buy their supplies, Congress had no money. There was no indigenous national currency, so Congress printed what it needed and asked the colonies to pay proportionate shares of their own taxes. Within five years Congress had circulated $200 million of these bills of credit, and few Americans would willingly accept them as payment for anything. "Not worth a Continental" became the slogan. As part of its measures in 1780 to put the government on a sounder footing, Congress devalued the currency, 40–1, so that the nominal debt shrank to only $5 million.

Meanwhile, officers were demanding the British system of half-pay for life for veterans. Despite repeated requests from Washington, Congress resisted this pension plan until October 1780, though it did vote death benefits for officer and enlisted families and half pay for life for those disabled in wartime.[46] Eventually it created a more generous pension system.

Tactics

As might be expected of a legislative body trying to manage a war, Congress swung between intrusiveness and desperate delegation, seeking but rarely finding an agreeable balance between civilian and military responsibilities. Fortunately for American democracy, George Washington accepted Congress' authority and deferred to its practices, despite frequent frustrations.

His first clear mission was to drive the British from Boston, which he accomplished in March 1776. The congressionally inspired invasion of Canada was conducted by other forces. While they succeeded in capturing Montreal, they were forced to retreat from Quebec in the spring of 1776. Washington recognized that the British were likely to attack New York, so he positioned his expanded army there, only to be defeated in a series of dispiriting engagements in the summer and fall of 1776.

Less than six months after confidently declaring independence, the frightened Congress fled to Baltimore on December 12. Two weeks later lawmakers voted to vest Washington "with full, ample and complete powers to raise and collect together, in the most speedy and effectual manner, from any or all of these United States, 16 battalions of infantry, in addition to those already voted by Congress" as well as "to arrest and confine persons who refuse to take the continental currency, or are otherwise disaffected to the American cause."[47]

So guilty did the delegates feel about their abdication of civilian control that three days later they issued a circular letter to the 13 states explaining "Congress would not have Consented to the Vesting of such Powers in the Military Department … if the Scituation of Public Affairs did not require at this Crisis a Decision and Vigour, which Distance and Numbers Deny to Assemblies far Remov'd from each other, and from the immediate Seat of War."[48] Once the crisis passed with Washington's victories at Trenton and Princeton, John Adams counseled against letting Washington retain too much power. As he told the delegates, "It becomes us to attend early to the restraining our army."[49]

Congress adopted the same desperation measures in June 1780, after the surrender of a large American force at Charleston, South Carolina, when it gave General Gates command of the southern army and empowered him "to take such other measures, from time to time, for the defence of the southern states as he shall think most proper."[50]

Congress returned to Philadelphia in March 1777, but had to flee in September when General William Howe occupied the city. The delegates relocated first to Lancaster, Pennsylvania, and then to York, where they stayed until Howe's evacuation in June 1778. Washington fought the British inconclusively at Germantown and Brandywine and then established winter quarters at Valley Forge.

The most important battle of 1777, and perhaps of the war, was fought at Saratoga, in New York, where British General John Burgoyne was defeated by forces led by General Horatio Gates. Thereafter, British infantry action was confined to the southern states – and the French government decided that the rebels had enough chance of success that they deserved their aid and support.

Congress had been seeking foreign alliances from the start of the conflict. It sent Silas Deane to France in 1775, following with Benjamin Franklin and John Adams in 1776. These and other American emissaries courted public opinion, negotiated treaties, and procured supplies. What had been a localized British–American conflict became a European war, with the Royal Navy threatened by the French fleet in Europe and the Caribbean and Gibraltar threatened by Spain.

When the British sent a peace delegation in 1778, the Congress spurned it, demanding recognition of American independence as a precondition to any talks. Despite the many positive developments, the war dragged on through inconclusive engagements in 1779 and into a major crisis in 1780. That year the British took control of the three most southern states, defeating American forces at Charleston and Camden, South Carolina. Congress devalued the currency and confronted angry debt holders and soldiers, including a mutinous Pennsylvania army that threatened to besiege the Congress in January 1781.

Fortunately the French responded with its fleet, some soldiers, and six million livres for the Continental army. Congress also moved to make the government more streamlined, professional, and efficient by creating executive departments for foreign affairs, finance, war and the navy. And on March 1, the Articles of Confederation went into effect, following a three-year delay as Maryland insisted that other states drop their claims to western lands, thus leaving them open for settlement as new states and territories.

The new government was still so weak and poor, however, that when the express rider arrived in Philadelphia on October 22 with word of the British defeat at Yorktown, there was not enough hard money in the treasury to pay him, so members of Congress each had to contribute a dollar of their own.[51]

War termination

Even then, the war was not really over, for British troops continued to occupy Charleston and still held New York, as they had since 1776. But the key American objective had been achieved: independence was not at issue in the peace talks.

Congress wanted to reduce the army in 1782, pending the conclusion of a formal peace treaty, but Washington and other officers resisted. It finally adopted a plan of voluntary retirement for officers, beginning in 1783.

Meanwhile, the most serious civil–military clash of the entire war occurred among Washington's troops at Newburgh, New York in March 1783. Although peace commissioners had been meeting during 1782, British envoys waited until October to indicate a willingness to grant independence. Preliminary articles of peace were signed in January 1783 and the formal British announcement of a cessation of hostilities was announced only on February 20. Meanwhile, the continental army was being cut back, but without the promises of substantial pensions desired by the soldiers. The army could not be disbanded because British troops still controlled, among other positions, New York – as they would until November 1783.

A junior officer circulated a paper among the disgruntled officers which threatened Congress with disobedience unless officers gained greater respect and remuneration from the legislature. The document also criticized Washington for siding with the lawmakers. A few weeks earlier, a group had petitioned Congress claiming: "We have borne all that men can bear – our property is expended – our private resources are at an end." These soldiers asked that their half-pay pensions be commuted to five years of full pay. Otherwise, they warned, "any further experiments on their patience may have fatal effects."[52] The latest circular threatened not to disband or not to fight unless their grievances were resolved. Washington responded by calling a general meeting. Addressing the officers, the general at first argued against the substance of the paper. Then he pulled out his spectacles to read a letter from a congressman explaining the financial problems. Few had seen him with glasses before. He explained, "I have grown gray in your service and now find myself growing blind." His gesture, the humanity of his appeal, turned the tide of sentiment, and some officers openly wept. The Newburgh Conspiracy evaporated.[53] The day Congress learned of these events, it voted full pay for five years for officers and full pay for four months for enlisted men. It left unresolved whether the payment would be in cash or securities with 6 percent interest. But the crisis had passed.[54]

Washington saved the day at Newburgh, as he had protected and deferred to the authority of Congress during the war. But the incident reminded the American politicians that they had to be wary in their dealings with the warriors. Those final months witnessed the disintegration of the Continental army as its members returned to civilian life. By the summer of 1784, by order of Congress, the army was cut to 80 men, left to guard military stores at West Point and Fort Pitt.[55]

In diplomatic and economic terms, the peace settlement was a victory for the new nation. Having lost the colonies, the British were eager to regain a profitable trading partner. Having been defeated in their attempts to conquer Canada, the newly united states now had uninhibited access to lands west of the mountains.

Lessons of the war

The Revolutionary War demonstrated that a disorganized group of colonials could come together and prevail against the greatest military power of the day. Their appeal was conservative in requesting rights that were fundamental to Englishmen and radical in calling for government by the consent of the governed. In a few months, these colonials went from letters and newspapers circulated by committees of correspondence to a representative congress making decisions and issuing orders that were actually obeyed. They fought a war without a real government, without the power of taxation that enables governments to raise funds for armies and navies, and without a bureaucracy or officer corps to fight for the independence their congress declared.

If one miracle was that such a hodgepodge succeeded, a second miracle was that its chosen military leader was a man of such integrity and devotion to political principle that he accepted and endured the frustrations and indignities of legislative control. As Richard Kohn argues, "George Washington never succumbed to temptation." He never used his authority or celebrity to challenge the Congress and the inefficient process it had created. Before, during, and after Newburgh he rejected calls for military insubordination. But as one observer noted in his journal, "The officers look upon Congress with an evil eye, as men who are jealous of the army, who mean them no good, but mean to divide and distress them. It is surprising with how much freedom & acrimony they declare their sentiments."[56]

Washington bridged the civil–military gap and set the mode of restraint and deference for future generations. Congress, too, in its own way, set the precedents for future conduct in wartime: hard work, close oversight, inadequate material support, and political responsiveness to public opinion.

More immediately, the war taught lessons for the new American leaders who were trying to make their independent government succeed. It reinforced their view that the government needed – for national security reasons at least – to be strong enough to tax in order to raise armies and navies, to be cohesive enough to make foreign treaties and alliances. It convinced them that they could create and sustain a Lockean government of separated institutions sharing powers while still being strong enough to preserve their national integrity. The war set the stage for peace; the Continental Congress set the model for the new government; and George Washington played the key role as a deferential commander-in-chief.

3 Lincoln, Congress, and the generals

The particulars of your plans I neither know or seek to know. You are vigilant and self-reliant; and, pleased with this, I wish not to obtrude any constraints or restraints upon you.

Abraham Lincoln to Lt. Gen U.S. Grant, April 30, 1864[1]

I can't tell you how disgusted I am becoming with these wretched politicians; they are the most despicable of men ... The Presdt [sic] is nothing more than a well meaning baboon.

General George McClellan[2]

I have done everything in my power here to separate military appointments and commands from politics ... but the task is hopeless.

General-in-Chief Henry Halleck[3]

[Army officers who] indulge in the sport [of politics] must risk being gored. They can not, having exposed themselves, claim the procedural protections and immunities of the military profession.

Secretary of War Stanton to Lincoln, January 1863[4]

There must be something in these terrible reports, but I distrust Congressional committees. They exaggerate.

Navy Secretary Gideon Welles[5]

We are here armed with the whole power of both houses of Congress. They have made it our duty to inquire into the whole conduct of the war; into every department of it. We do not want to do anything that will result in harm or wrong. But we do want to know, and we must know if we can, what is to be done, for the country is in jeopardy.

Senator Benjamin Wade, Chairman of the Joint Committee on the Conduct of the War[6]

The top item on Abraham Lincoln's desk when he entered the White House the morning after his swearing-in was a letter from the Union commander at Fort Sumter reporting that his dwindling supplies would last only another six weeks and expressing his professional opinion that only reinforcement by at least 20,000 men could save the fort. The new president promptly asked his civilian and military advisers what they thought should and could be done.[7]

Lincoln was then buffeted with conflicting advice on how to save the Union and whether to try to defend the fort in Charleston harbor. Radical anti-slavery members of his own Republican Party pressured him to assert control over federal facilities in the seceding southern states while his new Secretary of State was in secret talks with representatives from those rebellious areas. Navy officials recommended re-supplying and strengthening Fort Sumter, but army leaders considered it indefensible. Instead, they favored a mission to Fort Pickens in Florida, the only other major federal outpost in the south still in Union control. The cabinet was 5–2 against any re-supply missions as too provocative.[8]

Abraham Lincoln believed that it would help the Union cause if the Confederates fired the first shot, but he was unsure how to achieve that goal. In fact, he was woefully ignorant of how to be commander-in-chief since he had only "a few months' token service as a junior militia officer in the Black Hawk war of 1832, where his military experience included a (lost) wrestling contest with another captain for whose company would occupy a choice campground."[9]

Lincoln sought information and consulted widely and frequently with his cabinet and other officials. He pleaded with the senior army general to keep him informed. "Would it impose too much labor on General Scott to make short, comprehensive daily reports to me of what occurs in his Department?"[10] He even sent friends to provide first-hand reports on conditions in Charleston. Despite the pessimistic views of army leaders, he decided to send Fort Sumter a relief mission by sea under the command of his attorney general's brother-in-law. He also secretly approved an army-sponsored plan to send supplies to Fort Pickens. Bureaucratic foul-ups prevented both missions from being carried out as planned – a harbinger of events throughout his administration. Both the army and navy planned to use the navy's premier warship, the *Powhatan*, and conflicting orders were sent to its base in New York City. The ship sailed toward Florida, with its captain disbelieving last-minute orders from the president to go to South Carolina.[11] On April 10, Confederate forces demanded the surrender of Fort Sumter and two days later began the bombardment that started the war.

The Civil War severely tested the established patterns of civil–military relations. By war's end, Lincoln had a senior general he trusted, a loyal and effective Secretary of War, a strategy acceptable to most officials, and a Congress more supportive than disruptive. But that state of affairs was far from inevitable. In the early stages of the war, there were serious conflicts between the president and Congress, between each branch of government and senior military officers, and between career military men and the new volunteers. These conflicts were sometimes political, sometimes personal, sometimes over strategy, sometimes over minor tactical or technical matters. Normal disagreements were exacerbated by poisonous levels of distrust. Over time, however, the constitutional system worked. The president became the *de facto* as well as the *de jure* commander-in-chief; Congress raised the revenues, wrote the necessary laws, and approved the key appointments; and military commanders deferred to the civilian leaders even when they held them in contempt.

Reluctant dictator

As soon as he learned of the attack on Fort Sumter, Lincoln convened his cabinet for the first of many lengthy sessions on handling the war. The cabinet was a fractious group, not least because Lincoln offered positions to four of his rivals for the Republican nomination, several of whom remained convinced that they were better qualified than the backwoods lawyer from Illinois. Throughout his term these ambitious politicians maneuvered against each other and even against the president, hoping to succeed him as the Republican nominee in 1864.[12]

Lincoln had won election with only 40 percent of the popular vote, winning the electoral votes of all of the free states except New Jersey, which split its votes between Douglas and Lincoln, and none in the south or border states. His Republican party had been formed only six years before. And as one historian described it, "The so-called party comprised several groups, under chieftains personally hostile and full of jealousy and rivalry, who had come together upon one question only." What they agreed on was opposition to extending slavery into the new territories of the west. They disagreed, either as a matter of principle or as a question of political tactics, on whether slavery should be abolished where it then existed. Their 1860 platform, which Lincoln had quoted in his inaugural address, had declared "the right of each state to order and control its own domestic institutions according to its own judgment exclusively."[13]

Preserving the union without abolishing existing slavery remained Lincoln's goal in the immediate aftermath of the attack on Fort Sumter. He wanted to prevent additional secessions that could make Washington vulnerable or make military action against the rebels infeasible.

On April 15, he issued a proclamation calling on the states to mobilize 75,000 men in their militias for Federal service and summoning the Congress into special session starting July 4. The newly mobilized troops were to take back the forts and other property seized from the Union so that the laws could be properly executed. Lincoln also appealed "to all loyal citizens to favor, facilitate, and aid this effort to maintain the honor, the integrity, and the existence of our National Union."[14]

Two days later Virginia voted to secede, and two days after that Lincoln ordered a blockade of southern ports to help put down what he called an insurrection. He remained concerned about Maryland, which was torn by pro-slavery and pro-Union factions. To secure the lines of communication and to prevent pro-secession uprisings, Lincoln declared martial law in Maryland on April 27 and allowed detentions without trial by suspending the writ of habeas corpus, the first of eight similar actions during the course of the war.[15]

Lincoln took many acts of borderline constitutionality, hoping and expecting that Congress would later authorize his emergency measures – though the lawmakers waited until March 1863, to authorize his suspension of the writ of habeas corpus. In one dramatic case, Union soldiers arrested John Merryman, who had allegedly burned bridges and destroyed telegraph wires during the April, 1861 riots near Baltimore. The case was heard by the Chief Justice, Roger Taney, who ruled that Lincoln's order was unconstitutional, since only Congress had the power to suspend the writ. Lincoln refused to comply with the ruling. Taney had to be content filing a report. Merryman was released a few weeks later when military authorities concluded that he could never be convicted by a Maryland jury.[16]

Lincoln also had to take steps to rein in some abolitionist firebrands, such as General Benjamin F. Butler, who ruled escaped slaves "contraband of war" and refused to return them to their owners. When the popular Republican General John C. Fremont proclaimed slaves in Missouri free, Lincoln revoked the order and shortly thereafter relieved Fremont of command. The president was still worried that abolitionist actions might drive Kentucky to secede, and that, he feared, would doom the Union cause. The most Lincoln could accept was the law passed by the special session of Congress in early August. It allowed confiscation of property – including slaves – but only if they had been directly employed by Confederate armed forces.[17]

Meanwhile, the cabinet members undertook their duties in support of the war. Secretary of State William Seward notified foreign governments of the US action; Navy Secretary Gideon Welles sent orders imposing the blockade; and Secretary of War Simon Cameron began planning for the equipping of the additional troops.

On May 3, Lincoln called for an increase in the size of the regular army by 23,000 as well as 18,000 more sailors and a force of 42,000 volunteers for a three-year enlistment.[18] In the ensuing weeks, troops streamed into Washington. Lincoln and his cabinet members often reviewed them and met with their commanders. Both sides prepared for what they thought would be a short, decisive battle.

The most senior military officer, however, proposed a different strategy, one of limited means for limited ends. General Winfield Scott was an aging, infirm, and perhaps senile relic of a former era. Already 75 in 1861, Scott had been a general in the War of 1812, was a hero in the war with Mexico, ran for president on the Whig Party in 1852 while still in uniform, and remained loyal to the Union despite his Virginia birth. He was called "Old Fuss and Feathers." In the spring of 1861 he devised a plan to strangle the south with a naval blockade of the coasts and naval and ground force seizure of the Mississippi River. This plan, dubbed "Anaconda", had the advantage of limiting Union casualties and the disadvantage of requiring time to assemble the necessary forces.[19]

Lincoln and the politicians did not want to wait. They wanted to use the 90-day volunteers in some kind of battle, and believed that the capture of the new Confederate capital at Richmond, Virginia, would bring a quick end to the war. At a strategy conference on June 29, Lincoln told the field commander, General Irwin McDowell, who wanted more time for training, "You are green, it is true, but they are green, also; you are all green alike."[20]

When that first major encounter came, on July 21 along the creek called Bull Run near the Virginia town of Manassas – Union forces tended to name their battles after streams, Confederates after nearby towns – the outcome was a powerful setback for the Union. Federal forces fled in disarray, shocking members of Congress who had ridden out to observe the anticipated Union victory.

Three months later, after Confederate forces established defensive positions along the Virginia border and General George McClellan prepared for combat without actually launching any attacks, Union forces did move against Ball's Bluff on the Potomac River. Union forces suffered a quick and ignominious failure, including the death of Colonel Edward Baker, a close friend of the president and Senator from Oregon. These two defeats prompted the Congress, when it met in December, to establish an investigative committee.[21]

Congress was also primed to investigate problems in contracting and supply for Union forces. The man in charge of supply was Simon Cameron, a former Democrat who had become the Republican party boss in Pennsylvania and US Senator when Lincoln nominated him to head the War Department. Lincoln liked Cameron and wanted a Pennsylvanian in his cabinet, but tried to withdraw his offer of a position after being besieged with numerous reports of Cameron's corruptness. Cameron reportedly ran his political machinery with bribery and intimidation. Another Pennsylvania Republican, Congressman Thaddeus Stevens, when asked by Lincoln whether Cameron was an honest man, replied, "I don't think he would steal a red hot stove." Even the incoming Vice President, Hannibal Hamlin of Maine, said that naming Cameron would have an "odor about it that will damn us as a party."[22]

Cameron soon lived up to his sullied reputation. Facing wartime urgency, Cameron ignored existing legal requirements for competitive bidding and awarding contracts to low bidders. He favored suppliers and middlemen from his home state and paid dearly for poor quality goods. As two historians of the period concluded, "Cameron conducted the War Department as if it were a political club house; he used contracts freely to pay off old political debts and to shower additional favors on his henchmen."[23] In one celebrated case, the War Department paid $58,200 plus $10,000 for transportation to acquire one thousand horses for a Kentucky cavalry regiment – 485 of which had to be rejected as diseased and worthless.[24] Lincoln confided to his secretary that Cameron had proved to be "utterly ignorant ... Selfish and openly discourteous to the President[,] Obnoxious to the country [and] Incapable of either organizing details or conceiving and advising general plans."[25] The final straw came in December 1861, when Cameron, without consulting with the president or informing him of his plan, released a report to Congress and the press calling for the creation of an army of former slaves – a policy Lincoln strongly opposed at the time.[26]

Lincoln responded to these setbacks not by changing strategy, but by changing personnel. In the fall, he decided to change the leadership of the army and the war department. He accepted the resignation of General Scott and forced the resignation of Secretary Cameron. In their places, he put General George McClellan and Edwin M. Stanton.

Coalition of rivals

These events of 1861 show that the Union leadership was hardly unified. Republicans were divided between abolitionists and union preservationists who were willing to tolerate slavery confined to the south. Democrats were split between those supporting war to preserve the union and those favoring negotiations for a peaceful settlement, either with separation or with reunion keeping slavery intact. Many of the generals considered themselves Democrats, and they hoped for an agreement that avoided massive bloodshed. McClellan and his West Point compatriots tended to favor European-style wars of maneuver rather than decisive battles or strategies of annihilation of enemy forces. Radicals dominated the Congress, and Lincoln was left to juggle the many disparate views.

The mood in Washington in January 1862, was captured by Congressman Henry Dawes of Massachusetts, who wrote to his wife: "Confidence in everybody is shaken to the very foundation. The credit of the country is ruined – its army impotent, its Cabinet incompetent, its servants rotten, its ruin inevitable."[27] Everyone hoped that McClellan and Stanton would be the heroes who would turn things around.

George McClellan had a distinguished career at West Point and in the war with Mexico. He had resigned his commission in 1857, in order to become an official of railroad companies in Ohio and Illinois. He was made a major general after the war broke out and was given command of the Army of the Potomac after McDowell's defeat at Bull Run. A lifelong Democrat, he had a low opinion of the Republican administration. As he wrote to his wife, "I can't tell you how disgusted I am becoming with these wretched politicians; they are the most despicable of men ... The Presdt [sic] is nothing more than a well meaning baboon."[28] He wrote of being "bored and annoyed" at an October 1861 cabinet meeting. "There are some of the greatest geese in the cabinet I have ever seen – enough to tax the patience of Job", he wrote.[29]

Lincoln made a valiant effort to consult with his top general, frequently visiting his home in the evening to discuss strategy. But McClellan rebuffed his commander-in-chief. In one notorious case, on November 13, the general returned home from a wedding party and went to bed, deliberately ignoring the president and secretary of state, who had been waiting over an hour to talk to him.[30] Lincoln would spend the next year cajoling, pushing, reassuring, and supporting McClellan before finally deciding to replace him.

Edwin M. Stanton was another inauspicious choice, but one who turned out to be a loyal, devoted, and very effective cabinet officer. He was a pro-union Democrat from Ohio who had been attorney general in the final months of the Buchanan administration. He had a passing acquaintance with Lincoln in 1855, when he was involved in the McCormick reaper patent case, in which the Illinois lawyer had been retained in case the trial were heard in Chicago. Stanton was rude and snobbish to all of his underlings, but Lincoln held no lasting grudge from the encounter. Stanton openly disparaged the new president in 1861, referring to him as "the original gorilla." He also wrote to just-departed President Buchanan, "No one speaks of Lincoln or any member of his cabinet with respect or regard."[31]

The Ohio lawyer had many friends in that cabinet and Lincoln wanted to give prominent positions to pro-war Democrats, so Stanton was a welcome addition when the president lost confidence in Cameron. Stanton was also well regarded in Congress and, perhaps ironically, by McClellan. Soon after Bull Run the general turned to the lawyer as a legal adviser and friend, frequently using Stanton's house as a refuge from other officials, even the president. Ultimately, however, McClellan bitterly concluded that "His purpose was to endeavor to climb upon my shoulder and then throw me down."[32]

McClellan became general-in-chief in November, when Scott was forced into retirement. Stanton took over the War Department in January, when Cameron was reassigned as Minister to Russia. The general continued his preparations for a spring offensive, while the secretary of war seized effective control of his department and, more broadly, of the running of the war.

Stanton took office determined to improve administration and push the army into action. As he wrote to Charles Dana, "As soon as I can get the machinery of the office working, the rats cleared out, and the rat-holes stopped, we shall *move*. This army has got to fight or run away; and while men are striving nobly in the West, the champagne and oysters on the Potomac must be stopped."[33]

The new secretary seized control of communications, both with field armies and the press, by moving the telegraph office, which had been at McClellan's headquarters, next to his own. This action also meant that the president was a frequent visitor, walking next door from the White House and often staying for hours at a time. Stanton set aside two rooms for McClellan to use as headquarters, but the disgruntled general seldom used them. The secretary also created a separate military telegraph system which, by the last year of the war, employed more than 1,000 men and stretched over 5,000 miles of lines.[34]

Stanton tightened the administration of military contracting with a return to competitive bidding and closer oversight. Through old friendships and persuasive powers he won funds from Congress to refurbish his department's dilapidated building and to hire several dozen additional personnel. He also won passage of a law giving the president power to seize the railroads and telegraph for military purposes. In fact, the railroads had been very cooperative, but Stanton used the law as a lever to negotiate reasonable rates, standardized gauges and signaling, and military cargo priority. He then used railroads to engineer the rapid supply of Union forces during and after key battles, as demonstrated at the time of Antietam and later Chattanooga.[35]

The civilian secretary tried to forge close professional ties with McClellan and advised the general on ways to improve his standing with the cabinet. Early on, the two men spent entire days together, in apparent harmony. But eventually Stanton, wanting an alternative, disinterested military viewpoint, hired a retired general, Ethan Allen Hitchcock, who had a distinguished military record and had been commandant at West Point. Hitchcock was often amazed at how willingly and earnestly Stanton accepted his military advice.[36]

The secretary cultivated close ties to Capitol Hill. He welcomed frequent meetings with key legislators. He deflected one investigator who had been making wild charges about disloyal officials by meeting with one of the congressman in question, going over his bulging files, and then dismissing one officer and three clerks. He made a special effort to engage with the joint committee set up to investigate the conduct of the war, attending many of its secret sessions and even using it to elicit information and uncover fraud.[37]

Surprisingly, Stanton also forged an extremely close and loyal relationship with the president. Lincoln warmed to the man he called his "Mars", telling a journalist that his cabinet officer was "utterly misjudged." One of the army telegraphers called the president and his secretary the heart and the head of the war. Grant later observed that "Stanton required a man like Lincoln to manage him", that Lincoln dominated his subordinate by "that gentle firmness."[38]

Each could veto the acts of the other, but Stanton would ultimately defer if he was confident that the president had reached a firm decision. Lincoln himself described the arrangement. "I want to oblige everybody when I can; and Stanton and I have an understanding that if I send an order to him which cannot be consistently granted, he is to refuse it. This he sometimes does."[39]

Stanton's biographers report an incident which illustrates this relationship.

> Once when Lincoln sent a petitioner to Stanton with a written order complying with his request, the man came back to report that Stanton

had not only refused to execute the order but had called Lincoln a damn fool. Lincoln, in mock astonishment, asked: 'Did Stanton call me a damn fool?' Being reassured on that point, the President remarked drolly: 'Well, I guess I had better step over and see Stanton about this. Stanton is usually right.'[40]

Organizing for victory

When it came to fighting the war in 1862, the warriors and politicians clashed repeatedly. McClellan and much of the officer corps disagreed with the president and secretary of war over grand strategy, domestic politics, military professionalism, and the command and control of major military operations.

On many issues related to the war and slavery, Lincoln tried to preserve his freedom of action and avoid premature commitments by claiming, "My policy is to have no policy." But he had a clear vision of what he thought the army should do: attack, attack repeatedly, and destroy the Confederate army. He disparaged what he called "strategy", but what he meant was the Napoleonic war of maneuver. He favored decisive battles with Union victories as the best way to end the war quickly. What today's soldiers would call the enemy's "center of gravity", the capture of which would lead to its collapse, was to Lincoln the rebel army. "I think *Lee's* army and not *Richmond* is your true objective point", he wrote in 1863, expressing a view he held throughout the war after the initial battle at Bull Run. McClellan and his successors, until Grant, seemed to prefer wars of maneuver and the capture of political objectives like the Confederate capital.[41]

Domestic politics also divided the Republican civilian politicians from much of the military leadership. While some generals were viscerally anti-politician – General William T. Sherman complained to General U.S. Grant, "I am not a politician, never voted but once in my life, & never read a political platform"[42] – many were professed Democrats.

Of the 110 generals in the Union army in 1861, according to a Republican Senator, 80 were Democrats. According to a Republican congressman in 1863, four-fifths of the brigadier- and major-generals in the Union army were Democrats. As one historian has noted, "Most Union generals, through whatever mixture of conviction and self-interest, displayed rather than disguised their political leanings."[43]

Those political leanings should not be surprising, however, since most senior officers had risen in the ranks under Democratic administrations and with partisan sponsorship. Until Lincoln took office, Democrats had controlled the White House since 1828 except for two single terms won by war heroes – William Henry Harrison and Zachary Taylor – running as Whigs. Democrats had also controlled both houses of Congress for all but six of those years. Moreover, the Republicans were a new national party, having elected its first members to Congress only in 1854.

The newly empowered Republicans remained suspicious of the officer corps, and even critical of West Point. Many viewed the military academy as "the hotbed in which rebellion was hatched", and they decried the many regular army officers defected to the Confederacy – about one in every four in the army in 1861. Republicans claimed, however, that no enlisted men turned traitor.[44] The distrust between career soldiers and the militia leaders, rooted in the Framers' suspicions about a standing army and continuing through most of American history, had political overtones in the Civil War.

In the mobilization for war, there were essentially Republican and Democratic armies. Mostly Democratic officers led the regular army regiments, while the newly formed volunteer units were often peopled and led by avowed Republicans who were willing to fight for their political beliefs regarding slavery and the Union. Of course, many pro-war Democrats were commissioned to lead volunteer units, but they too were taking up arms for the sake of their political views. Major General Jacob D. Cox, founder of the Republican party in Ohio and never before in the military, explained the rise of political generals.

> In an armed struggle which grew out of a great political contest, it was inevitable that eager political partisans should be among the most active in the new volunteer organizations. They called meetings, addressed the people to arouse their enthusiasm, urged enlistments, and often set the example by enrolling their own names first.[45]

Lincoln claimed that "in considering military merit … I discard politics."[46] But in fact he was quite adroit in building a bipartisan administration and army with careful attention to political affiliations and factors. The general-in-chief after McClellan, Henry Halleck, complained, "I have done everything in my power here to separate military appointments and commands from politics … but the task is hopeless."[47] What the president and Stanton did do, however, was to quash those officers who tried to play politics against the administration. As Stanton wrote to Lincoln in January, 1863, "[Army officers who] indulge in the sport [of politics] must risk being gored. They can not, having exposed themselves, claim the procedural protections and immunities of the military profession."[48]

Warriors and politicians also clashed over their respective roles and responsibilities, by way of differing views of military professionalism. Lincoln went out of his way to show deference and respect for military commanders, such as by going to see Scott and McClellan rather than summoning them to the White House. His letters to his commanders were unfailingly polite, even when remonstrating them or issuing clear orders. In a letter to General Joseph Hooker, for example, he praised the officer's abstinence from politics as well as his ambition and self confidence. But he also pointed out, "there are some things in regard to which I am not quite satisfied with you", and went on to criticize, as we shall see, Hooker's call for a dictatorship in Washington.[49]

On paper, Lincoln subscribed to the notion that military operational plans were beyond his purview. Writing to Grant in 1864, he declared, "The particulars of your plans I neither know or seek to know. You are vigilant and self-reliant; and, pleased with this, I wish not to obtrude any constraints or restraints upon you." Only a few days later, however, he ordered specific changes in Grant's plans for the Red River campaign. In fact, as Eliot Cohen has demonstrated, Lincoln remained "deeply immersed in the details of military operations", exercising strong oversight, though he did it more by questioning, prodding, and suggesting than by direct orders.[50]

The commander-in-chief also made several visits to the front lines to confer with his generals and to observe the condition of the men and their equipment. He and Stanton also sent their own bureaucratic spy, Charles Dana, who was ostensibly investigating military pay problems, but in fact was instructed by Stanton that "your real duty will be to report to me every day what you see." Dana was even given a special cipher to use in his reports.[51]

Generals like McClellan, however, resented political intrusions, either by the president or the investigative congress. Few of the congressional fire-brands had any military experience, yet they gratuitously offered their advice on strategy and tactics. The commanders resented the pressure to launch attacks before their troops were trained and ready to their professional standard. The ritual complaint from the politicians became, why don't they attack? Many of the West Point professionals also disliked the presence of so many newly commissioned generals who had political connections but little military experience. These cultural clashes were not unique to nineteenth century America, but they did at times infringe upon the conduct of the war.

In one famous incident, Lincoln dismissed from service a politically well-connected major, John Key, who was overheard declaring that the army wanted a negotiated peace and was avoiding major battles. "That is not the game", Key said. "The object is that neither army shall get much advantage of the other; that both shall be kept in the field till they are exhausted, when we will make a compromise and save slavery." When Key sought reinstatement, the president refused, saying "I had been brought to fear that there was a certain class of officers in the army, not very inconsiderable in number, who were playing a game to not beat the enemy when they could, on some peculiar notion as to proper way of saving the Union .... I dismissed you as an example and a warning to that supposed class."[52]

In January 1862, Lincoln held several meetings to discuss the conduct of the war. On January 6, he met with the new congressional committee investigating the conduct of the war and heard their criticisms of McClellan and their demands for decisive action. He said he had no knowledge of McClellan's plans or the reasons for delay, but that he had no intention of interfering with the commander. Afterward, he wrote to McClellan, who had been confined to his sickbed for several days, urging him to meet with the committee members as soon as possible.[53]

On January 10 he began a series of meetings with his cabinet and senior generals. At one point he visited the Quartermaster General, Montgomery Meigs, and told him, "The people are impatient; [Treasury Secretary] Chase has no money, and he tells me he can raise no money; the Gen[eral] of the Army has typhoid fever. The bottom is out of the tub. What shall I do?"[54] McClellan finally showed up on January 13, but still refused to give details of his plans for fear of a leak. The same day, Lincoln replaced Cameron with Stanton, and the new secretary of war began holding lengthy meetings with the congressional committee.[55]

Responding to the political pressures for action, Lincoln then prodded McClellan on January 27 by issuing General War Order No. 1, which commanded all Union armies to make a coordinated advance on all fronts by Washington's Birthday, February 22. Four days later he issued a special War Order No. 1 to the Army of the Potomac, directing it "after providing safely for the defense of Washington," to seize Manassas Junction and advance toward Richmond by that date.[56]

McClellan objected in a 22-page letter, revealing that he preferred to attack Richmond from the east. Lincoln sought the views of McClellan's division commanders and found eight in favor and four opposed, but only two of the four supported the president's idea of a direct assault. "We saw ten generals afraid to fight", commented Stanton.[57] But Lincoln acquiesced in the judgment of the men in the field.

On February 19, Stanton corralled McClellan to meet with some members of the congressional investigating committee. When the general explained that one reason for delay was to secure a line of retreat, Senator Benjamin Wade of Massachusetts exploded. The Army of the Potomac, he said, could "whip the whole Confederacy if they were given the chance; if I were commander, I would lead them across the Potomac, and they should not come back until they had won a victory and the war ended, or they came back in their coffins."[58] The general noted that Stanton did not once speak up in his defense.

By early March, however, with McClellan still preparing but not advancing, Lincoln came under renewed pressure from Congress and his advisers to discipline his top general. The committee members urged the removal of McClellan, but had no one to propose in his place. "Anybody will do for you", Lincoln told Senator Wade, "but I must have somebody."[59] Stanton agreed with the congressional recommendation for a reorganization of the army into *corps d'armée* instead of the existing division structure. On March 8 Lincoln endorsed McClellan's plan for the peninsula campaign but ordered the reorganization of the army. He also conditioned his approval on McClellan's leaving enough forces behind to secure Washington. On March 11, he took away his commander's title as general-in-chief, leaving him only in charge of the Army of the Potomac.[60] A month later, he warned the general

Figure 3.1   Abraham Lincoln and General George McClellan at Antietam, 1862 (Library of Congress)

that the country was watching him, that "it is indispensable to *you* that you strike a blow. I am powerless to help this."[61]

From March until Henry Halleck was promoted to general-in-chief in July, Lincoln and Stanton effectively ran the war. They faced a difficult task since there was no unity of command, but eight separate commands reporting to Stanton. The amateur generals did reasonably well, coordinating operations in various theaters, including an offensive in the west. Halleck turned out to be indecisive, however, forcing Lincoln and Stanton to maintain close control.[62]

Meanwhile, McClellan's move toward Richmond was stalled and then turned back by the new commander of the Army of Northern Virginia, Robert E. Lee. Anxious and shaken, McClellan wired a hysterical message to Stanton. "If I save this army now, I tell you plainly that I owe not thanks to you or to any other persons in Washington. You have done your best to sacrifice this army."[63] Lincoln responded with a promise of reinforcements, but faced continued pressure to replace his failing commander.

Lee then moved north, winning a second battle at Bull Run at the end of August and attacking into Maryland in September. Desperate to defend the capital, Lincoln overruled his cabinet by putting McColln in charge of forces around Washington. After the bloodiest single day of the war, in the battle at Antietam Creek, Lee headed south, allowing the Union to claim a victory. Lincoln ordered McClellan to follow Lee and deliver a knockout blow, but the Union general claimed logistical problems.

New team, new strategy

These events – the continuing, inconclusive, deadly war with no immediate prospect of victory – helped convince Lincoln to change his war aims, using the sense of victory after Antietam as the occasion to announce it. Until then, the president had insisted that his only goal was to restore the Union. He avoided the issue of slavery. But by the late summer of 1862 he decided to announce his intention to proclaim the emancipation of slaves in the south, at least in those areas which had not returned to the Union by January 1, 1863. He knew this would be popular in Republican areas, and he hoped to strengthen his party in the 1862 congressional elections. He also had to deal with the practical problems raised as Union forces moved into rebel territory and had to do something about the slaves they encountered.

Lincoln also realized that McClellan did not favor the kind of vicious, all-out war that the president believed was necessary to defeat the rebels. The two men made clear their differing views in July, when they met at Harrison's Landing, Virginia. The general gave the president a long letter, arguing that the war "should be conducted upon the highest principles known to Christian Civilization." He opposed "confiscation of property, political executions of persons" and "forcible abolition of slavery."[64] Lincoln and the Congress were moving in the opposite direction, both with a new confiscation act liberating the slaves of those who supported the rebellion and with orders by General John Pope, approved by Stanton, ordering his army to live off the country, to not worry about protecting the private property of rebels, and to arrest all disloyal males and females. As Stanton told a journalist who asked about the treatment of captured guerrillas, "Let them swing."[65]

Immediately after the 1862 elections, Lincoln finally ousted McClellan, turning command over the General Ambrose Burnside, the first of several officers who tried and failed to achieve a decisive victory over the next year and were promptly replaced. After suffering heavy casualties at Fredericksburg, Lincoln gave command to General Joseph Hooker. But the president gave the new commander an explicit warning:

> I have heard, in such a way as to believe it, of your recently saying that both the the Army and the Government needed a Dictator. Of course it was not *for* this, but in spite of it, that I have given you the command, Only those generals who gain successes, can set up

dictators. What I now ask of you is military success, and I will risk the dictatorship.[66]

Within five months, however, Hooker had been defeated at Chancellorsville and was refusing to defend Harper's Ferry as Lee moved north. Hooker resigned in protest, and Lincoln selected General George Meade to take command – just two days before the two armies stumbled into the giant battle at Gettysburg. Once again, the Union prevailed, Lee retreated, and the Union commander failed to attack the withdrawing troops. Lincoln wrote a tough letter to Meade – "Your golden opportunity is gone, and I am distressed immeasurably because of it" – but then decided not to send it. Meade, learning of the president's dismay, offered his resignation but was persuaded by General Halleck to withdraw it.[67]

Meade held important commands for the duration of the war. But he seemed to have no grand plan for victory, and Lincoln turned instead to a newly victorious general in the west, U.S. Grant, who did. Grant believed in, and practiced successfully, a war of annihilation of the enemy. He was willing to suffer heavy casualties in order to defeat the enemy. As he told one officer, "The art of war is simple enough. Find out where the enemy is. Get at him as soon as you can. Strike him as hard as you can and as often as you can, and keep moving on."[68]

Lincoln put Grant in command of the western armies in October, then brought him back to Washington in March 1864, to give him supreme command of the Union armies, with the newly revived rank of Lieutenant General. Grant pushed on, heedless of heavy casualties, against Lee's forces. General William T. Sherman moved from Tennessee across Georgia, taking his scorched earth campaign directly to southern civilians, and capturing Atlanta on September 2.

Relations among the civilian and military leaders were surprisingly good during 1864. General Halleck dismissed reports of high level quarrels as "all 'bosh.'" One of Lincoln's secretaries said that "the stories of Grant's quarreling with the Secretary of War are gratuitous lies. Grant quarrels with no one."[69] And Grant himself wrote an extraordinary letter to Lincoln in May:

> From my first entrance into the volunteer service of the country to the present day I have never had cause of complaint, never have expressed or implied a complaint against the administration or the Secretary of War for throwing any embarrassment in the way of my vigorously prosecuting what appeared to be my duty. Indeed, since the promotion which placed me in command of all the armies ... I have been astonished at the readiness with which everything asked for has been yielded, without even an explanation being asked.[70]

Despite this outward harmony, however, Lincoln was acutely conscious of the impending presidential elections. McClellan was preparing to run against the president for the Democrats and the influential *New York Herald* was promoting Grant as a candidate. Lincoln may have named Meade to replace Hooker because Meade had been born abroad and was considered ineligible to run for president. Only when Lincoln had received a letter from Grant pledging that nothing could persuade him to be a candidate did the president support the enactment of a law reestablishing the rank of Lieutenant General, a measure pushed in the Congress as a reward to Grant.[71]

Congress at war

In the nineteenth century, Congress was still a part-time legislature, typically meeting only three months per year, from early December until March 3. Every other year's session was lame-duck, peopled by members elected two years before and meeting after the latest balloting. Lincoln accelerated the convening of the new thirty-seventh Congress by calling a special session in July of 1861 rather than waiting for the normal time in December. The Senate alone had met for three weeks following Lincoln's inauguration in order to receive and act on nominations for the cabinet and lesser posts, including military officers. But the Senators had finished their work and adjourned two weeks before the attack on Fort Sumter.

Returning on July 4, the new thirty-seventh Congress spent a busy month responding to Lincoln's call with a burst of legislative activity. Republicans had controlled the House of Representatives during the second half of Buchanan's presidency, then gained majorities in both houses in the 1860 elections. Lincoln's party had a 33–15 lead over the Democrats in the Senate, with three from other parties, and a commanding 108–44 majority in the House, with 31 from other parties.[72]

Legislators took seriously their constitutional powers to raise and support armies and to provide and maintain a navy, as well as to set the rules for the armed forces. Senator Benjamin Wade of Massachusetts expressed the Legislative Branch view of things when he said that the President might be Commander-in-Chief, "but Congress, the legislative power sitting superior to him or any the magistrate in the nation, may regulate, modify, and direct whatever principles they please [that] their chief commander shall act upon and execute."[73]

While the president enforced civilian control through his chain of command, Congress asserted its own civilian control through its powers of lawmaking and funding. Congress also had enormous influence over the selection of military personnel, starting with its authority to nominate men to attend the academies at West Point and Annapolis, the entry points for commissioned officers. While congressmen did not have explicit patronage power over military appointments, as they did over most civilian positions, they frequently recommended officers for key assignments in their states and took personal interest in their careers. As two historians of the patronage system concluded, "Congressmen or Congressional delegations usually gave the President the names of those whom they wished appointed as brigadiers, major generals, and lesser officers."[74]

Many in Congress were more radical than the president, more willing to make the war about slavery rather than simply preserving the Union. On July 9, for example, the House passed a resolution declaring that soldiers had no duty to capture and return fugitive slaves. After wrangling over more extreme measures, Congress finally passed, on August 6, a compromise measure confiscating only that property used "in aid of the rebellion" – that is, only slaves actually employed in arms or labor against the Union could be freed. In the Senate, Henry Wilson of Massachusetts, chairman of the military affairs committee, met resistance to his measure retroactively approving Lincoln's call for volunteers, increase of the regular army, blockade of southern ports, and suspension of the writ of habeas corpus. After much debate, the Senate approved all but the language relating to the writ.[75] To fund the war, it enacted America's first income tax.

With the Senate in session, the president submitted list after list of military nominations, most of which were routinely and promptly confirmed – over 10,000 in the course of the war. The military affairs committee acted without partisan splits on appointments. But its chairman, Senator Wilson of Massachusetts, did refuse to confirm any officers who had returned fugitive slaves to their masters.[76]

While passing laws to organize and equip the rapidly expanding army, Congress also decided to increase its oversight of the process. In July the House established a special committee to investigate reports of fraud and mismanagement in government contracting. That committee later exposed scandals in Missouri under the regime of General Fremont. Senator Wilson welcomed visits by officers and enlisted men who wished to tell his committee of their views and problems.[77]

Although Congress was out of session from early August until December, some members continued to push for offensive actions. After the Union defeat at Ball's Bluff in October, for example, three Senators harangued General McClellan and then met with Lincoln to press their views.[78]

The union defeats at Bull Run and Ball's Bluff prompted legislators in both houses to create an investigative committee when Congress reconvened in December. A New York congressman introduced a resolution calling for information to be provided regarding Ball's Bluff. In the Senate, one member proposed a committee of inquiry into both recent defeats and then, when others wanted to add additional topics to the committee's agenda, Senator Grimes of Iowa proposed a joint committee to examine all aspects of the war, with "the power to send for persons and papers." Senator Sherman of Ohio noted that voting appropriations was easy, "but if we ignore the high duty imposed upon us as representatives of the people to investigate the conduct of the war and of all the officers of the Government, we neglect the chief duty that is now imposed on us." Both houses agreed, and the Joint Committee on the Conduct of the War (JCCW) was established on December 20, with three Senators and four Representatives, including one Democrat from each chamber. Senator Benjamin Wade of Massachusetts was named chairman. None of the original members had any prior military experience, and all but one were lawyers. Radicals had a 4–3 majority over moderates.[79]

The JCCW had the tools available to any congressional committee – oversight, subpoena, publicity, presumptive right of consultation – and it used them vigorously. Some historians see the committee as a hindrance to the war effort, treating several senior officers unfairly and trying to impose its strategic ideas on the administration.[80] That was certainly the view of two men who later became president – Woodrow Wilson and Harry Truman – and who fought to prevent creation of such an intrusive committee during the two world wars.

I believe that the JCCW should be seen as an ordinary and legitimate instrument of congressional prerogatives. It had an important oversight function, but its members had their own political motivations, and they used their committee positions to advance themselves and their views. The president and secretary of war conferred with committee members frequently, not only because of any threat of investigation but also because these men represented important segments of public opinion, whose support was ultimately vital for the war effort. Some senior commanders resented being called before the committee – an attitude not uncommon even today – but that is an important feature of the American system of civilian control.

Two facts in particular defend the advantages of having such a committee: it worked hard and it worked in secret. Committee members met almost daily when Congress was in session, gathering information and conducting hearings. It held 272 official sessions during three and a half years. Its members initiated meetings with the president at least eight times, and with Secretary Stanton even more often. And although the committee's 11 reports were highly critical of many aspects of the war, these reports were released only after weeks and months of secret sessions. There was no parade of leaks to shape news coverage and public opinion.[81]

Members traveled widely to gain first hand impressions and to understand what they were investigating. Subcommittees went to Boston, New York, Annapolis, Illinois, and to the battlefields in Virginia, Kentucky, and Tennessee. Besides investigating military disasters, the committee looked into several operations on which it filed no report. It also looked into many allegations of contracting and supply problems. A further proof of respect for the JCCW, lawmakers frequently referred press allegations to the committee and requested investigations.[82]

On the other hand, it is true that the committee had its favorites, like General Fremont, whom it defended despite significant incriminating inform- ation. And it had its targets, like McClellan and General Charles P. Stone of Ball's Bluff, whom it pursued unmercifully.[83] It also had a perhaps naïve strategy – attack, attack, always attack – which was attractive to civilians sitting in Washington. But these views were no different from those of many in the cabinet, elsewhere in Congress, or in the press.

On several occasions, the committee was the conscience pushing Lincoln toward emancipation or the "bad cop" he could cite when politely urging generals to take the offensive. Its very records provide key documentation for our understanding of the war and the many confusions attendant to its conduct. Commanders were probably more careful because they anticipated questions from the legislators. Speeches by its chairman, drawing on its reports, were widely circulated by the Republican party during the 1864 presidential campaign.[84]

Navy Secretary Gideon Welles reflected a critical view of the JCCW when he said, "There must be something in these terrible reports, but I distrust Congressional committees. They exaggerate." The members defended themselves and explained their purpose in an 1863 report: "Your committee therefore concluded that they would best perform their duty by endeavoring to obtain such information in respect to the conduct of the war as would best enable them to advise what mistakes had been made in the past and the proper course to be pursued in the future." Chairman Wade explained to McClellan:

> We are here armed with the whole power of both houses of Congress. They have made it our duty to inquire into the whole conduct of the war; into every department of it. We do not want to do anything that will result in harm or wrong. But we do want to know, and we must know if we can, what is to be done, for the country is in jeopardy.[85]

Congressional oversight was not omnipresent, however, for even during some of the most important periods of the war the legislators were out of session for extended periods. Most members were away from Washington during August 6 to December 2, 1861; July 17 to December 1, 1862, March 14 to December 7, 1863; and July 4 to December 5, 1864. In other words, Congress was absent during the Shenandoah Valley and Antietam campaigns in 1862, during the musical chairs of generals in 1863, and during Grant's long, bloody campaign of 1864.

One of the most difficult issues faced by Congress was the question of conscription. In July 1862, the legislators approved amendments to the Militia Act reiterating the obligation of all able-bodied males 18–45 years of age and requiring up to nine months' federal service. Using this new law, Lincoln on August 4 announced a draft of 300,000 men for nine months for all those states which had not met their quotas of volunteers for three-year terms. Practical problems prevented this measure from ever having real effect, so the lame-duck Congress on its final day, March 3, 1863, passed a comprehensive conscription bill. This measure required house-to-house canvasses for draftees, but allowed men to avoid service by finding a substitute or by paying a commutation fee of $300.[86]

This law came about through the normal legislative process of pulling, hauling, and compromise. Both bills, in 1862 and 1863, became vehicles for amendments dealing with emancipation and military service for blacks. Shifting majorities passed or defeated amendments trying to deal with these topics, along with the underlying conscription issue.[87] Senator Wilson, chairman of the Military Affairs Committee, offered a floor amendment, previously rejected by his committee, for the $300 commutation fee. An important factor behind Wilson's support of this fee, in addition to pressure from wealthy constituents, was to help highly industrialized Massachusetts maintain its labor supply. Later he persuaded Stanton to increase enlistment bonuses so as to minimize the need for draftees. The draft riots of 1863 and other public opposition drove Congress in 1864 to amend the law, repealing the commutation fee except for conscientious objectors. On another occasion, Wilson won enactment of a measure granting equal pay for black and white soldiers, and making it retroactive to the date of enlistment.[88] These actions display Congress in action on the details of major legislation. Members were following their individual policy and political judgments; the executive branch was not the key player.

As things turned out, the major impact of the draft law was to stimulate volunteer enlistments. In the first draft call of 1863, 255,373 were called; 117,986 hired substitutes; 86,724 paid the commutation fee; and 4,316 failed to show; only 46,347 – 18 percent – actually entered the ranks.[89] Overall, only six percent of the 2.7 million men who served in the Union army during the Civil War were directly drafted.[90]

The politics of war

Elections strongly influenced the course of the war. Lincoln's victory in 1860 drove many southern states to secede. The prospect of congressional elections in 1862 led the president and congressional Republicans to push for a strong offensive to end the war or at least demonstrate Union resolve. The sense that Antietam was a Union victory, as Lee retreated into Virginia, reassured Lincoln enough to announce his planned emancipation proclamation. But the Republican losses in the 1862 elections made Lincoln more radical on war aims and tactics, and perhaps more desperate to find a winning general. In 1864, Lincoln was unsure of winning re-nomination until the Baltimore convention in June and fearful of defeat at least until the confidence-boosting fall of Atlanta in September.

In 1862, the Republicans held on to 33 of 52 Senate seats, but saw their lead in the House drop from 108–44 – plus 34 of other parties – to 85–72 – with 27 from other parties. These results could deny them a working majority.[91]

Stanton reacted to these setbacks by working to guarantee a strong Republican turnout in the 1863 state elections and in the 1864 presidential contest. He made sure that Ohio defeated a leading peace Democrat running for Governor, for example, by arranging for Ohio troops to vote in the field and allowing war department clerks to travel home with free railroad passes. Lame-duck Democrats tried to pass a bill censuring Stanton and forbidding military officers from interfering in civil elections, but the measure failed.[92]

In 1864, Stanton pressured military officials to help Republican state agents and to thwart the Democrats. Entire regiments were furloughed home to crucial states. As Charles Dana commented, "all the power and influence of the War Department … were employed to secure the re-election of Mr. Lincoln."

Stanton knew how strongly the men in uniform supported the president: Lincoln got 53 percent of the votes overall, but a rousing 78 percent of those of Union soldiers.[93]

Political considerations also influenced military goals and strategy. They help explain why Lincoln moved to the radical position on freeing slaves and using them in the army. They help explain why northerners embraced Sherman's attacks on the people of Georgia and why they accepted the heavy casualties under Grant, which led to victories over Lee. Congress reflected the divisions within the country, and Lincoln steered a course through them.

At the end, however, there was still basic split – between Lincoln and the moderates who favored a benevolent reconstruction and the radicals who demanded southern capitulation and black empowerment. The president used a pocket veto to kill the Wade–Davis bill in 1864, which would have imposed a congressional plan antithetical to Lincoln's approach. For example, it would have required a majority of each seceded state to take an oath of past as well as future loyalty in order to reestablish their own local governments. Lincoln favored a prospective loyalty oath and a 10 percent threshold of citizens taking the oath.[94]

As the Confederate forces seemed on the verge of surrender, Lincoln took special measures to ensure that his more lenient approach was followed. On March 3, 1865, he specifically ordered Grant not to "decide, discuss, or confer upon any political questions" with General Lee. "Such questions the president holds in his own hand; and will submit them to no military conferences or conversations." When Sherman, shortly after Lincoln's assassination, offered generous terms to General Joseph Johnston – including provisions on the recognition of southern governments, referral of measures to the Supreme Court, and a general amnesty – Stanton ordered the deal revoked, an action which led the angry Sherman to refuse to shake the War Secretary's hand during a grand review of Union troops a few weeks later.[95]

Assassination and aftermath

The struggle over control of the military continued even after the end of the war and the assassination of the president. Indeed, Andrew Johnson was impeached and nearly removed from office because he refused to obey the law giving Congress the power over the appointment of the Secretary of War and other officials. The underlying dispute was that Johnson favored a more forgiving policy toward the former rebels, while the radical Republicans in Congress insisted on more punishment for southern whites and more empowerment for southern blacks. As the occupying force, the US Army was caught in the cross-pressures.

At the apex of the power struggle was Secretary of War Stanton, who sided with the radicals. Asked to resign by President Johnson in August 1867, Stanton refused, relying on the Tenure of Office Act, passed over Johnson's veto, which prohibited the removal of cabinet officers until their successors had been confirmed by the Senate. He did, however, step aside and let General Grant act as interim secretary until December, when the reconvening Congress passed a resolution supporting him. Stanton then encamped in his office and refused repeated presidential orders to surrender power. On the very days that Johnson tried to force the issue, impeachment resolutions were filed in the House and reported by Committee in February 1868. Stanton remained at his post until May, when the Senate fell one vote short of convicting and ousting the president.[96]

Stanton resigned; Grant was chosen as Republican candidate for president in the fall elections; and Reconstruction proceeded as intended by the Congress. The era of congressional dominance of government, briefly interrupted by the demands of Civil War, resumed. It was destined to last for over three decades, until Theodore Roosevelt came to power. In the interim, the army was punished for having been the implementer of Reconstruction. A key feature of the settlement of the disputed presidential election of 1876, which awarded Rutherford B. Hayes the electoral votes to become president, was the removal of US troops from the southern states and passage of the *posse comitatus* law, which still forbids the use of troops for domestic law enforcement.

The legacy of congressional involvement in the war was also negative. When Congress declared war against Germany in 1917, President Woodrow Wilson vigorously opposed any effort to create the equivalent of the Joint Committee on the Conduct of the War. In time, however, the Senate Foreign Relations Committee became the focal point for skeptical oversight and ultimately the engine of defeat of the Versailles peace treaty. In the Second World War, then Senator Harry Truman, mindful of the precedents, actively worked to limit his committee, the Special Committee to Investigate the National Defense Program, to matters of military contracting. He did not try to oversee the strategy or conduct of the war.

The Civil War poisoned American civil–military relations so much that it took several generations for the warriors and politicians to recover from its effects.

4 Managing the Vietnam War

Now, I don't need ten generals to come in here ten times and tell me to bomb. I want some solutions, I want some answers.

> Lyndon Johnson to Army General Harold Johnson[1]

Maybe we military men were all weak. Maybe we should have stood up and pounded the table …. At times I wonder, 'Why did I go along with this kind of stuff?'

> CNO Admiral David McDonald[2]

It is high time, we believe, to allow the military voice to be heard in connection with the tactical details of military operations."

> Senate Armed Services Subcommittee, August 1967[3]

I don't want any more of this crap about the fact that we couldn't hit this target or that one. This is your chance to use military power effectively to win this war, and if you don't, I'll consider you responsible.

> Richard Nixon to Admiral Thomas Moorer, December 1972[4]

Lyndon Johnson inherited a war along with the presidency in November 1963, a war he was never sure how to win but dared not to lose. He also inherited a group of advisors, civilian and military, who clashed over the most basic questions of the use of military force. On Capitol Hill, a sympathetic Congress supported administration policies until the costs mounted and the internal disagreements surfaced. The new president had been a loyal and enthusiastic supporter of John F. Kennedy's policies. He had traveled to Vietnam and proclaimed President Ngo Dinh Diem the "Winston Churchill of Southeast Asia."[5] He endorsed the deployment of 16,000 US military advisors as a necessary measure to block the advance of Communism. As a seasoned politician, Johnson was particularly concerned about avoiding the outcomes which befell Harry Truman, who tolerated the Communist takeover of China, sent American troops into ground combat in Korea, ignored warnings of provoking Chinese intervention, had to fire his popular but insubordinate military commander, and then lost the battle for public opinion regarding his military policies. In all of his subsequent decisions, one can see Johnson's preoccupation with maintaining military, congressional, and public support for his conduct of the war in Vietnam. In his first days as president, Johnson told his advisors, "I am not going to be the president who saw Southeast Asia go the way China went." But he also made clear that Vietnam was not his highest priority: reelection was. As he told the Joint Chiefs at a reception just before Christmas 1963, "Just get me elected, and then you can have your war."[6]

The biggest threat to Johnson was Senator Barry Goldwater (R-Ariz), the popular and outspoken conservative, an unabashed anti-communist who favored "a new winning strategy" in Vietnam and hinted that he would unleash the military to do what they thought best.[7] He also had opposed Kennedy's agreements with the Soviet Union on nuclear weapons testing and was willing to delegate use of nuclear weapons to military commanders. He easily won the Republican presidential nomination in July 1964, setting the stage for a titanic struggle with the new president.

Despite the ongoing conflict in Southeast Asia, Johnson was determined to be the peace candidate. "The United States intends no rashness and seeks no wider war", he declared. He also warned, "We don't want American boys to do the fighting for Asian boys. We don't want ... to get tied down in a land war in Asia."[8] In disavowing belligerent intentions, Johnson was following the practice that helped Woodrow Wilson in 1916 and Franklin Roosevelt in 1940

Declaration of war

In the spring of 1964, Johnson discussed with his advisors the possibility of seeking congressional endorsement of his policies. Such action had the diplomatic advantage of demonstrating American unity and the political advantage of removing Vietnam as a partisan issue in the upcoming elections. "By God,", Johnson declared, "I'm going to be damn sure those guys are with me when we begin this thing."[9] Consultations continued with key congressional figures during the summer. The measure was modeled on those previously passed by Congress in 1955 regarding Formosa (Taiwan) in 1957 regarding the Middle East, and in 1962 regarding Cuba. In those instances, the joint resolutions were seen as warnings to deter hostile actions more than as authorizations for major combat.

On August 2, probably in response to US covert actions against North Vietnam, torpedo boats fired on the US destroyer *Maddox*. When a similar attack was reported two days later – though the evidence later seemed quite ambiguous – Johnson decided it was necessary to retaliate, and to ask for congressional support. He ordered air strikes – 64 sorties against North Vietnamese patrol boat bases and a fuel complex – and sent the draft resolution to Congress for immediate action.[10]

Figure 4.1   Lyndon Johnson meeting with Joint Chiefs of Staff, 1964 (LBJ Library)

Angered by the apparent attacks and determined to show toughness and unity in an election year, Congress quickly passed the administration's resolution by nearly unanimous votes – 414–0 in the House, 88–2 in the Senate. The measure declared that "the Congress approves and supports the determination of the President, as commander in chief, to take all necessary measures to repel any armed attack against the forces of the United States and to prevent further aggression." It also proclaimed that "the United States is therefore prepared, as the President determines, to take all necessary steps, including the use of armed force, to assist any member or protocol states of the Southeast Asia Collective Defense Treaty requesting assistance in defense of its freedom."[11] In a face-saving measure of dubious legality, Congress included a provision saying that the resolution could be terminated by a non-vetoable concurrent resolution of both houses of Congress.

Later on, officials pointed to the Gulf of Tonkin resolution as the "funct-ional equivalent" of a declaration of war.[12] State Department lawyers argued that the resolution was not necessary to carry out the war because of the inherent powers of the president and the ratification of the 1954 SEATO treaty that committed the signatories to mutual defense against communism. Nevertheless, repeal of the resolution became a goal of antiwar congressmen, at least as a symbolic action against continued US participation in the war.

The military and legislative actions in August muted Vietnam as a political issue in the following weeks. In the final balloting, Johnson trounced Goldwater, winning 61 percent of the vote and all but six states. He also gained huge, better than 2–1 Democratic majorities in the Congress, setting the stage for what he called the Great Society.[13] But while Congress busied itself with voting rights, anti-poverty and medicare legislation, national security officials turned their attention to the deteriorating situation in South Vietnam.

Maxwell Taylor, the former JCS Chairman, went to Saigon as Ambassador in July 1964 and soon began sending gloomy cables about the political and military capacities of the South Vietnamese government. He was also troubled by the disagreements among his country team. "We criticize the Vietnamese for their rivalries", he said, "but we're not exactly setting an example."[14]

After the US election, he returned to Washington for key meetings with Johnson and his advisors. On December 1, the president approved the first part of a two-phase plan that recommended increased covert operations against North Vietnam followed a month later by a moderate level of air strikes on the North. Johnson even resisted reprisal raids after a Christmas Eve attack on an American troop billet that killed several soldiers. He held off until a second attack on US personnel came on February 7. After approving two days of reprisal raids, Johnson then weighed more sustained bombing campaign, finally launching Rolling Thunder on March 1, 1965.

Two theories, two wars

From the start, US military and civilian leaders had a fundamental disagreement over the nature of the conflict in Vietnam and how to deal with it. Most of the civilian officials believed that the chief problem was the weakness of the South Vietnamese government, political and military, and that North Vietnamese aid to its allies in the south was illegal but not decisive. As President Kennedy had said regarding the South Vietnamese in a September 3, 1963 interview, "In the final analysis, it is their war. They are the ones who have to win it or lose it."[15] Military leaders, by contrast, continually emphasized the role of external support and argued that major attacks on the north were the necessary and perhaps sufficient condition to win the struggle in the south.

Civilian and military leaders also clashed on the use of force. McNamara and his whiz kids had already won the intellectual debate over nuclear deterrence and war-fighting with their notions of escalation ladders, second strike capability, and counterforce and countervalue targets. Each use of force was intended to signal something – resolve, restraint, willingness to escalate, etc. Since the human cost of any use of nuclear weapons was seen as so horrendous, civilian leaders were determined to try to minimize their actual use through withhold options and firebreaks. Faced with a limited war in Southeast Asia, they translated their game theory notions of signaling from the nuclear realm and applied them to conventional conflict.

In a policy memo by McGeorge Bundy, sent in the heat of his visit to Vietnam at the time of the attack on US barracks in Pleiku in February 1965, the national security advisor recommended "a policy of *sustained reprisal* against North Vietnam" as "the best way of increasing our chance of success in Vietnam."[16] He noted that the policy could fail but would "set a higher price for the future" that could deter others. He specifically followed the logic of the game theorists by recommending "that the level of reprisal be adjusted rapidly and visibly to both upward and downward shifts in the level of Viet Cong offenses. We want to keep before Hanoi the carrot of our desisting as well as the stick of continued pressure. We also need to conduct the application of force so that there is always a prospect of worse to come."[17]

Military leaders saw few reasons for restraint and believed, in theory and practice, that massive attacks on enemy forces and leadership were the best and only sure way to compel them to cease their aggressive acts. As early as January 22, 1964 – long before the Gulf of Tonkin attacks and reprisals in August – the Joint Chiefs sent a memo to McNamara urging fewer restraints on US military activities.

> In order to achieve that victory [over the "externally directed and supported insurgency in South Vietnam"], the Joint Chiefs of Staff are of the opinion that the United States must be prepared to put aside many of the self-imposed restrictions which now limit our efforts, and to undertake bolder actions which may embody greater risks.[18]

The Chiefs recommended a US military takeover of conduct of the war and even US aid programs as well as aerial bombing of the north "using US resources under Vietnamese cover."[19]

They repeated their recommendations five times more prior to the Gulf of Tonkin attacks. In May, for example, they urged air strikes on airfields, ammunition and petroleum, oils and lubricants (POL) storage sites, major railway and highway bridges, and outlined ways to destroy entirely the north's industrial base. After the reprisal raids in August, they called for "significantly stronger military pressures" on the north and specifically rejected the idea "that we should be slow to get deeply involved."[20]

On November 14, 1964, the Chiefs spelled out their contrasting views on the use of force.

> The Joint Chiefs of Staff do not concur with a concept of "tit-for-tat" reprisals nor with Ambassador Taylor's recommendation that the United States and the Government of Vietnam [GVN] jointly announce such a policy which ties our action to equivalency. "Tit for tat" is considered unduly restrictive, inhibits US initiative, and implies an undesirable lack of flexibility both as to the nature and the level of response.[21]

During 1964, the Chiefs' support for air strikes on the north was a means of avoiding a ground force commitment in the south. Angered and frustrated by the experience of the Korean War, they did not want to fight another land war in Asia. But even after the deployment of large numbers of ground combat forces, they continued to believe and argue that the war could be won only by major attacks on the north.

Intellectually and bureaucratically, the United States ended up fighting a very compartmentalized war. Strategic air operations, including strikes on the north and in Laos and Cambodia, were controlled by the Pacific Command in Hawaii. The war in the south directed by the commander of what was called MACV – Military Assistance Command, Vietnam – with separate sectors for army and marine operations. Some operations, air and ground, had narrow military goals, but many were for psychological or diplomatic reasons. The air war on the north, in particular, became caught up in the diplomatic maneuvering over peace talks. Target lists grew or shrank to "signal" American responses to North Vietnamese behaviors, and bombing pauses were touted as giving peace a chance to work. The ground war in the south followed its own logic, largely separate and distinct from the diplomatic dance that influenced the air war.

Ground combat commitment

Ironically, the deployment of the first combat troops was made in order to support the air war on the north. Some 3,500 marines were sent to Danang on March 8, 1965, in order to protect the base which had been sending aircraft to strike in the north. But with the Saigon government in continued disarray and its military actions faltering, US officials saw the logic of sending more ground troops. McGeorge Bundy summarized the evolution of US thinking in a memo to Johnson on July 24, 1965.

> [I]nitially we all had grave objections to major US ground force deployment. Even those in favor, (like my brother Bill), wanted to try other things first, and none of us was prepared to urge on Westmoreland things he was not urging on us. Then when we got major bases of our own, largely for air action, we moved quite promptly to protect them. These deployments did not give us bad reactions, and it became easier for Westmoreland to propose, and for us to accept, additional deployments.[22]

Even Lyndon Johnson felt the need to do something different. He berated his Army Chief of Staff, General Harold Johnson, as he sent him to Vietnam in March, 1965. "Now, I don't need ten generals to come in here ten times and tell me to bomb", the president complained. "I want some solutions, I want some answers."[23] When, several days later, the Chiefs for the first time recommended direct combat use of US troops, the president was ready and agreeable.

Maxwell Taylor, then ambassador to Saigon, later reflected: "It was curious how hard it had been to get authority for the initiation of the air campaign against the North and how relatively easy to get the marines ashore. Yet I thought the latter a much more difficult decision and concurred in it reluctantly."[24] In practice, US civilian leaders – and the Congress – paid more attention to the air war throughout the region than to the ground war in the south. The commanders had a much freer rein to conduct military operations there, subject only to the troop ceilings which they periodically requested increasing.

The buildup was massive and relentless. In October 1963, there had been 16,732 US military personnel in Vietnam, mostly military advisors to South Vietnamese forces and support units. At the end of 1964, the figure had risen to 23,300. During 1965, the number surged to 184,300. It jumped to 385,300 by the end of 1966 and to 485,600 by the end of 1967, peaking at 543,482 in 1969. At its height, an additional 82,000 US military personnel were supporting the war from offshore and in Thailand. There were also 72,000 troops from other nations involved in the war.[25]

Under General William Westmoreland, they launched major operations to "search and destroy" enemy forces. Earlier emphasis on "pacification" took a back seat to large unit operations throughout the country. These attacks were supported by huge numbers of air strikes, dropping more than four times the tonnage of munitions targeted against the north and the resupply lines – the "Ho Chi Minh Trail" – snaking through Laos and Cambodia. The south was also where the United States suffered its heaviest casualties. Fewer than 400 Americans had died in action prior to the Gulf of Tonkin attacks and reprisals. Another 1,369 died in 1965; 5,008 in 1966; 9,378 in 1967; and 14,592 in the peak year of 1968.[26]

Dissension and debate

The human and material costs kept mounting, but the indicators of progress were inconclusive. Since Westmoreland's search and destroy operations did not seize and hold territory, the best measure of success became the enemy body counts, but they grew unreliable and were disbelieved by the entire chain of command. The interdiction campaigns against enemy supply lines were massive in input but inadequate in results: the North Vietnamese and Viet Cong forces in the south needed only about 15 tons of supplies each day, an amount that could be carried by just a few trucks.[27]

Throughout 1965 and 1966 and into the summer of 1967, the pattern was the same. The Chiefs pressed to strike additional targets in the north; a few were added; then they pressed to expand the list further. Westmoreland sought more troops; McNamara traveled to Saigon and got him to agree to a lower number; the president approved the reduced request.[28]

Meanwhile, there were antiwar demonstrations in Vietnam and America; peace plans from all quarters; bombing pauses and escalated attacks – all inconclusive. Most notable were: a 37-day bombing pause in December 1965–January 1966; the first US air attacks near Hanoi and the port city of Haiphong in June 1966; and major ground operations near Saigon, near the Cambodian border, in the Central Highlands and in the Mekong Delta.

Many US civilian officials grew disillusioned with the war in the spring and summer of 1967. Robert McNamara vigorously defended past decisions and current operations, but opposed major additional escalation and gave hints of a change of heart. The Chiefs kept pushing for stronger action and resisting any cutbacks or ceilings on military activities. But a CIA analysis in May 1967, reached a very bleak conclusion: 'Short of a major invasion or nuclear attack, there is probably no level of air or naval actions against North Vietnam which Hanoi has determined in advance would be so intolerable that the war had to be stopped.'[29]

Westmoreland and the Chiefs were seeking 200,000 more men for Vietnam, a call-up of reserves, and fewer restrictions on attack on the north. On May 19, 1967, McNamara gave a long memo to the president opposing the military's recommendations and urging only 30,000 more troops. Besides opposing most of the measures sought by the military leaders, McNamara also offered judgments on American public opinion.

> Most Americans do not know how we got where we are, and most, without knowing why, but taking advantage of hindsight, are convinced that somehow we should not have gotten this deeply in. All want the war ended and expect their President to end it. Successfully, or else. This state of mind in the US generates impatience in the political structure of the United States. It unfortunately also generates patience in Hanoi.[30]

Frustrated with the progress of the war and angry at the civilian leaders, the Chiefs vented their feelings on Capitol Hill. While McNamara and JCS Chairman General Earle Wheeler were traveling to Vietnam, they met with Mendel Rivers (D-SC) and some members of his House Armed Services Committee, where they reiterated their rational for expanding the war.[31] Military leaders also convinced Senator John Stennis (D-Miss) and other members of the Senate Armed Services Committee to hold hearings on the air war. In the course of eight days of hearings in August 1967, the Preparedness Investigating Subcommittee heard from all the senior military leaders and from McNamara. Although the hearings were held behind closed doors, declassified transcripts were released in September, shortly after the Subcommittee's devastating report.

McNamara was confident and forceful in his testimony, ready to argue the futility of attacking every target not previously approved by the president. He claimed that all but 57 of the 359 targets recommended by the JCS had been approved, 85 percent, and that destruction of most of those remaining would have little impact on the war effort. In a few cases, he pointed out, the targets were justifiably off limits because of the risk of provoking a confrontation with the Soviet Union or China. He also said, quite disingenuously, "I don't believe that there is this gulf between the military leaders and the civilian leaders in the executive branch."[32]

The hearings demonstrated otherwise, of course. And Lyndon Johnson was so concerned about their impact that he acted in advance to approve an expanded target list as well as more troops for Vietnam. At least 29 targets were added to the approved list in the month before the hearings, and only one target recommended by the JCS after July 20 was disapproved.[33] In an August 16 meeting, Johnson told McNamara, "I would like to be able to say that we have hit six out of every seven targets requested."[34]

Johnson also, for the first time in the war, added General Wheeler to the short list of officials who participated in the "Tuesday Lunch" sessions where bombing targets were decided. While military critics contend that Johnson "picked" targets for attack, in fact the president de-selected some from the recommended lists, usually because of proximity to the Chinese border or Soviet supply venues or because heavy defenses made the costs of attack too high compared to the military benefit.

The Stennis panel concluded that the air campaign against the north had not achieved its objectives because of "the fragmentation of our air might by overly restrictive controls, limitations, and the doctrine of 'gradualism' placed on our aviation forces ..." It complained that "civilian authority consistently overruled the unanimous recommendations of military commanders and the Joint Chiefs of Staff for a systematic, timely, and hard-hitting integrated air campaign against the vital North Vietnam targets ...." The subcommittee concluded, "It is high time, we believe, to allow the military voice to be heard in connection with the tactical details of military operations."[35]

McNamara's testimony was the last straw for the Chiefs. They thought that the defense secretary had misled the Congress about the effectiveness of the air war thus far and prospectively. Within hours of McNamara's hearing, they met secretly in General Wheeler's office. The JCS chairman demanded total secrecy and then suggested that they should resign en masse at a press conference the next day. After several hours of discussions, the senior officers reached a consensus in favor of the unprecedented action. But early the next morning Wheeler called them together again and announced his change of heart. "We can't do it", he said. "It's mutiny."[36]

General Harold K. Johnson and Admiral David McDonald also considered resignation in protest during the war. But the CNO lamented, "Maybe we military men were all weak. Maybe we should have stood up and pounded the table .... At times I wonder, 'Why did I go along with this kind of stuff?'"[37]

Within three months, however, Lyndon Johnson had arranged the removal of Robert McNamara, although the longest-serving defense secretary did not actually leave the Pentagon until the end of February 1968. He had lost the confidence of the president as well as of the Chiefs.

While some writers wish that the Chiefs had carried out their resignation plans and think that that might have shocked the public into supporting their wider war policies, a well-documented and well-received analysis by a highly regarded army officer blames the Chiefs for different reasons. H.R. McMaster, in *Dereliction of Duty*, laments the "five silent men" who never really developed a good alternative strategy. "The Chiefs' failure to [render their best advice] and their willingness to present single-service remedies to a complex military problem, prevented them from developing a comprehensive estimate of the situation or from thinking effectively about strategy."[38]

Congress and the politics of the war

Congress also never stood up to Lyndon Johnson, never dissented in an effective way against the war. One reason was party loyalty: Democrats controlled Capitol Hill and the White House, so they saw enormous political risks in challenging the president's policies. They also knew Johnson personally, especially the Senators, and empathized with his dilemmas. Johnson also made a practice of including congressional leaders in frequent Vietnam policy meetings, making it harder for them to criticize outside what they had acquiesced to while inside. They also knew that American public opinion, in spite of the noisy antiwar protesters, continued to support the war.

Republican supporters of the war were never as visible or outspoken as some Democratic critics, but they were an important factor keeping Congress in line. Johnson told the Senate's Republican leader, Everett Dirksen (R-Ill.) in February 1965, "I'm getting kicked around by my own party in the Senate, and getting my support from your side of the aisle."[39] A year later, however, Johnson expressed concern that Sen. Stennis was getting inside word about future troop increases and mused to his advisors, "Maybe we consult with 'em too much."[40]

Nevertheless, there were some critics and several attempts to use legislative actions to shape military strategy. Probably most significant were the dueling hearings by the Senate Foreign Relations and Armed Services Committees. J. William Fulbright's Committee held nationally televised hearings on several occasions starting in February 1966 where it grilled administration witnesses and gave a megaphone to outside critics. The Stennis panel in 1967, by contrast, gave voice to the Chiefs and their criticisms of the policy of restraint. But they met in secret and garnered only moderate attention when their report and transcripts were released.

Lyndon Johnson's mentor and close political ally, Richard Russell (D-Ga.) was chairman of both the Armed Services Committee and the defense appropriations subcommittee. Russell opposed deeper involvement in Vietnam before the Gulf of Tonkin incident, then became a sturdy supporter of the war. In June 1965, he told a Georgia audience:

It was a mistake to get involved there in the first place; I have never been able to see any strategic, political, or economic advantage to be gained by our involvement …. Whether or not the initial decision was a mistake is now moot. The United States does have a commitment in South Vietnam. The flag is there. US honor and prestige are there. And, most important of all, US soldiers are there.[41]

Many members of Congress shared Russell's view. They rallied round the flag in 1964 and were reluctant to undercut public or military morale thereafter.

When Johnson announced the major deployment of troops to Vietnam in July 1965, there were, by one credible estimate, only about 10–12 Senators and 35–40 Representatives who were actively opposed to the use of large-scale US forces in the conflict. Another analyst concludes that "in the Senate a majority was either downright opposed to Americanization or ambivalent; perhaps more important, the number of committed hawks that spring [of 1965] was astonishingly small." By early 1966, almost half the Democratic Senators and one-fourth of the House Democrats were openly raising concerns about further escalation I the war.[42]

Despite their doubts, members of Congress were willing to make speeches and provide appropriations supporting the war. They also defeated amendments intended to limit the conduct of military operations. Of the 94 votes taken by Congress on measures directly related to the war between 1966 and 1972, only nine came while Johnson was president.[43] A 1966 effort to repeal the Gulf of Tonkin resolution got only five votes in the Senate. In 1967, Senators trying to pass a non-binding sense of Congress measure opposing attacks in North Vietnam and any increase in US troop levels beyond 500,000 lost out to supporters of an amendment declaring Congress' "firm intentions to provide all necessary support for members of the armed forces of the United States fighting in Vietnam" as well as supporting a negotiated settlement "which will preserve the honor of the United States."[44]

Although two key Democratic leaders in the Senate were critical of the war, the Democratic leadership and key chairmen in the House were supporters. Its Armed Services Committee, headed by Rep. Mendel Rivers (D-SC), was also a reliable source of support. A group of members traveled to Vietnam in the spring of 1966 and reported confidently that "we are moving steadily toward victory over the Vietcong." A respected Vermont Republican, Senator George Aiken, offered a different assessment. In October, 1966 he argued that the United States had already won the war in the sense of avoiding defeat and that we should declare victory and pull out our forces.[45]

Just before the 1966 elections, a magazine survey of members four 58.5 percent favoring existing policy in the war, 26.4 percent for stronger military action, and 15.1 percent for de-escalation and negotiations. House Republicans, led by Gerald Ford (R-Mich.) and Melvin Laird (R-Wisc.), tried to make the war an issue in the elections by releasing a report calling the war a stalemate and by arguing that the administration was engaged in "deception and confusion."[46] Although the war was only one of several issues cutting against Democrats, the elections gave them a three-seat loss in the Senate and a 47-seat loss in the House. They still retained majorities of 64–36 and 248–187.

Several key members of Congress pressed openly for more troops and an expanded target list during 1967, culminating with the Stennis subcommittee hearings and report. The administration was moving in the same direction, in part to preempt the criticism. As White House counsel Harry McPherson later recalled, "Like an acid, [the war] was eating into everything. It threatened to wipe out public awareness of Johnson's great achievements; it had already corroded his relationships with members of Congress." At a private dinner in May, Sen. Russell told the president, "We've just got to finish it soon because time is working against you both here and there."[47]

Instead of confronting the war directly, opponents launched the first of several indirect attacks on presidential policies, which later culminated in the enactment, over Richard Nixon's veto, of the War Powers Act of 1973. The 1967 measure was the "National Commitments Resolution", a non-binding declaration that any promise to use force abroad requires "affirmative action by Congress." The measure had been prompted by anger of the administration testimony that the Gulf of Tonkin Resolution was the "functional equivalent" of a declaration of war. Russell joined Fulbright in support of the new resolution, but it was not brought to a vote.[48]

Johnson took several steps in the fall of 1967 to try to stop the erosion of support in Congress and the country. He approved a larger target list, summoned Westmoreland back to Washington to trumpet good news about the war effort, and had more meetings with congressional leaders. He also announced the replacement of McNamara.[49]

The president also indicated to the Joint Chiefs that he was willing to increase pressure on the communists. In an October 17, 1967 report, the Chiefs complained that "progress has been and continues to be slow, largely because US military power has been retrained in a manner which has reduced significantly its impact and effectiveness." They recommended 10 additional steps, many acceptable to McNamara, but also operations in Laos and Cambodia, which the president rejected. Johnson also complained that the Chiefs had offered only suggestions for action outside South Vietnam and for things already disapproved.[50]

Turnaround after Tet

Three months later, Johnson's carefully orchestrated pattern of carrots and sticks, peace feelers and air strikes, encouraging reports and optimistic forecasts, was blown away by the nationwide Viet Cong offensive begun on the January 30 Tet holiday. While analysts later concluded that the ultimate outcome was a severe defeat for the insurgents, the images in America of its embassy under attack and the long, block-by-block fight for the ancient capital of Hue triggered a shift in US public opinion. Tet marked the crossover point, when public opposition to the war first exceeded public support.[51] The trends were evident throughout 1967 and would continue inexorably until the end of the war.

The loss of public support for the war effort coincided with a renewed push by the Chiefs for a more aggressive policy, including deployment of 206,000 additional troops to Vietnam. With McNamara leaving, military leaders thought that Johnson would be more receptive to their proposals. Since they were not surprised by the 206,000 figure, they thought Johnson would not be either. But he was, and he asked his advisors to convene his outside group of "wise men" for a review. This group included many committed hawks like former Secretary of State Dean Acheson and General Omar Bradley, who had previously reassured the president that he was on the right course.

This time, however, they had a different view. Meeting with Johnson on March 26, McGeorge Bundy told the president that "there has been a very significant shift in most of our positions since we last met. … Dean Acheson summed up the majority feeling when he said we can no longer do the job we set out to do in the time we have left, and we must begin to take steps to disengage." Johnson asked for individual comments and was shocked by what he heard. He called his top advisors aside and asked, "Who poisoned the well with these guys?"[52]

And they were joined by Johnson's old friend and new secretary of defense, Clark Clifford, in raising doubts about the war. Clifford later wrote about his consultations with the Chiefs. "The military was utterly unable to provide an acceptable rationale for the troop increase. Moreover, when I asked for a presentation of their plan for attaining victory, I was told that there was no plan for victory in historic American sense."[53]

In response to these views, Johnson changed his plans in many ways. He approved only a limited troop increase of 13,500. He announced that he would not run for reelection. He launched a new peace offensive, including an end to the bombing of the north, and stayed with it until peace talks began in Paris in May. He replaced Westmoreland with General Creighton Abrams, who was more disposed to pacification efforts than large-scale search and destroy missions.[54] And despite some renewed attacks on the north in July, he halted all attacks on November 1, hoping to encourage the peace talks and help Hubert Humphrey defeat Richard Nixon for the presidency. Lyndon Johnson's war was at an end.

Nixon's plan

Richard Nixon won the presidency with a narrow 500,000 popular vote margin over Humphrey. He had been vague about the Vietnam war during his campaign, pledging to "end the war and win the peace in the Pacific."[55] While many observers inferred that he had a "secret plan" for Vietnam,

Nixon's approach was modeled on Eisenhower's approach to Korea in the 1952 campaign – criticizing the lack of success thus far and suggesting a fresh approach without specifying details. Once in the White House, he received quite varied suggestions from his advisors. Senior military leaders in Washington recommended the removal of Johnson's restraints with expanded attacks on North Vietnam and across the border in Cambodia. As General Wheeler told him, everything possible was being done in Vietnam "except the bombing of the North."[56] The US commander in Vietnam, General Creighton Abrams, had been changing the US military role and wanted to continue building up South Vietnamese military capabilities. The new Secretary of Defense, former congressman Mel Laird, agreed with Abrams largely for domestic political reasons: he wanted to "Vietnamize" the conflict and bring US troops home as rapidly as possible. Henry Kissinger, the national security advisor, envisioned a multi-layered strategy that involved the Russians and Chinese as well as the Vietnamese.

Nixon believed that it helped his diplomacy to be perceived as willing to take extreme measures, what he himself called the "madman theory." As he told his chief of staff, H.R. Haldeman, "I want the North Vietnamese to believe I've reached the point where I might do anything to stop the war."[57] The new president centralized control over all aspects of the war inside the White House and under Kissinger, even to the extent of trying to maintain back channel links to Abrams and the Chiefs that excluded Laird. He distrusted Laird, viewing him as too willing to shape policy to conform to the restraints of public opinion.[58]

In fact, Laird devised the strategy which best served Nixon's political, diplomatic and military goals – Vietnamization in the south, allowing withdrawals of US troops, and more aggressive action against the north, which kept the Chiefs happy and supportive. In his first meeting with the Chiefs, the new defense secretary announced his four primary goals: to end US involvement in Vietnam, to end the draft, to cut the defense budget, and to repair civil–military relations. He then – and repeatedly thereafter – forced the Chiefs to choose between money for Vietnam operations and money for US military modernization.[59] After only a few weeks in office, for example, Laird announced a $1.1 billion cut in the planned $79 billion defense budget for the coming year and told the military they would have to reduce the number of their favored B-52 bombing operations. He later told General Abrams that "the major constraint on US involvement was now economic."[60]

Laird maintained his own direct contact with Abrams and reinforced the US commander's efforts to reduce the American combat role in the conflict. Traveling with Wheeler to Vietnam in early March 1969, Laird told Abrams, "I think we've got some time, and we've got to make the best use of the time that we possibly can." He also said that "we have a program to reduce the U.S. contribution, not only in the form of men, but in casualties and material and in dollars ...."[61]

While Laird pressed the military to support US troop withdrawals and Vietnamization, Nixon adopted many of their recommendations for military escalation. In response to increase attacks in February 1969, he ordered air attacks on enemy positions in Cambodia – but ordered such tight secrecy that the US military chose to maintain two sets of books on the operations. When this "secret bombing" was investigated exposed and investigated by Congress in 1973, it led to an impeachment charge against the president.[62]

On April 10, 1969, Nixon approved the basic policy planning document for the conflict, NSSM 36, which ordered "the preparation of a specific timetable for Vietnamizing the war." It assumed that enemy force levels would remain about the same and that there would be "no de-escalation of allied military efforts, except that resulting from phased withdrawals" of troops. On May 14, Nixon proposed the simultaneous withdrawal of US and North Vietnamese forces from the south. Hearing no favorable reply, on June 8, during a meeting with South Vietnamese President Thieu, Nixon announced the first unilateral US troop reduction – 25,000 men. That action was coupled with the president's decision three days earlier to resume air attacks on the North for the first time since just before the 1968 US elections. Nixon told Thieu in July that the two leaders should have a plan for continued US troop cuts, "but let us keep it secret among ourselves."[63]

In mid-summer, Laird engineered a change in the formal mission statement for Abrams and MACV. Under the Johnson administration, the purpose of US support was "to defeat the externally directed and supported communist subversion and aggression" and to attain "a stable and independent noncommunist government." Despite objections from the Chiefs and other commanders, Laird insisted that US policy had changed and ordered a new mission statement on August 15. The revised document made no mention of defeating the enemy or of attaining an independent government. Instead, it declared the US objective to be "to allow the people of the Republic of Vietnam to determine their future without outside interference." To that end, Abrams was ordered to assist the south's armed forces "to take over an increasing share of combat operations." In persuading Nixon that this was consistent with administration policy, the secretary also promised that no public announcement would be made of the change. Just before a planned, nationwide antiwar demonstration in October, however, Laird revealed that US military policy had changed to give highest priority to Vietnamization.[64]

To Nixon and Kissinger, military operations were a means to reassure Saigon and to pressure Hanoi in order to make progress in the peace talks, which they had supplemented with secret exchanges starting in August 1969. To Laird, they were a tactic that had to be limited for budgetary and domestic political reasons yet maintained at some level to keep US military support of the administration. To military leaders, however, they were the key to what they still believed was a possible victory over the communists. General Wheeler complained to General Abrams during an October meeting,

It seems almost impossible to get the secretary of state, the secretary of defense, equally or more important the president, to realize that they are dealing from a position of military strength. And I *mean* military strength. Not just a *marginal* position of strength, but a very *substantial* position of strength.[65]

In short, the military thought the US was winning while the civilians were concerned about not losing. At the same time, the intelligence community at the same time was concluding that "the Communists retain a substantial capability to sustain military operations" and that the Viet Cong infrastructure "continues to function effectively."[66]

The military unleashed

As the United States withdrew troops, it became more dependent on airpower to influence the war. The drawdowns also put pressure on the military to act before additional forces were sent home. From a peak of 543,000 in April, 1969, US troop strength in Vietnam dropped to 484,000 in December, to 335,000 at the end of 1970, to 158,000 at the end of 1971, and to only 24,000 at the end of 1972.[67]

In September, 1969 Nixon announced a second American troop withdrawal of 35,000 men and secretly ordered planning for a wider air war in case negotiations were unsuccessful. The Chiefs' plan, named Duck Hook, called for mining the north's ports and harbors and a four-day series of strikes against military and economic targets in the north. The president ultimately decided against the attacks because of likely domestic turmoil and opposition from allies.[68] Instead, on November 3, Nixon made a defiant nationwide address, proclaiming his desire for an honorable peace, explaining his policy of Vietnamization, troop withdrawals, and negotiations, and calling for support from the "silent majority" of Americans to counter noisy antiwar demonstrators. He also tried to reduce domestic opposition to the war by suspending draft calls in November and December and by signing a bill establishing a draft lottery. On December 15, he announced a further troop withdrawal of 50,000.

As US troop levels fell, military leaders pressed for action in border areas and along infiltration routes in order to ease pressure on the South Vietnamese forces. In February 1970, Nixon approved orders for secret air strikes in Laos. In response to increased enemy activity in April, he accepted military advice to send US ground forces into Cambodia. Knowing of Laird's opposition to such attacks because of concerns over the likely domestic US reaction, Nixon pointedly excluded his defense secretary from key planning sessions when he met with the acting JCS Chairman, Admiral Thomas Moorer. Later Nixon told Laird, "we must play a tough game" to buy time for troop withdrawals.[69] Despite his misgivings, Laird displayed strong public support of the highly controversial operation, which triggered widespread

US protests and prolonged fights in Congress over antiwar legislation. As the attacks in Cambodia continued during May, Nixon also approved an expanded target list and the heaviest air raids into the north since he had taken office.

Despite its outward show of unity, the Nixon administration was riven internally by distrust and suspicion. The president told some aides of his distrust of Kissinger and Laird and some top military officers. Nixon and Kissinger made deliberate attempts to bypass Laird and deal directly with Abrams and the Chiefs. Kissinger's military deputy, Colonel and later General Alexander Haig, had his own secret communications and suspicions.[70] In response to press leaks, Nixon ordered wiretaps on several NSC staffers and Laird's military assistant.

It was in this climate in September 1970 that a young navy yeoman assigned to clerical duties on the NSC staff became the key figure in a JCS spy ring. Charles Radford purloined and copied for his navy superiors, including Admiral Moorer, the most sensitive documents crossing the desks of Haig and Kissinger. On one occasion, traveling to China with Kissinger, Radford even took documents from Kissinger's briefcase and passed them on to his uniformed bosses. He was discovered and reassigned in December 1971, when he was suspected of leaking documents to columnist Jack Anderson, but the administration kept the scandal secret for over a year.[71] At first, Nixon wanted to "use this as a device, of course, to clean out the Joint Chiefs' operation." But he also saw the advantages of keeping Admiral Moorer indebted to him, so he relented. "We can't touch him [Moorer]", Nixon told his aides, "because it hurts the Joint Chiefs. The Joint Chiefs, the military, et cetera – not to be viewed as our enemy."[72]

Secrecy and suspicion led to another scandal. The commander of the 7th Air Force, General John D. Lavelle, objected to restrictive rules of engagement that forbade his pilots flying over North Vietnam from striking certain air defense targets unless enemy radars had been activated. Knowing that the administration had labeled most of its attacks "protective reaction strikes", he believed he should be able to react protectively whenever over enemy territory, and not just when the rules provided. He also thought he had winks and nods from his superiors to act as he did. It was later determined that Lavelle's pilots had conducted at least 28 unauthorized strikes in North Vietnam in a four-month period – nearly one fourth of the officially acknowledged "protective reaction strikes" at that time. He was removed from command and retired – without the real reason being made public. In fact, the investigation leading to Lavelle's dismissal had begun when a young air force sergeant complained to his Senator that he had been ordered to falsify records to conceal operations over the north.[73]

Congress emboldened

Antiwar members of Congress seized upon these reports of secret bombing and unauthorized air strikes and other scandals to publicize problems in the war and to try to drum up public support for legislation to restrict its conduct. Pro-war lawmakers defended administration policy and used their more senior legislative positions to smother objectionable amendments.

Senior members of the defense committees were mostly strong supporters of the war, and they heard from their military contacts the largely optimistic reports from the field. They were satisfied that the Nixon administration was listening to the senior military and adopting many of their proposals. They could deflect antiwar pressures from constituents by endorsing the administration's troop reductions and peace talks efforts, while accepting Nixon's escalatory moves as unfortunate but necessary to end the war more quickly.

Nixon made a point of briefing key congressional figures such as Senators Russell and Stennis, but they were known supporters of the war. Kissinger reports that only a handful of key leaders – none a critic of the war – were briefed about the spring 1969 bombing in Cambodia because "This was at that time the accepted practice" for classified operations. He also notes that "Not one raised the issue that the full Congress should be consulted."[74]

With Russell weakened by a terminal illness, Stennis became the administration's point man in the Senate in 1970. Nixon personally met with him in advance of the Cambodian invasion in April 1970 and again before the US supported South Vietnamese attacks into Laos in February 1971.[75] In return, Stennis was a stalwart opponent of restrictive legislation, often on the Senate floor throughout month-long debates in the early 1970s, corralling votes and making procedural motions to protect the administration's policies.

Fulbright was marginalized because his committee had no real jurisdiction over legislation related to the war. That rested in Stennis' Armed Services Committee, which also had more pro-war Senators than Foreign Relations. The Arkansas Senator was also upstaged by a bipartisan group of even more outspoken opponents of the war, who authored the key antiwar amendments that became the battlegrounds in 1970–3.

One of the most important figures was the Senate Majority Leader, Mike Mansfield (D-Mont.), a longtime student and professor of Asian affairs. Mansfield sent private advisory letters to Nixon, as he had done to Johnson, and at first was supportive of the Republican Administration's peace efforts. He told Nixon in October 1969 that "we would do our best to protect his political flanks as far as the Democrats are concerned" if the president took steps to reduce US troop levels and pressured the Saigon government in peace talks. He also offered "my personal assurances" that "I will not criticize in any way, shape or form but, on the contrary, will give articulate public support" to presidential decisions to end the war rapidly. Nixon believed that Mansfield was offering him a politically useful "last chance to end 'Johnson's and Kennedy's war'", but that it would still be wrong to end the war "on any terms I believed to be less than honorable."[76]

Mansfield was torn in several ways by the Vietnam issue. He headed a sharply divided Democratic caucus in the Senate; he strongly supported Nixon's opening to China and wanted administration support for his own visits to Beijing; yet he became disillusioned with the administration's escalatory moves and finally shifted into the antiwar camp after the Cambodian invasion. He then took the lead an offered a series of amendments calling for US troop withdrawals promptly after an agreement on the return of POWs. Several passed the Senate and were modified or dropped in conference with the House. All were toothless in the sense of merely declaring the "sense of Congress" but still were strongly opposed by the Administration.[77]

The House of Representatives was more supportive of the war than the Senate throughout the conflict. The Speakers, John McCormack (D-Mass.) and his successor, Carl Albert (D-Okla.), not only defended the war but used their positions to derail antiwar efforts. At no time while US combat troops were stationed in Vietnam did more than 40 percent of the members vote for antiwar legislation.[78] The strong pro-war sentiment in the House, coupled with the Administration's pressure, prevented enactment of any Senate-passed measures that would have had a significant impact on the conduct of the war.

There were 85 rollcall votes on the war during the Nixon administration. Each victory, or even close call, gave hope to antiwar factions and heartburn to the administration. Perhaps the most significant impacts came indirectly. The likelihood of congressional opposition may have tempered some military decisions and forced more diplomatic overtures. The increasing size and speed of US troop withdrawals was certainly viewed by Laird as politically necessary to counter antiwar forces in Congress. The defense secretary also feared that other defense programs would suffer as Congress cut defense spending as a surrogate for ending the war. General Wheeler shared this view. As he told General Abrams in October 1969, "In my more cynical moments I even suspect that some of these expenditure limitations are designed basically to force a reduction in our efforts here in Vietnam."[79]

In December 1969, the Senate passed and the House later agreed to an amendment which seemed innocuous but proved significant – a prohibition on introducing US ground combat troops into Laos or Thailand.[80] That prevented US infantry support for faltering South Vietnamese troops during their February, 1971 attacks into Laos. And the fact that the amendment failed to contain a restriction applying to Cambodia paved the way for the US invasion in April 1970.

Legislation on the draft also was a surrogate for the debates on the war and a vehicle for indirectly impacting US force levels. Complaints about the unfairness of the draft system – especially the sense that rich, white college boys were avoiding military service while others were doing the fighting and dying – led many Republicans take the lead in supporting a volunteer armed force. Nixon eliminated many of the remaining grounds for deferments and urged congressional approval of a lottery system, which was enacted late in 1969. He also appointed a commission which in 1970 recommended an end to the draft. In 1971, however, the Administration needed a two-year extension of the draft. The measure eventually passed overwhelmingly, in part because it contained vague language urging an end to the war and absolute ceilings on the number of draftees.[81]

Congress also began work on measures to prevent future Vietnams, particularly a bill to reassert Congress' war power by specifying conditions under which troops could be sent into combat and procedures for congressional authorization or disapproval. These efforts had the active participation of Sen. Stennis as well as several antiwar Senators. The final version was not enacted until 1973, after US involvement in the war was over. Overwhelming majorities of both houses overrode Nixon's veto of the War Powers Resolution in November, 1973. Legislation also passed in the early 1970s to restrict overseas sales of US weapons and to give Congress more information and a greater role in such sales.

Democrats were emboldened by the public support for their antiwar legislation, particularly after the Cambodian invasion in the spring of 1970. They also gained nine members in the House in the 1970 elections, including several prominent antiwar activists. While some war critics like Sen. Albert Gore, Sr. (D-Tenn) also lost, the net effect was a slight increase in war opposition in the new Congress.

Democrats had many political incentives to criticize the war, and antiwar Republicans had local support for their positions even though they opposed the Republican president. But they were also boxed in by Nixon's ostensible support for peace talks and troop withdrawals, which they also favored. The administration's trump card, which was highly important to the general public and acknowledged by antiwar factions, was the question of US prisoners of war. All lawmakers demanded a return of the captives and conditioned their own end-the-war legislation on the POW issue. Any such conditions, of course, required negotiations which only the executive branch could conduct.

Air strikes and peace talks

In June 1971, just after the Senate passed the Mansfield amendment requiring a US troop withdrawal in nine months, provided that American POWs were released, Nixon told Kissinger that he felt compelled to withdraw troops, but that if the North Vietnamese failed to give him an agreement. "I'm gonna … bomb those bastards so that they lack the capability to take over South Vietnam." He also said that "you've gotta remember that everything is domestic politics from now on."[82]

To build support for his reelection, Nixon announced further US troop cuts in November 1971 and again in January, April, and August 1972. He also revealed that Kissinger had been holding secret peace talks with the North Vietnamese. But he broke off the talks when the North Vietnamese seemed intransigent at diplomacy and ready to renew their military offensive in the South.

The Easter Offensive in 1972, the largest enemy action since the 1968 Tet offensive, led to the capture of the northernmost provincial capital and saw communist gains throughout the border provinces. The Chiefs pressed the president to remove the longstanding restrictions on key targets in the north. Admiral Moorer pleased with Nixon to "let us make these bastards pay for the American blood they've spilled." He argued with Laird, who warned that the operation risked Soviet cancellation of the politically important summit in Moscow two weeks later. Moorer countered that "we've let them get away with this long enough." Years later, Moorer told a reporter that the Chiefs were "ready to walk out the door" if Nixon didn't approve the expanded operations. "We thought we had a real chance to break their backs – we weren't going to throw it away like Johnson did."[83]

Despite the diplomatic risks, Nixon ordered the mining of Haiphong harbor and six other ports, as well as a major series of air strikes in the North, called Linebacker, targeting bridges, power plants, and petroleum storage facilities. He also nominated Moorer, who had been acting chairman for several months, to a regular term as JCS Chairman. The Soviet Union protested, but did not cancel the summit. In July, public and private peace talks resumed.

Just before the elections, Kissinger held a dramatic news conference announcing that "peace is at hand." In fact, the United States and North Vietnam were very close to an agreement, but it was unacceptable to the South Vietnamese. Nevertheless, the public sense of progress helped to propel Nixon to a landslide victory over George McGovern, as the president won 61 percent of the popular vote and every state but Massachusetts and the District of Columbia.

Kissinger resumed talks with the North Vietnamese and Al Haig went to Saigon to try to get South Vietnamese concurrence in the agreement. "You should point out composition of our new Senate to Thieu", Kissinger cabled. "No matter what happens, there will be a fund cutoff if we do not move in this direction." Nixon feared the same outcome. But he sent the South Vietnamese leader a secret letter promising renewed US military support if necessary. "You have my absolute assurance that if Hanoi fails to abide by the terms of this agreement it is my intention to take swift and severe retaliatory action."[84]

Renewed peace talks, and continued South Vietnamese unhappiness, led to a breakdown in negotiations in December. Once again, Laird argued against increased military action and for signing the agreement immediately. He warned Nixon, "We believe that you will no longer get the support of

Congress for continuation of the war if our POWs are not returned to the US promptly." Further delay or escalatory action, he argued, "will destroy the remaining flicker of support you now have from both the Senate and the House."[85] The president, however, gambled that massive force might break the deadlock.

On December 18, Nixon ordered Linebacker II, the most intense air assault of the war, a 12-day series of B-52 and tactical aircraft strikes at the full range of North Vietnamese targets. An NSC memo said, "The plan includes new targets not previously attacked and is designed to accomplish the maximum psychological shock." Nixon told Moorer, "I don't want any more of this crap about the fact that we couldn't hit this target or that one. This is your chance to use military power effectively to win this war, and if you don't, I'll consider you responsible."[86]

On December 30, with signals from Hanoi of renewed willingness to talk, the United States halted bombing north of the twentieth parallel. The Paris talks resumed, and on January 15, 1973, Nixon halted all US offensive military action. A week later, the two sides initialed a ceasefire agreement, later signed on January 27. The agreement called for an internationally supervised ceasefire throughout the north and south; release of all American POWs and removal of all US military personnel within 60 days; a declaration that the South Vietnamese people had a right to self-determination; and a ban on infiltration of troops and war supplies into the south.[87] Nixon proclaimed the agreement "peace with honor."

The dramatic return of American POWs started on February 12, 1973. When the last of the 587 prisoners was released on March 29, the remaining 2,500 US combat troops were withdrawn from Vietnam as well. That marked the psychological end of the war. In fact, however, US air strikes continued in Laos and Cambodia – and Congress objected. In May the House voted for the first time to cut off money for military operations in Southeast Asia, and the Senate followed suit in June. Congress had no stomach for more bombing – or more killed or captured pilots. Meanwhile, the president was turning all his energies to deal with the burgeoning Watergate scandal, which forced him to fire his top two aides in April and to endure the start of months of televised hearings in May. On June 29, the president agreed to language requiring an end to all offensive military operations by August 15.[88]

The direct American role in the war ended on that date, but the conflict continued. The South Vietnamese forces received US military aid, though in amounts cut sharply by Congress, but many of their top officers turned out to be corrupt or incompetent. The North Vietnamese and their allies in the south mounted a major offensive in 1975 that led to the collapse of the south's forces and government. Saigon fell on April 30 as the last American helicopters fled the scene.

Bitter lessons

The Vietnam war ruptured American politics not only while it raged but for many years thereafter, poisoning even the presidential elections in 2004. That conflict remains for many a litmus test of patriotism and a reminder of the painful consequences of disagreement over a major war.

Vietnam veterans have been prominent in Congress, in both liberal and conservative quarters. They were crucial in building support for restoration of diplomatic relations with Hanoi and the signing of trade agreements. Their views on use of force questions are given special weight.

Perhaps the deepest wound from Vietnam came in civil–military relations. A generation of officers who fought in the jungles or risked their lives overhead resolved: "never again." They believed that their civilian masters had rejected their advice and had misused or even abused their precious people with a flawed strategy. They also believed that those who fought had been left abandoned by the politicians who sent them to fight, left to face hostility from home. They resented returning to a country that blamed them for the war they had loyally and bravely fought. While some officers dispute the wisdom of the large unit, search and destroy, ground operations, most believe that the United States forces never lost a battle. America lost the war, however, because of public opposition at home – opposition stimulated by the news media and reinforced by antiwar activists in the streets and in Congress.

Given this critique, US officers took a series of steps to prevent another Vietnam. General Creighton Abrams, recalled from Saigon to be Army Chief of Staff, restructured his forces so that no major conflict could be conducted without calling up the reserves. He knew that Lyndon Johnson had refused to call up reservists precisely because he feared it would increase domestic opposition to the war. He wanted that risk to be part of any future calculation about going to war.

Army officers in particular drew upon Soviet military literature to fashion a new way of looking at war. Instead of the old distinction between strategy and tactics, they added a middle ground – the operational level of war – in which military officers and their well-considered doctrine should prevail, and into which the civilians should not venture. What Eliot Cohen calls the "normal theory" of civilian control, which has become dominant in the US military since Vietnam, calls for civilians to give clear and attainable political objectives and then to leave the military aspects to those in uniform.[89]

Military leaders were joined in their critique of Vietnam by political officials who shared their anger. Caspar Weinberger, in particular, codified what became known as the Vietnam syndrome with a 1984 speech laying out six "tests" which should be met before US troops were sent into combat. These included: a "vital' national interest; "a clear intention of winning"; "clearly defined political and military objectives"; and "before the US commits combat forces abroad, there must be some reasonable assurance we will have the support of the American people and their elected representatives in Congress."[90]

These conditions were intended to prevent US involvement abroad in discretionary wars with limited objectives. They seemed to allow only Second World War-type, unconditional surrender conflicts. And, in fact, the US military largely resisted involvement in every major operation from Lebanon and Kuwait through Somalia, Haiti, Bosnia and Kosovo. Only with the strong public support for action after 9/11 and the mission of regime change in Afghanistan and Iraq did the US military again enthusiastically embrace major war abroad. And when a skilled and deadly insurgency developed in Iraq, US officials went to great lengths to catalog the many ways in which Iraq was not another Vietnam. At the same time, the same officials began issuing body counts of insurgents killed and enunciated a strategy of training Iraqi forces to fight the insurgency and withdrawing US forces as soon as the political and military situations allowed. Whatever the lessons of Iraq, they will likely hang heavy over the US military for years to come. Perhaps there will even be an "Iraq Syndrome."

Part II

The challenge of rearmament

5 John Adams and the politics of rearmament, 1798

if you must have an army I will give it to you, but remember it will make the government more unpopular than all their other acts.

John Adams, 1798[1]

In what both John Adams and Thomas Jefferson later called an atmosphere of "terrorism," the United States greatly expanded its army, created its navy, re-established the Marine Corps, and imposed tough laws on foreigners and policy critics. In the process, the president and Congress each tried to fashion policies consistent with their institutional and political needs. And the whole issue of military command and control got caught up in a vicious power struggle.

The crisis erupted in the spring and summer of 1798, but it had been brewing at least since 1793. When revolutionary France declared war on Great Britain and other European states, President George Washington proclaimed official neutrality, hoping to avoid involvement in the conflict. His action also postponed a domestic fight between supporters of France, led by Thomas Jefferson, and supporters of Great Britain, led by Alexander Hamilton.[2]

By the start of Washington's second term, two distinct political factions were jelling into political parties. On one side were farmers and southerners like Jefferson and James Madison who acknowledged the need for a central government but wanted to keep it limited. They were distrustful of bankers and businessmen, and especially of any standing army. True to their own revolutionary heritage, they admired the French upheaval as an extension and vindication of what they had achieved in North America.

The other faction was led by men from northern cities who favored a central government active and powerful enough to encourage and secure the development of a continental nation, linked by commerce and trade. While they welcomed political independence from Great Britain, they wanted to continue close economic and cultural ties. They also welcomed a national military establishment as a means of protecting the nation and its economic interests.

When the British began seizing US ships carrying goods to or from French ports in 1794, the two countries verged on war. Washington cooled the war fever by naming Chief Justice John Jay to try to negotiate a settlement of outstanding issues. Jay succeeded many months later, but his treaty was a compromise, obtaining some British concessions, such as a promise to evacuate western frontier forts by June 1796, but also granting US concessions limiting trade. The fight over the treaty lasted for many months in 1795, culminating in a Senate vote of 20–10 – just enough to meet the two-thirds requirement – for conditional approval, provided that a section were deleted that limited the size of US ships trading in the West Indies and banned re-export of many tropical products. Washington was so torn over the public controversy that he waited seven weeks before deciding to proceed with ratification of the amended treaty.[3]

As the leading historians of the Federalist period, Stanley Elkins and Eric McKitrick, have concluded, "The outpouring of popular feeling over the Jay Treaty, as has long been understood, was more directly responsible than anything else for the full emergence of political parties in America, and of clearly recognized Federalist and Republican points of view on all political questions."[4] The split was sharp in the presidential elections of 1796, when Adams bested Jefferson by only three electoral votes, 71–68, thus creating an awkward situation where the legal successor to the president was the head of the opposition.

John Adams began his presidency with the best of intentions, but with two actions that proved significant political blunders. Concerned about deteriorating relations with France, he sought Jefferson's help in recruiting Madison for a three-man delegation to Paris. Even before Madison declined, as expected, Adams' own cabinet was in an uproar over both the idea of sending a mission and the fact that they had not been consulted in advance. The new president thought he was demonstrating smooth continuity by asking Washington's cabinet to stay on, but what he got was internal opposition from men who were personally and politically much closer to Alexander Hamilton. Former Treasury Secretary Hamilton, by then practicing law in New York, had tried to engineer Adams' defeat by his own Federalist running mate in 1796 and later came to rival the president in power and influence over the Executive Branch. Adams later said that his greatest mistake as president was to retain the Washington cabinet.[5]

The French Government had been angered by the Jay Treaty and by the extent of American trade with Great Britain. It pointedly decreed in July 1796 that it would seize US vessels attempting to trade with the British in the Caribbean. Several ships were seized in the subsequent months. Meanwhile, the French minister in Philadelphia openly sided with Jefferson in the presidential elections, and the outraged Federalists began calling the Republicans the French Party.[6]

Adams used his inaugural address on March 4, 1797, to warn of foreign interference in American politics, of votes that "can be obtained by foreign

Figure 5.1 John Adams (Library of Congress)

nations by flattery or menaces, by fraud or violence, by terror, intrigue, or venality." He also listed as the "natural enemies" of the Constitution: "the spirit of sophistry, the spirit of party, the spirit of intrigue, the profligacy of corruption, and the pestilence of foreign influence, which is the angel of destruction to elective governments." While speaking of his "personal esteem for the French nation, formed in a residence of seven years chiefly among them, and a sincere desire to preserve the friendship which has been so much for the honor and interest of both nations," he pledged to continue Washington's policy of neutrality.[7]

Ten days later, the new president learned that the French had spurned Washington's minister to Paris, Charles C. Pinckney. Officials refused to accept his credentials and ordered him to leave the country. Adams decided to summon Congress to a special session, starting May 15. At that time, Adams told the members of the "indignities" suffered by Pinckney and promised "a fresh attempt at negotiation." He then asked for several additions to US defenses – a strengthened navy, coastal fortifications, more artillery and cavalry, but only a provisional army, not an expansion of the existing force.[8]

These recommendations reflected Adams' considered approach to war and diplomacy. He doubted that a French invasion was likely. As he wrote to Elbridge Gerry, "Where is it possible for her to get ships to send thirty thousand men here? We are double the number we were in 1775. We have four times the military skill and we have eight times the Munitions of War. What would 30,000 men do here?" But he believed that a military buildup was necessary to convince France to negotiate.[9]

He thought that the US coast and commerce could best be protected by a strong navy, a view not shared by his mostly pro-army advisers. A few years later, he noted, "Floating batteries and wooden walls have been my favorite system of warfare and defense for this country for three and twenty years." But he admitted making few converts to this view.[10]

Although Adams believed in a strong Executive, he openly deferred to Congress on particular details, asking the legislators to write laws so sailors could defend themselves and to "prevent the resources of the United States from being converted into the means of annoying our trade." He did not offer specific legislative proposals of his own at that time.[11]

The politics of defense

The Fifth Congress was sharply divided along partisan lines. The Federalists had a 22–10 margin in the Senate, but only a narrow margin in the House, one that fluctuated with member departures and absences. The Republicans were more sensitive to their minority status because they had had effective control of the House during all of Washington's second term. They were now united in their disdain for Adams and their opposition to anti-French military preparations. They decried Adams' message as tantamount to declaration of war. But they accepted the idea of a new three-man delegation to Paris and accepted Adams' nominations once the independent-minded Elbridge Gerry was added.[12]

When the Congress began debating defense matters, Adams lost control, for his own party thought he had not gone far enough and the opposition considered even modest measures the first step on the road to war. In the ensuing fight, the Secretaries of State and Treasury, encouraged by Hamilton, pushed for such unprecedented steps – a provisional army of 25,000, new taxes, embargo on French trade, and laws allowing expulsion of aliens

– that the Republicans succeeded in blocking any augmentations. By the time Congress adjourned on July 8, the only defense measure approved was additional funds to complete the three frigates already under construction under legislation passed in 1794.[13]

The members of Congress believed that they had the experience as well as the Constitutional duty to make independent judgments on defense matters. Half of the Representatives and 60 percent of the Senators were veterans of military service. The popularly elected House members were slower to approve provocative measures than the Senators, who were chosen by state legislatures – until the furor over the XYZ affair in the spring of 1798. While Federalists tended to support Adams and Republicans to oppose, coastal Republicans joined with the Federalists to support shipbuilding. In the 1797 debates, the House voted to limit presidential authority by forbidding the newly authorized frigates to be used in convoys, but the Federalist-dominated Senate opposed. When the House feared loss of all shipbuilding funds, they agreed to compromise by approving the ships without the restriction.[14]

The partisan differences on military matters are striking and perhaps surprising 200 years later. The Federalists favored a strong central government and a military force capable of defending US interests on the high seas and against Indians and Europeans in nearby colonies. Many who had served in the Revolutionary War, like Washington and Hamilton, doubted the effectiveness of the state-based militia. The Republicans, remembering Cromwell's dictatorship in England, feared standing armies as threats to liberty and insisted on Constitutional provisions making it difficult to raise or maintain a national army and giving Congress alone the power to declare war. As Madison argued, "War is the parent of armies; from these proceed debts and taxes; and armies and debts and taxes are the known instruments for bringing the many under the domination of the few." Republicans also resented the comparative high cost of military forces, which even in 1796 accounted for over one fourth of total federal expenditures, and for over half the funds spent on items beyond interest on the national debt.[15]

Given their differing views toward Great Britain and France, the American partisans did not see a common external threat against which to rally. They were happy with neutrality toward European affairs and in agreement with Washington's advice against entangling alliances. And as political fissures widened, each side increasingly distrusted the motives of its opponents.

As a result, and as the Framers probably intended when they created a government of separated institutions sharing powers, there was gridlock rather than consensus and compromise. Only 718 men were in the US Army in 1789; there was no navy or marine corps, since they had been disestablished after the Revolutionary War. Congress agreed to increase the army to deal with Indian threats on the borders, but military operations were usually supplemented by militia units. Washington pushed for an expanded regular army of 5,000 men for a frontier legion. In 1796, a law was passed setting a regular force, constabulary in nature, of a little over 3,000 men.[16]

To deal with contingencies, the Federalists in 1794 proposed a provisional army primarily to deter a British attack. The Republicans countered with a plan for a select corps of militia. Neither was approved. What did gain congressional favor, however, was a small program of six frigates to deal with pirates along the Barbary Coast. When news arrived in 1796 of a treaty with Algiers, the Republicans in Congress quickly passed legislation cutting the procurement from six to three and reducing the army's authorized strength while mandating regiments with small companies. Left in place, however, was basic law providing arsenals, stores, small units manning isolated frontier posts, with artillery and engineers in coastal forts, plus a tiny cavalry for patrol and communications.[17]

After four months home in Quincy, Adams returned to Philadelphia in November 1797, for the regular session of Congress.[18] He used his first annual message, now called the state of the union address, to reiterate his call for defensive measures, arguing that nothing had changed to render them unnecessary: "… the law of nations has lost so much of its force, while pride, ambition, avarice and violence have been so long unrestrained, there remains no reasonable ground on which to raise an expectation that a commerce without protection or defense will not be plundered." He said he was awaiting word from the delegation sent to Paris, but he doubted that "permanent tranquility and order" would soon return to Europe.[19]

In the subsequent weeks, Congress remained deadlocked over military measures. In February 1798 the House on three occasions voted down Republican attempts to repeal the tax passed earlier to complete the three frigates. Meanwhile in France, the Directory issued a new decree against American shipping and the US delegation received demands for bribes before talks could begin. These developments, when news later reached America, sparked an intense new crisis and transformed political attitudes toward rearmament.[20]

XYZ affair

On March 4, Adams received the first of several dispatches from the mission sent months before to France. The American envoys reported that the French had refused to receive them and had demanded bribes as a precondition for any negotiations. The French also insisted that Adams apologize for seeking an increase in US naval strength and that the Americans extend a large loan to France in addition to the bribe of about $250,000.[21] Letters also reported the recent decree closing French ports to any ship that had visited an English port and allowing seizure of neutral ships carrying anything produced in Great Britain.[22]

Once the reports were decoded, Adams consulted his cabinet. Half the members favored a declaration of war. One suggested seizing Louisiana, another urged an alliance with Great Britain. After hearing from Hamilton, who urged an attitude of "calm defiance" along with specific military measures, Secretary of War McHenry passed along a full-scale rearmament proposal. Hamilton suggested arming merchant vessels, building 20 sloops of war and 10 ships of the line, plus an eight-fold increase in the regular army, to 30,000 men, and a provisional army of another 30,000. The former Treasury Secretary prudently insisted that revenues be raised to cover the costs.[23]

At first Adams agreed with the idea of formally declaring war and began drafting a message for Congress with that recommendation. But he became persuaded that such action might endanger the American envoys. What he sent to Congress on March 19 was a simple report that he had "no ground of expectation" that the commission would succeed. He renewed his plea for increased defensive measures "with promptitude, decision, and unanimity."[24]

Congress reacted along party lines, the Federalists pressing ahead with military measures and the Republicans suspecting that Adams was exaggerating the threat. To calm any war fever, Jefferson suggested that Congress adjourn and go home to consult with their constituents, hoping to build support for peace He advised that to "do nothing, & to gain time, is every thing with us."[25]

On March 27, Representative Richard Sprigg of Maryland, a Republican, offered a series of resolutions questioning the need for war but supporting "adequate provision" for seacoast protection and internal defense. As debate proceeded, William Branch Giles of Virginia complained that the president was "pursuing hostile measures, and keeping back all information." Federalist John Allen of Connecticut then proposed that the president be asked to provide the diplomatic papers to Congress. His colleagues agreed, for it was difficult to debate the possibility of war without knowing as much as the president regarding French actions.[26] The Republicans were upholding the prerogatives of Congress; they did not expect that Adams would have withheld information so helpful to his argument.

On April 2, the House voted overwhelmingly – 65 to 27 – to demand the papers relating to the mission to France. Adams complied the very next day. After three days of closed-door debate, the Members voted to publish copies of the dispatches. The impact on public opinion was swift and overwhelming. As Elkins and McKitrick wrote, "The opposition in Congress to all intents and purposes collapsed." Moreover, Federalists would see electoral gains, especially in the South, throughout the rest of 1798 and into 1799.[27]

America united to defend its honor, support the president, and prepare for possible war. On April 9, Congress began debating the administration program introduced by Samuel Sewall of Massachusetts. It was a comprehensive bill, providing for three new army regiments for a total strength of 3,000 men; a Provisional Army of 20,000; and a direct tax on land, houses, and slaves to pay the costs. Republicans objected even to the first reading of the administration's bill and managed to prolong debate for a month. Their main target was the idea of a standing army, which they labeled a "system of terror."[28]

Hamilton joined the public debate with a series of essays in early April challenging the patriotism of the opposition. He charged the Republicans with "unremitting efforts to justify or excuse the despots of France, to vilify and discredit our own government ... to distract the opinions and to dampen the zeal of our citizens ... [and] to divert their affections from their own to a foreign country."[29]

Adams surged in popularity. His public appearances were greeted with wild applause, and he began wearing a military uniform and sword. On one occasion a supporter cheered that he had stood up to the "cutthroat, frog-eating, treaty-breaking, grace-fallen, God-defying devils, the French."[30]

Climate of fear and suspicion

In fact, there were many French sympathizers in America. Many refugees from the revolutionary turmoil lived in coastal cities and were politically active. Foreign Minister Talleyrand himself had lived in exile for two years. George Rogers Clark, renowned Indian fighter, still held a commission as a general in the French army and considered himself more loyal to Paris than to Philadelphia. The XYZ dispatches included a boast by M. Y that the "French party in America" would blame the Federalists for failed negotiations – and the Federalists believed that the Republicans were foreign agents. Prominent people talked of 100,000 Americans joining to support an invading French army. There were reports of a plot by the United Irishmen to aid France in overthrowing the US government as well as rumors of treasonous correspondence between opposition Virginia congressmen and the Directory in Paris. It was only a short logical step to the conclusion that the elimination of Republicans was a necessary measure against France in a time of war.[31] These fears spawned the Alien and Sedition Acts that same year.

There is no modern evidence to prove a conspiracy, but Federalists at the time firmly believed it. They argued that France won her battles in Europe by allying with parties in enemy nations. They witnessed pro-French demonstrators in the streets of Philadelphia and heard the revolutionary rhetoric. They were concerned that France might occupy Louisiana and other Spanish colonies and then dismember the United States. Southerners especially feared that France might invade with a black-led army, fresh from the Caribbean, which could incite a slave rebellion.[32]

The spring of 1798 was a turbulent time in America. Party divisions were deep; suspicion was rampant; fear of violence was widespread and credible. In an exchange of letters in 1813, Jefferson wrote that "the character of the times" that season was "terrorism", but he claimed that it was "felt by one party only." Adams cited numerous examples of what he called "Terrorism" against Federalists. In addition to the rebellions by Shay, Whiskey distillers, and Fries, he cited the situation during the XYZ crisis, "when I myself judged it prudent and necessary to order Chests of Arms from the War Office to be brought through bye Lanes and back Doors ... to defend my House."[33]

In April, Adams learned of a letter found near his house telling of a plot by émigré Frenchmen and American accomplices to burn down Philadelphia and kill its inhabitants. A second warning letter arrived ten days later, and then a third. In fact, there were four serious fires in Philadelphia between mid-April and June, 1798, with arson strongly suspected in two of them. There was also street rioting in May between pro-French and pro-British groups of young men. Public concern was so widespread that Jefferson wrote Madison that "many weak people packed their most valuable movables to be ready for transportation."[34]

The threat of terrorism and domestic subversion was palpable and powerful in 1798, though at this distance it seems grossly exaggerated. Nevertheless, it proved a strong impetus to congressional action to counter the perceived threats, both internal and external. Jefferson noted that feelings ran so high that, "Men who have been intimate all their lives cross the street to avoid meeting and turn their heads another way, lest they should be obliged to touch hats."[35]

This climate of fear triggered support for military rearmament and political repression. By the time it adjourned on July 19, the Fifth Congress had approved legislation quadrupling the size of the army and increasing the navy's fleet more than tenfold. It also re-established the marine corps and created a separate navy department. It authorized a 10,000 man provisional army in case of emergency. While not formally declaring war, Congress voted an end to American treaties with France and a full trade embargo as well as authorizing the navy to attack and seize French ships.[36]

Congress showed its seriousness of purpose by voting, for the first time, for a direct tax on land, houses, and slaves to raise the needed $2 million to pay for the military buildup. The measure imposed a levy of 50 cents for each slave and a graduated tax on houses – from 40 cents for one valued at $200 to 30 cents per hundred dollars' valuation for a $500 house.[37] This was widely felt among the population and the cause of later blowback. It was a change from previous practice, for the 1794 shipbuilding program had been financed by tariffs, excises on whiskey, snuff and sugar, and a luxury tax on owners of carriages.[38]

The final bill passed with substantial Republican support, 60–11, thus demonstrating the political pressure for standing up to France. But in recognition of its Constitutional prerogatives, Congress kept tight rein on how the president might use his new authorities. It limited the Provisional Army to only eight months, until the next planned session of Congress, and only in case of war, invasion, or "imminent danger." Southern Republicans thought it was better to have a fixed number of regular troops rather than a larger standby force. The president was not given authority to take preliminary steps such as appointing officers for the provisional army. Nor was he allowed to begin licensing privateers.[39]

In creating the Navy Department, Congress demonstrated its oversight powers. Many members were angry that the War Department had taken three years to build the three frigates first authorized in 1794. A House committee investigated the matter and issued a report charging "enormous expenses and unaccountable delays." When the opportunity arose in 1798, Congress established a separate Navy Department so that shipbuilding would get a higher priority. And it did. When Benjamin Stoddert became the first secretary at the end of June, there were only three ships in service and none at sea at the time. Within a month, the first US ship, the Ganges, went on patrol against the French. By the end of 1798, the navy had 20 ships, and 33 by the end of 1799.[40]

In addition to military and diplomatic measures against the French, the Federalists enacted political sanctions against French sympathizers at home. Adams signed the Alien and Sedition Acts into law and tarnished his reputation forever thereby, but the impetus for the laws themselves came from Congress. Adams fueled the firestorm by repeatedly branding his opponents as in league with France, but his legislative allies made it an urgent cause. As Senator Theodore Sedgwick of Massachusetts said when he first learned of the XYZ dispatches, "It will afford a glorious opportunity to destroy faction."[41]

The large number of immigrants coming to the new republic prompted consideration of legislation providing for naturalization. Federalists sought to stop or reduce the flow of new people because they seemed predisposed to support the Republicans. They tried to prevent foreign born people from voting or holding office, but lost that provision by a 2–1 vote. In mid-June, 1798, Congress narrowly passed – by a single vote in each house – a new Naturalization Act extending the residency period for naturalization from five to 14 years.[42]

This set the stage for other legislation dealing with foreigners. On June 25, Congress passed a measure extreme in intent but never invoked in practice. The Alien Act allowed the president "at any time during the continuance of this act" – that is, whether there was peace or war – to deport any aliens "he shall judge dangerous to the peace and safety of the United States, or shall have reasonable grounds to suspect are concerned in any treasonable or secret machinations against the government." No court hearing or even a specified reason was required for the deportation. The law expired in 1800 without ever having been invoked.[43]

On July 6, the Alien Enemies Act became law. The original version had called for a vast system of registration, surveillance, and individual permits. The target was the "wild Irish" who had pro-French sympathies and were drawn into Republican politics. Even Federalists recognized that the provisions were excessive, however, so they modified the legislation to limit the expulsions to cases of war or invasion and to permit judicial review. Thus changed, the bill attracted Republican support.[44]

Even the Sedition Act was modified to little more than the existing common law on sedition, but it was used for politically motivated prosecution. The original House bill made mere threats to defame punishable. The original Senate measure said there could be treason in peacetime, named France as the enemy, and made giving aid and comfort to an enemy punishable by death. Eventually the Senate struck references to treason and France. And the final Senate bill reflected common law practice regarding sedition. The House added provisions requiring proof of malicious intent and allowing truth as a defense. It also permitted juries to determine both facts and law.[45]

The final version made it unlawful

> to combine or conspire together, with intent to oppose any measure or measures of the government ... [or to] write, print, utter or publish ... any false, scandalous and malicious writing ... against the government of the United States, or either house of the Congress of the United States, or the President of the United States, with intent to defame ... or bring them into contempt or disrepute ...[46]

It is arguably significant that the final text prohibited criticism of the President and Congress, but not of the Vice President.[47]

Hamilton's views reflected the shifting mood on this bill. At first he said the "spirit of patriotism" could be used to crush the opposition so that "there will shortly be national unanimity." Later he urged caution: "Let us not be cruel or violent." And eventually he pleaded, "let us not establish a tyranny", warning that the sedition act might "endanger civil War."[48]

Struggle for control of the army

Although Adams had not pressed for expansion of the army, he moved quickly to implement the new law. On June 2, without even consulting his cabinet or the former president, he nominated George Washington as commander, hoping thereby to unify the country and intimidate the French. Enjoying retirement at Mount Vernon and doubting the likelihood of a French invasion, Washington was at first reluctant to accept. When he finally relented on July 8, he insisted that he be allowed to name his chief subordinates.[49]

This posed a problem for Adams because, even more than a war with France, he feared that Alexander Hamilton would become de facto head of the army and a threat to his administration. His animosity went deep, at one point calling Hamilton an "instrument of hell."[50] While both men were committed Federalists, sharing a common view of executive power and the national interest, they were political rivals. And with three of Adams' cabinet members routinely seeking and accepting Hamilton's advice on policy questions, the former Treasury Secretary was the guiding force behind many of the administration's actions. He remained close to Washington and expected to be named second in command.[51]

In fact, Hamilton had been Washington's young adjutant in the Revolutionary War and was a longtime proponent of a national army. He had chaired the Continental Congress' military committee in 1783 when it reported a plan for peacetime army of 3,000, supplemented by elite reserve in case of war or invasion, much like the later provisional army. While the plan was killed by Gerry and other New Englanders who fiercely opposed the idea of any standing army, Hamilton continued to press similar ideas in subsequent years.[52]

When Washington accepted Adams' nomination, he sent a list of proposed general officers with Hamilton's name first. "Oh no", Adams declared, "it is not his turn by a great deal."[53] He then engaged in a series of maneuvers to try to avoid making Hamilton Washington's chief deputy. He argued for restoring all revolutionary war generals to their prior rank, which would have made them senior to Hamilton. Eventually he was pressured into including Hamilton, but then left Philadelphia for Quincy without signing any of the commissions.[54]

Adams saw these maneuverings by Hamilton and his supporters as a threat to civilian control as well as to his own authority. He called the cabinet intrigue a "combined plot" to "appoint him [Hamilton] general over the president." And when it was over and Hamilton had prevailed, Adams called his rival "the most restless, impatient, artful, indefatigable and unprincipled Intriguer" in the United States.[55]

Hamilton and Secretary of War McHenry set to work organizing the new army.[56] As Adams had believed, "I have always cried Ships! Ships. Hamilton's hobby horse was Troops! Troops!" The newly named major general got involved in the minutia of military organization and training. He designed uniforms for Washington and other officers, designed huts for different ranks and even conducted experiments to determine the ideal length and speed of marching steps.[57]

Since the new army had political as well as military purposes, Hamilton insisted on the ideological purity of senior officers and blocked Adams' efforts to name some Republicans as generals. The plan for 12 regiments meant that he could pick nearly 400 officers, a potent force of future supporters.[58]

Adams concluded that he had lost control of the government. "With all my ministers against me, a great majority of the Senate and other House of Representatives, I was no more at liberty than a man in prison, chained to the floor and bound hand and foot."[59]

As a result, he decided to change course – and spent the rest of his term trying to avoid a full-scale war with France. He became more willing to see hopeful signs in the peace overtures emanating from Paris. There were various reports of French willingness to end the crisis. And the French defeat at the Battle of the Nile made it even less likely that France would take on America.[60]

Despite his proclamation in June that "I will never send another minister to France without assurances that he will be received, respected, and honored as the representative of a great, free, powerful, and independent nation", he suggested to his cabinet in October that he might announce his intent to nominate a minister to France "in order to keep open the channels of negotiation." Meeting resistance, he created only a small loophole – that he would not send a new minister "without more determined assurances he would be received."[61]

When Congress convened on December 8, Adams appeared with Generals Washington, Hamilton, and Pinckney arrayed behind him. He spoke of "the ultimate failure of the measures which have been taken by the Government of the United States toward an amicable adjustment of differences with" France. But he pointed to evidence that "it is averse to a rupture with this country, and that it has in a qualified manner declared itself willing to receive a minister from the United States for the purpose of restoring a good understanding." He declared, "It must therefore be left with France (if she is indeed desirous of accommodation) to take the requisite steps."[62]

With regard to the military measures previously adopted, Adams saw nothing "which ought to change or relax our measures of defense." He repeated his view that "An efficient preparation for war can alone insure peace." And he renewed his call for an increased navy "to guard our coast and protect our trade."[63]

Congress eventually approved an increase in the navy, but it also agreed to Hamilton's proposal for restoring and tripling what was called the Eventual Army, since the authority for a Provisional Army had lapsed. The legislature approved a force of 30,000 men in 25 regiments that could be used in case of war or invasion. Meanwhile, Hamilton and McHenry continued recruiting men and appointing officers for the New Army of regulars. Adams tried to slow things down, often sitting on matters requiring his clearance.[64]

The last straw for Adams was a report from Senator Sedgwick in early February 1799, that the Senate was considering giving Washington the new, never previously used rank of "General." Adams exploded. "What, are you going to appoint him general over the President?"[65] He was concerned about the former president dominating his successor, but even more concerned that Hamilton might succeed to the title and the power. He warned Sedgwick, "… if you must have an army I will give it to you, but remember it will make the government more unpopular than all their other acts."[66]

Two weeks later, without prior notification to his cabinet or Congress, Adams nominated William Vans Murray to be minister to France. Federalists and Republicans alike were "thunderstruck." He agreed to add two Federalists to the delegation as a concession to Congress, and all three were promptly confirmed. With the old Congress gone, and the sixth not scheduled to meet until December, Adams delayed sending the new envoys to France for eight months, perhaps waiting for the completion of additional navy ships.[67] The delegation concluded a treaty with France in September 1800, just before elections ousted Adams and the Federalists in Congress from power.

Support for the military buildup collapsed even before the treaty was signed, a casualty of domestic opposition to the direct tax, the idea of a standing army, and the Alien and Seditions Acts. Congress voted in February 1800 to suspend enlistments for the new army and cancelled the law for a provisional force. In fact, less than half the authorized number ever enlisted in the new army. They spent the summer of 1799 scattered, and the fall constructing winter encampments. They did little serious training. Washington lamented the failure to create the larger standing force several months before his death. "The golden moment is passed", he said, "and probably will never occur again."[68]

This rearmament controversy was repeated several times in later American history. Although the circumstances varied – different enemies, different domestic political dynamics, different degrees of harmony and discord – the underlying institutional forces operated in similar ways. The president always had the initiative, but Congress imposed its own conditions and viewpoints.

6 Franklin Roosevelt and the politics of rearmament

After all, if Italy and Japan have developed a technique of fighting without declaring war, why can't we develop a similar one?

Franklin Roosevelt, December, 1937[1]

You might say that the Army played politics in this period [spring of 1940]. That is a crude expression. Actually, we had regard for politics. We had regard for the fact that the President did not feel assured he would get the backing of the people generally and in the Middle West particularly and had to move with great caution.

General George C. Marshall[2]

Anyone who reads the hearings will note that the principal discussion is not what is in the bill, but what ought to be in the bill in order properly to meet the situation which confronts us.

Senator Carl Hayden (D-Ariz), May, 1940[3]

By forceful leadership, persuasive rhetoric, crafty diplomacy, and stealthy military actions, Franklin D. Roosevelt turned a withdrawn, isolationist United States into an arsenal for democracy and a fighter against fascism. In a later age, with a less sympathetic press and a less deferential Congress, he might well have been impeached for his conduct, which in several instances was of questionable legality and Constitutionality. Instead, he succeeded in rearming a reluctant nation and sending its soldiers and sailors, step by step, into combat. The verdict of history is in his favor, but the trials he endured were difficult, and the outcome never certain.

America in the 1930s was far from a world power, but was instead a sideline observer of the battles developing in Europe, Asia, and Africa. The US military was a pitiful force, labeled by General George C. Marshall "a third-rate power." The US Army in 1939 ranked nineteenth in size, between Portugal and Bulgaria, and was forty-fifth in terms of the percentage of the population under arms. Its units were mostly under strength, and it did not even have enough ammunition for target practice. About a third of the army's budget went for engineering projects in US rivers and harbors and maintenance of the Panama Canal. The navy had fallen below the ceilings set by the naval disarmament treaties of the 1920s and was building only about one fourth as many new ships as the other naval powers until Roosevelt directed some job creation money to the navy in 1933. As late as 1939, total military spending – including those funds for domestic water projects – accounted for only 12 percent of total federal spending.[4]

Isolationism was the only "ism" most Americans embraced. They didn't want to be infected by the Communism of Soviet Russia or the Fascism of Mussolini's Italy and then Hitler's Germany. They wanted to stay safe, protected by two large oceans. They were sympathetic to underdogs – Haile Selassie vainly resisting Italy's invasion of Ethiopia and Chiang Kai-shek struggling against Japan's invasion of China – but not to the point of getting involved in another foreign war.

Congress mirrored public opinion. Convinced by revisionist historians that merchants of death had driven America into the deadly trenches of the First World War, Congress built a fortress of neutrality laws making it next to impossible to be lured into another distant conflict. The legislative branch also nearly surrendered its war-making authority to the outcome of a national referendum.

Shielded from foreign wars and preoccupied with the continuing effects of the depression, the American people were largely indifferent to the collapse of the Versailles Treaty in Europe and the ineffectiveness of the League of Nations. Franklin D. Roosevelt, however, was concerned though he waited until he was safely reelected in 1936 before beginning to warn his countrymen of the gathering dangers abroad.

On October 5, 1937, with Japan fighting in China, a civil war raging in Spain, Ethiopia having been conquered by Italy, and Hitler and Mussolini proudly proclaiming a Rome–Berlin axis, Roosevelt spoke in Chicago about "the epidemic of world lawlessness." He noted that epidemics of diseases usually led to a community effort to "quarantine" the patients. All he proposed was a "search for peace", but the public reaction to his meta-phor of containment was overwhelmingly negative. The very next day he backtracked, telling a press conference that he planned nothing more than the speech itself – no change in the neutrality laws, no economic sanctions. He later told his speechwriter, "It's a terrible thing to look over your shoulder when you are trying to lead – and to find no one there."[5]

Despite this initial setback, Roosevelt set about to mobilize public opinion and US resources to defend America – and its beleaguered friends – against the new aggressors. As he told William Allen White two years later, "My problem is to get the American people to think of conceivable consequences without scaring the American people into thinking that they are going to be dragged into this war." In fact, he managed masterfully to keep public opinion in step with his rearmament program and his progressively less neutral foreign policy. In 1937, for example, a near majority – 46 percent – of Americans said they favored an increase in funding for the army and navy, compared to 33 percent for no change and 21 percent for a decrease. But another poll that year found overwhelming opposition – 95 percent to 5 percent – to taking part in "another European war" and a 1936 survey found Americans by a 4–1 margin unwilling to fight even if a foreign power tried to seize land in Central or South America. Nor were they willing – 37 percent for, 56 percent against – to require military service for young men.[6]

While the president was the champion of rearmament and the leader of the effort to untie the isolationist restraints on US foreign policy, he found willing allies in Congress and among opinion leaders, and eager subordinates in the armed forces. Together, they outmaneuvered and defeated the opposition and persuaded a reluctant populace that the costly rearmament and military aid to beleaguered Britain would make it easier for America to remain at peace.

Congress and the politics of isolationism

At the very time when Roosevelt hinted at collective action to quarantine aggressors, the Congress was moving in a different direction – debating a proposed Constitutional amendment requiring a national referendum before Congress could declare war. The vote in the House of Representatives in January 1938, fell just nine votes short of the number needed to bring it out of committee for floor debate.[7] The 209–188 vote suggests there was a majority in support of the measure, but far short of the two-thirds necessary to approve a Constitutional amendment.

Congress wanted to make it difficult to get involved in a war. During the mid-1930s there was a strong public reaction against the First World War, fueled by a congressional investigation designed to show that American involvement in that conflict had been driven by munitions manufacturers, the "merchants of death." When newly inaugurated Franklin Roosevelt proposed legislation granting the president discretion in imposing arms embargoes, Congress instead enacted a mandatory embargo. The first of five neutrality acts prohibited the export of "arms, ammunition, or implements of war"; barred US ships from carrying arms to belligerents; and restricted travel by American citizens on ships of belligerent countries.[8]

When that law was set to expire in 1936, Congress extended it for another year and added language prohibiting Americans from making loans or extending credit to belligerents. In 1937, the legislators passed an act specifically forbidding the export of arms, ammunition, and implements of war to Spain, which did not fall under the existing law since it was torn by a civil war. In May 1937, Congress voted for a third neutrality act, imposing a rigid embargo on both countries at war and those experiencing civil strife. The revised law added a prohibition on the arming of US merchant vessels.[9]

Isolationist sentiment was strong in the Midwest and Mountain states and included large numbers of both Republicans and Democrats. The disparate coalition included liberal pacifists, pro-Soviet Communists, pro-German and Italian fascists, anti-British Irish, anti-Catholic and anti-black bigots, and virulent Roosevelt haters.[10] All agreed with the slogan adopted by one of the leading isolationist groups, "America First."

Support for military programs was consistent but restrained. Budget requests were modest, compared with other government expenditures. In fact, benefits to veterans exceeded expenditures for the current armed forces from 1923 until 1938. During the 1930s the House of Representatives usually voted for some cuts in presidential requests for the army and navy, and the Senate then partially restored the funds.[11]

The strongest early support for rearmament came from the naval affairs committees, especially Congressman Carl Vinson (D-Ga.), who ultimately served as chairman – or ranking minority member – of the defense committee for 42 years. Although his committee could only authorize shipbuilding, subject to appropriations, he steered several bills through Congress during the 1930s. The Vinson–Trammel Act of 1934 called for adding ships up to the existing treaty limits. Another act early in 1938 provided for additional substantial increases in the US Navy.[12]

Roosevelt and Vinson teamed up to push money into shipbuilding. In 1933 the president directed the Public Works Administration to spend $238 million – 7 percent – of the emergency relief funds passed by Congress on construction of two aircraft carriers, four cruisers, 20 destroyers and four submarines – ships which proved vital in the war effort after the destruction of battleships at Pearl Harbor. In contrast, when Roosevelt assigned a mere $2.5 million from the same bill to manufacture munitions for the army, the pacifist outcry was so strong that the next Congress specifically prohibited the use of relief funds for munitions.[13]

The former Assistant Secretary of the Navy himself showed a clear preference for maritime power until after the outbreak of war in Europe. At one meeting, General Marshall pleaded, "At least, Mr. President, stop speaking of the Army as 'they' and the Navy as 'us'."[14] Roosevelt articulated, and probably shared, the view that ships guaranteed commerce and thus were more peaceful than ground troops. Building navies was not warlike compared to building armies, in his view. By the late 1930s, he developed an enthusiasm for air power, both land-based and sea-based. And he argued that building airplanes was another good way to avoid getting into war. Many in the Congress shared these views and were more willing to fund ships and aircraft than ground forces and their equipment. American public opinion also showed a strong preference for air and naval power.

As early as 1935, with majority opinion in favor of a larger military, the figures supporting a larger air force – which did not become a separate service until 1947 – were regularly much higher than for the army and navy. In one instance, the results were 48 percent favoring higher appropriations for the army, 54 percent for the navy, and 74 percent for the air force. Air power retained its favored status throughout the years before Pearl Harbor.[15]

Military leaders

Senior officers accepted the support they got from their civilian leaders, even though funding fell short of their perceived requirements. Time and again they reminded congressional committees that they were not allowed to ask for more than the president and his Budget Bureau had approved. But Congress sometimes restored a portion of the Budget Bureau cuts from the service proposals during the mid to late 1930s.[16] After war broke out in Europe, Roosevelt was more willing to let his service chiefs go directly to Congress with their requests. When they took the lead, he risked less of his political capital, and the Congress viewed the issues less politically.

The hero of the rearmament effort, and of the later war as well, was George C. Marshall. Strong-willed but self-effacing, Marshall had spent the interwar years studying the army's junior officers and marking some of them for the senior commands they eventually received when war came. He cultivated key members of Congress as well, offering them credible testimony and appropriate deference. He also gained invaluable experience outside the army when he was dispatched to set up and supervise some 19 camps for young men in the Civilian Conservation Corps. His CCC work helped him better plan the mobilization of millions of men when the army expanded under the draft.[17]

Marshall understood the strength of isolationist sentiment in the nation and the constraints it imposed on the military. "We had to move cautiously", he later told his biographer. "If I had ignored public opinion, if I had ignored the reaction of Congress, we would literally have gotten nowhere. I had to be very careful, I felt and I still think, not to create the feeling that I, as the leader of the military portion of affairs at that time, was trying to force the country into a lot of actions which it opposed." He was deferential toward the legislative branch, but was such an honest and straightforward witness that he built a "fruitful collaboration" with "a friendly and trusting Congress."[18]

His stature on Capitol Hill not only enabled him to succeed in gaining support for conscription and extra funds for the army, but also allowed him to overcome patronage pressures to retain superannuated officers. When he became Chief of Staff in 1939, he spoke of his plan to revitalize the army. "I've made a little list", he said. "I'm going to put these men to the severest tests which I can devise in time of peace. ... Those who stand up under the punishment will be pushed ahead. Those who fail are out at the first sign of faltering." When Marshall sought legislative authority to remove older officers, some of them persuaded the Chairman of the House Military Affairs Committee to pigeonhole the bill. Marshall then found an ally in Senator James Byrnes (D-So.Car.), who added language to an appropriations bill giving Marshall what he needed. When he subsequently removed a high ranking National Guard officer, the state's congressional delegation demanded a meeting. Marshall told them, "it seems to me that you are only considering one constituent and ignoring all [your] other constituents who are members of the division." He told the group, "if he stays, I go, and if I stay, he goes." The congressmen backed down.[19]

Marshall was admired on Capitol Hill and in the White House for his willingness to speak truth to power. In November 1938, at a White House meeting where Roosevelt told senior officers that he favored more money for airplanes, the bulk of which would be sent to European allies, the president asked Marshall whether he agreed. "I am sorry, Mr. President", the general replied, "but I don't agree with that at all."[20] His reply shocked his colleagues, but it made a favorable impression on Roosevelt.

Five months later he was summoned to the White House and told he would be named Chief of Staff of the Army. Once again, Marshall told the commander-in-chief that he wanted to be able to speak his mind freely. "Is that all right?" he asked. When Roosevelt gave the predictable affirmative reply, Marshall continued, "You said *yes* pleasantly, but it may be unpleasant." Later on, Marshall picked his battles carefully. "I never haggled with the President. I swallowed the little things so that I could go to bat on the big ones. I never handled a matter apologetically and I was never contentious." Nevertheless, the general felt that the president "rather hesitated about taking me into his confidence." And Roosevelt's untidy management style led Marshall to doubt the president's abilities until his decisiveness after Pearl Harbor.[21]

The Chief of Naval Operations, Admiral Harold "Betty" Stark, was also well regarded by the president and congressional leaders. Logical and methodical, he and Roosevelt had been friends since the First World War, and he had developed close ties with Capitol Hill during his navy career. It helped, of course, that the president had a special fondness for the navy.[22] In addition to these service chiefs, Roosevelt developed close ties with the head of the army's rapidly expanding air corps, General Henry "Hap" Arnold, and Admiral Ernest King, whom he made commander of the Atlantic Fleet and eventually successor to Stark as CNO. He also brought back from retirement Admiral William Leahy, first making him ambassador to Vichy France and then, in 1942, Chief of Staff and head of the Joint Chiefs of Staff.

The major tension in the military establishment was not between senior officers and their civilian superiors, or between them and the Congress, but rather it was the long and bitter clash between the top two civilians in the War Department. In 1936, Roosevelt had named Harry Woodring, a former Democratic governor of Kansas as Secretary of War. The following year, he appointed Louis Johnson as Assistant Secretary, the number two slot. A lawyer who helped found the American Legion and later served as its national commander, Johnson was bright, energetic, and the polar opposite of the isolationist Woodring. They clashed, profoundly and often, in personality and over policy. By 1939, *Time* magazine could report: "Only when absolutely necessary do they speak to each other. When official business requires them to communicate, they do so in writing or through harried subordinates. Mr.

Johnson despises Mr. Woodring. Mr. Woodring distrusts and despises Mr. Johnson, who for 27 months has gunned for Mr. Woodring's job."[23]

Roosevelt tolerated the open hostility because his management style was to assign tasks without regard to formal authorities or official lines of command. He also found it difficult to fire once-favored subordinates, even when they were disloyal or incompetent. If need be, the president would just work around them by going directly to others. In this case, Roosevelt bypassed Woodring and put Johnson in charge of airplane production and assigned foreign sales of aircraft to Britain and France to the Secretary of the Treasury, Henry Morgenthau.[24]

Marshall was caught in the middle, agreeing with Johnson on policy issues but still feeling primary loyalty to Woodring. One reason he became Chief of Staff, he thought, was that both Woodring and Johnson mistakenly thought that the other opposed Marshall's promotion.[25] Roosevelt waited until June 1940 to resolve the conflict by replacing both the Secretary of War and the Secretary of the Navy with prominent, pro-interventionist Republicans.

The gathering storm

Roosevelt recalled Congress to a special session on November 15, 1937, but only to deal with his domestic legislative proposals – wages and hours standards, agriculture and conservation. He was under fire from conservative Democrats who opposed these measures, as they had his plan to expand the Supreme Court so he could appoint more justices friendly to the New Deal. Facing domestic defeats, Roosevelt turned his attention to foreign affairs. When Japanese aircraft attacked the US gunboat *Panay* and three US merchant vessels in the Yangtze River near Nanking, the president asked Congress for funds to expand the US Navy, citing his "growing concern" about the world situation. "I do not refer to any specific nation or to any specific threat against the United States. The fact is that in the world as a whole many nations are not only continuing but are enlarging their armament programs", he wrote.[26]

Early in January 1938, he convened White House meetings with congressional leaders to discuss a defense buildup. In his subsequent January 28 message to Congress, Roosevelt called American defenses "inadequate" and asked for $28 million more for the navy and $17 million for the army. He argued that "we must keep any potential enemy many hundred miles away from our continental limits." At the same time Roosevelt launched secret discussions with the British, sending a navy captain for staff talks with the Royal Navy. In May, Congress passed a 10-year, $1 billion authorization for naval expansion for a "two ocean navy."[27]

Public opinion supported the start of rearmament. Roosevelt's international policy was endorsed, with 50 percent approving and only 15 percent disapproving in July 1938. And as the Munich crisis developed in September, surveys found majorities expressing a willingness even to pay more in taxes for a larger army – 53 percent, navy – 54 percent, and air force – 74 percent.[28]

Immediately after the agreement dismembering Czechoslovakia and putting the Sudetenland under German control, Roosevelt gave a radio address warning that Americans must continue to arm. "There can be no peace if national policy adopts as a deliberate instrument the threat of war", he declared. While publicly reiterating his desires for peace, he began secret talks with the British regarding ways to circumvent the neutrality act so that he could funnel US weapons to Britain even in the event of war. He also moved toward an Atlantic-first naval strategy by shifting the annual fleet exercise from the Pacific to the Caribbean and ordering the Pacific fleet to sail to the 1939 New York World's Fair.[29]

But his new obsession was air power. He suggested increasing American aircraft production from 2,600 to 15,000 per year. On November 14, 1938, he held a major meeting with his army advisors – the one where Marshall openly disagreed with his priorities. The president argued, "A well-rounded ground army of even 400,000 could not be considered a deterrent for any foreign power whereas a heavy striking force of aircraft would." He wanted an American air force of 10,000 planes and production capacity for 20,000 a year. He saw little need to spend money on pilots, crews, ground service and maintenance facilities, since the bulk of the planes would be sold abroad. He said he could not "influence Hitler with barracks, runways, and schools for mechanics." Eventually, he modified his plans so as to have a more balanced force of ground and air units, and a scaling back of production goals to 6,000 per year.[30]

This was the first of more than 20 cases between 1938 and 1945 when Roosevelt overruled the recommendations of his military advisers. That was, of course, his Constitutional prerogative, but it underscores the fact, as the official US Army history of the Second World War puts it, that "Roosevelt was the real and not merely a nominal Commander-in-Chief of the armed forces. Every President has possessed the constitutional authority which that title indicates, but few Presidents have shared Mr. Roosevelt's readiness to exercise it in fact and in detail and with such determination."[31]

Even before the new 76th Congress convened in January 1939, Roosevelt approached the Chairman of the Senate Foreign Relations Committee, seeking support for changes in the neutrality act. This proved politically impossible until after the German invasion of Poland, but it was a key legislative priority for the president throughout the year. Meanwhile, he tried to move American opinion to see the world as he saw it – with Nazi aggression as the principal threat, one which endangered America as well as Europe.

Sometimes he went too far. In a January 31 meeting with members of the Senate Military Affairs Committee, he warned that war in Europe was imminent and that, even if our oceans protected us, the economic consequences could hurt us. If Hitler dominated Europe, it would imperil the peace and safety of the United States. "That is why the safety of the Rhine frontier interests us", he said. "Do you mean our frontier is on the Rhine?" a senator asked. "No, not that", he replied. "But practically speaking, if the Rhine frontiers are threatened the rest of the world is, too." Roosevelt was angry at the leaks regarding his comments, denouncing them as a "deliberate lie", but the damage had been done. The incident boosted isolationist sentiment.[32]

Roosevelt also launched a peace offensive, asking Hitler and Mussolini in April to disavow specifically any intention to attack 31 listed nations. Hitler mocked the proposal, but it helped Roosevelt persuade the nation of his own sincerity in seeking peace, even as he obtained funds for increased armaments.[33]

Public opinion moved slowly as Roosevelt pushed. In a January 1939 survey, American respondents gave support to the idea that the United States must stand firm to prevent Hitler or Mussolini from taking any more territory by a 56 percent to 31 percent majority. But the only nation a majority said they were willing to defend with US forces was Canada – 73.1 percent – compared to only 27.8 percent for defending England and only 22.1 percent for defending France. Opposition to a draft was still strong – 37 percent for, 63 percent against.[34]

In one of the most significant developments in US civil–military relations, Roosevelt on July 5, 1939 transferred the Joint Board of the Army and Navy to the Executive Office of the President, where he could oversee and direct war planning and conduct. Later on, he created a chiefs of staff committee of the four most senior officers, so that they could interact with their British counterparts. Although Admiral Leahy continued to press for a formal document authorizing the Joint Chiefs of Staff, Roosevelt said it "would provide no benefits and might in some way impair flexibility of operations."[35] In other words, it might cause problems for Roosevelt's very fluid management style.

War in Europe

The same day Germany invaded Poland, General Marshall and Admiral Stark assumed their new positions as service chiefs, eager to continue the rearmament plans already authorized by the president and Congress. As required by the neutrality act, Roosevelt ordered an arms embargo. But in a nationwide radio address, he said, "This Nation will remain a neutral nation, but I cannot ask that every American remain neutral in thought as well." He also said America would continue searching for peace.[36]

On September 8, Roosevelt declared what he called a "limited national emergency" and ordered small increases in military personnel – 17,000 for the army and 5,000 for the navy. He recalled the Congress for a special session on September 21 and pleaded with the legislators to change the neutrality act. "I regret that Congress passed that [original 1935] Act", he said. "I regret equally that I signed that Act." He said he favored keeping US ships and citizens out of the war zones, but that victims of aggression should be able to buy armaments on a cash and carry basis.[37]

American opinion still opposed a draft and direct US participation in the European war. But 58 percent favored repeal of the neutrality act if it would help England and France but not Germany. And support continued strong for increased military spending. At the end of October the Senate voted 63–30 to revise the act, and the House followed a few days later with a 243–141 vote. The fourth neutrality act dropped the mandatory embargo and allowed arms sales on a cash and carry basis. But it still made it unlawful for US vessels to carry passengers or any articles to belligerent states, unlawful for US citizens or ships to go to or through combat zones, and unlawful to travel on ships of belligerents. It also banned the arming of US merchant vessels.[38]

The start of war in Europe stimulated additional measures to increase US military capabilities. Chairman Vinson, with Roosevelt's backing, introduced another naval expansion bill, authorizing $1.3 billions for ships over the next four years. The army's head of congressional liaison found strong support on the Hill for more funds and recommended: "I firmly believe that now is the time to ask for *everything* the War Department needs. We will get it. Let us strike while the iron is hot." Despite those favorable prospects, the president decided to ask for only another $120 million for the army.[39]

When Congress reconvened on January 3, 1940, Roosevelt devoted his state of the union address to foreign affairs. He reiterated America's search for peace but warned against ignoring the current realities of war. During the winter of what was called the "phony war", some members of Congress began pushing for cuts in defense spending. The House Appropriations Committee, for example, cut the president's request for the army by 9.5 percent in early April.[40]

Then Germany invaded Denmark and Norway on April 9, demonstrating Hitler's appetite for all of Europe. The next day, Marshall met with a group of Senators in a session arranged by Senator Byrnes and industrialist Bernard Baruch. As they talked long past midnight, Marshall pleaded his case for rearmament in what Baruch termed "a turning point in convincing … critics of preparedness." Events in Europe also led to a sea change in congressional opinion after the invasion of Belgium and the Netherlands on May 10. Henry Cabot Lodge (R-Mass.) told General Arnold "it is the general feeling of Congress, and as far as I can gather, among public opinion throughout the country, to provide all of the money necessary for the National Defense, and so all you have to do is ask for it."[41]

May 1940 marked the tipping point in American public opinion. That month found a 50–50 division on the question of the draft. Thereafter, support shifted to 2–1 in favor. That month found 86 percent to 14 percent for a doubling of defense spending, including if necessary a special tax to pay for the buildup –76 percent for, 24 percent against. Nevertheless, Americans were still opposed – 18 percent for, 74 percent against – to allowing American ships to carry war supplies to Britain.[42]

Working with Treasury Secretary Morgenthau, Marshall arranged for a meeting with Roosevelt on May 13. The general urgently sought an extra $657 million for the army, but his own civilian superiors disagreed among themselves. When Morgenthau defended Marshall's proposals, Roosevelt turned them down, telling his advisors, "I am not asking you, I am telling you." When Morgenthau told the president, "I still think you are wrong", he replied, 'Well, you filed your protest." He also rejected the suggestion that Marshall be allowed to go to the Hill on his own.[43]

The Treasury Secretary then asked Roosevelt, "Will you hear General Marshall?" At first Roosevelt, in a bantering mood, said, "I know exactly what he would say. There is no necessity for me to hear him at all." Then Marshall walked over the Roosevelt and asked directly," Mr. President, may I have three minutes?" "Of course, General Marshall", came the reply.[44]

The Army Chief of Staff then poured forth his concerns and frustrations, detailing the army's critical requirements for more money and better organization. He concluded, "If you don't do something … and do it right away, I don't know what is going to happen to this country." The surprised president gave the general part of what he sought and asked him to return a few days later with a more detailed list of requirements. This was the moment that "broke the log jam", in Marshall's view.[45]

On May 16, Roosevelt went before Congress with a huge military spending request – $1.2 billion in addition to his January request of $1.8 billion. He warned of the short flight times from Atlantic islands to US shores and asked for capacity to produce 50,000 planes a year. He sought to increase the army from 227,000 to 255,000 men and to provide weaponry for a mobilization force of 750,000. But he didn't call for conscription.[46]

When General Marshall and Admiral Stark went before Congress in the following days, they found a changed atmosphere. The Senate Appropriations Committee held three hours of hearings and reported a comprehensive spending bill. The naval affairs committees rushed to passage a bill increasing the number of the navy's planes from 3,000 to 10,000 and providing for 16,000 pilots. Congress also lifted army manpower levels by another 25,000 – to 280,000.[47]

The atmosphere was one of fear and urgency as German troops surged toward the English Channel and toward Paris. To restore American confidence, Roosevelt gave one of his biennial fireside chats on May 26. He detailed the improvements already achieved in military capabilities, the increased numbers of soldiers and sailors, of planes and tanks and anti-aircraft guns. He pledged, "it is my resolve and yours to build up our armed defenses. We shall build them to whatever heights the future may require."[48]

Five days later he asked Congress for an additional $1.3 billion for defense and for authority to call up the National Guard. Marshall asked an increase in the army to 325,000 and Congress boosted the figure to 375,000. Stark asked for a 70 percent increase in the size of the fleet, and Vinson spearheaded another naval expansion bill that authorized 13 battleships, six carriers, 32 cruisers, 101 destroyers, and 39 submarines.[49] On July 10, Roosevelt sent Congress another supplemental spending request for defense, seeking an additional $4.8 billion. These additional sums were finally enacted in early September.

Congress's new-found enthusiasm for military spending reflected a sea change in American public opinion as Nazi troops marched into Paris. Support for the $2 billion increase in defense was overwhelming – 86 percent for, 14 percent against – even when the pollsters mentioned a special tax to pay for it. Opinion was still evenly divided, however, on the idea of a draft and still strongly opposed to changing the neutrality laws so that US ships could carry war supplies to England.[50]

Meanwhile, the army staff was developing plan for a fully equipped force of 500,000 men by July 1941 and one million by January 1942. Marshall knew he needed a draft to reach those numbers, but the president was reluctant to endorse such a proposal. In fact, Roosevelt was preoccupied politically by the issue of running for a third term. He wanted the Democratic convention to draft him, without having formally to seek the nomination. So Marshall consulted with outside advocates of conscription, led by New York lawyer Grenville Clark. Although Marshall indicated that the army could not yet give public support to the proposal, he sent three officers to help prepare a bill. The bipartisan Burke-Wadsworth bill was introduced on June 20, two days before the French surrender to the Nazis.[51]

As Marshall later explained, "You might say that the Army played politics in this period. That is a crude expression. Actually, we had regard for politics. We had regard for the fact that the President did not feel assured he would get the backing of the people generally and in the Middle West particularly and had to move with great caution."[52] Once the bill was before Congress, Marshall felt free to testify, stressing that the War Department supported the measure.

Although until August 2 Roosevelt himself did not openly endorse the draft – which he always insisted on calling a "muster" to connote the rallying of Minute Men[53] – he took other steps to shape opinion in its favor. On June 22 he finally replaced his discredited secretaries of war and navy with two prominent Republicans – Frank Knox, the GOP candidate for Vice President in 1936 and Henry Stimson, who had been Secretary of War under Taft and Secretary of State under Hoover. Both favored conscription. It also helped that the 1940 Republican nominee for President, Wendell Willkie, endorsed the draft in his acceptance speech. Public support for the draft rose from 50 percent in May to 64 percent in June to 71 percent in July.[54] The final bill did not pass until September, and only with amendments limiting service to 12 months and forbidding use of troops outside the Western Hemisphere.

While the military leaders were pleased to get the ever-rising appropriations, they disagreed with several of the president's other decisions in the summer of 1940. Roosevelt ordered all-out military aid to Britain after the fall of France. The services protested, arguing that Britain was probably doomed and that the transfers would leave the United States stripped of necessary arms. They also protested Roosevelt's order transferring B-17 bombers to Britain and ordering that the fleet be kept at Pearl Harbor, supposedly to deter the Japanese.[55]

Congress also, though for different reasons, worked to restrict Roosevelt's ability to help Britain. The Senate Naval Affairs Committee Chairman, David Walsh (D-Mass.), was angry at learning of a plan to send 20 newly built torpedo boats to Britain. He called a hearing, at which the navy admitted there were also discussions under way with Britain regarding the sale of destroyers. Walsh went to the floor of the Senate, angrily denounced the plans to send American equipment abroad, and offered an amendment, readily adopted, banning the disposal of any equipment unless the service chief certified that such material "is not essential to and cannot be used for the defense of the United States." Chairman Vinson pushed a similar amendment through the House, though his motivation was anger at Roosevelt's veto of a bill designed to force the removal of some of the navy's senior officers and the protection of some naval aviators. Vinson's amendment prohibited the selling, disposal or scrapping of ships "without the consent of Congress."[56]

Arsenal of democracy

During August 1940, Churchill repeatedly pressed Roosevelt for the sale of 50 aging destroyers, but the president resisted. Churchill offered to lease some British bases in the Atlantic and Caribbean but insisted that the actions not be linked. At first, Roosevelt felt that he lacked legal authority for the deal without congressional approval, but Attorney General Robert Jackson wrote a memorandum arguing that the president had authority to transfer the destroyers. Once the acquisition of bases was added into the deal, the civilian leaders were confident that the gains to US defenses made certification by Admiral Stark easy. Jackson met with Marshall and Stark on August 22. After extensive discussion, the officers were ready to certify the transfers of the destroyers and some army equipment. Stimson also worked to obtain informal word that Willkie would support the deal. When Roosevelt announced the arrangements, he met with widespread support. Only a few diehard isolationists like Senator Walsh still denounced the plan.[57]

Late in the presidential campaign, two weeks after the first draft lottery and with Willkie surging to 4 percent below Roosevelt in opinion polls, the president used a major speech in Boston to reiterate his hatred for war and his promise, "Your boys are not going to be sent into any foreign wars." Every time before, and thereafter, Roosevelt had added the words "except in case of attack." When his speechwriter raised the point, the stubborn president countered, "If we're attacked it's no longer a foreign war."[58] The Boston statement was the one thrown back at him time and again later.

Roosevelt won reelection and then had to deal with the plans being developed by US military leaders and the worsening situation in Europe. Coordinating with Marshall, Admiral Stark recommended on November 12 what was called Plan Dog – the "D" option – calling for a defensive posture in the Pacific while building up offensive strength in the Atlantic. Stark also argued that US naval assistance alone would probably not defeat Hitler and that the United States would "need to send large air and land forces to Europe or Africa, or both."[59] Roosevelt was not ready to sign on to such a strategy, but he did authorize secret military staff talks with the British.

American involvement in the war seemed increasingly inevitable. Stimson noted "a basic agreement" on that point among himself, Knox, Marshall and Stark after a December 16 meeting. In a long cabinet meeting on December 19, the secretary of war told Roosevelt that the United States needed to begin stopping German submarines that threatened British ships. "Well, he said he hadn't reached that yet."[60]

What he had decided to do, however, was to seek congressional authorization to send massive amounts of military equipment to Britain, called Lend-Lease on the dubious proposition that the items would be returned after the war. One of the leading isolationists, Senator Robert Taft (R-Ohio), quipped, "Lending arms is like lending chewing gum. You don't want it back."[61]

Nevertheless, Roosevelt performed a series of public relations master strokes. In a news conference on December 17, he compared the assistance to lending a neighbor a garden hose to fight a fire. In a December 29 fireside chat, he said that the United States must be "the great arsenal of democracy" and that "there is far less chance of the United States getting into war if we do all we can now to support the nations defending themselves against attack by the Axis." The phrase, "arsenal of democracy", had been suggested by Frenchman Jean Monnet.[62] On January 3, 1941, Roosevelt's budget message called for a near tripling of defense expenditures in the coming year. Three days later, in his state of the union address to Congress, he linked arming the allies to the achievement of a world founded on "four freedoms" – of speech and religion and from want and fear.[63] These various steps helped to build strong public support for lend-lease, better than 2–1 in most polls.[64]

House Speaker Sam Rayburn arranged for the Lend-Lease bill to be numbered H.R. 1776 and then worked tirelessly to orchestrate prompt and favorable House action. He got numerous opposition amendments ruled out of order and corralled the votes to defeat 19 other restrictive amendments. In the Senate, the Democratic leadership, which felt compelled to refer the measure to the isolationist Foreign Relations Committee, arranged to add two lend-lease supporters to the panel. Senate passage by a 60–31 vote was helped by Willkie's endorsement of the bill and by acceptance of an amendment making it clear that only weapons built with lend-lease funds could be shipped abroad, not those funded by regular defense appropriations. Seven billion dollars were approved for the aid program at the end of March, and within two months over 60 percent of the funds had been allocated to specific programs.[65]

Congress then faced the military manpower question. While the initial draft lottery had gone smoothly, the draftees then began to barrage their congressmen with complaints about primitive encampments and inadequate equipment, such as broomsticks for rifles. Many looked forward eagerly to the end of their one year obligation in the coming October.

Army planners had opposed the one-year limitation and built the new divisions on the implicit assumption that the draftees would be in their units beyond 12 months. Otherwise, the forces would disintegrate. Marshall and Stimson recognized the problem and began urging the president to ask Congress for an extension of the draft. When Roosevelt's reluctance was evident, Marshall decided on a different approach – to use his own prestige to make the case. He turned his previously routine annual report into a hard-hitting brief for draft extension. He detailed the eight-fold growth of the army over two years, and the problems that necessarily created. He noted that in all but two regular army divisions, the number of draftees ranged from 25 percent to 50 percent. The loss of these men after 12 months would be devastating.[66]

Marshall failed to brief congressional leaders in advance, however, so the release of his report provoked an angry response even from such friends as Speaker Sam Rayburn, who had earlier gone on record opposing a draft extension as a violation of the moral contract with the draftees.[67]

Despite his reelection victory and the deceptively large Democratic majorities in Congress, Roosevelt was still a divisive politician. Antipathy toward him was still deep. When one Democratic Senator had complained that, by his court-packing scheme and efforts to purge conservatives from the party, Roosevelt was "his own worst enemy", his colleague bitterly replied, "Not while I'm alive, he isn't." The president was quite willing to let his subordinates do the heavy lifting on Capitol Hill. Thus, he allowed Marshall to take the lead on draft extension, waiting until July 21 to endorse the idea – and then putting the onus on Congress. Without extension, he said, the army would disintegrate. "The responsibility rests solely with Congress." Roosevelt also backed off pushing for repeal of the amendment restricting use of the draftees to the Western Hemisphere, giving "the laboring oar" instead to Marshall.[68]

Public opinion opposed the draft extension as well as the repeal of the Western Hemisphere restriction. Only 27 percent favored a two-year requirement; 65 percent wanted only one year. Over half the people favored the restriction throughout 1941 polling. A congressional aide with four decades' experience reported that the fear of the bill was the worst he had ever seen, that a vote for it was viewed as political suicide. The army's legislative liaison staff forecast a 5–1 vote against the bill.[69]

Marshall had an uphill fight, but he reached out to members of both parties, talking them through the accomplishments thus far and the problems remaining. He sensed that members viewed him as a nonpolitical expert on military matters. He made personal appeals to Republicans, at one point meeting with a group until past midnight. One congressman explained his continued opposition: "You put the case very well, but I will be damned if I am going along with Mr. Roosevelt." Marshall shot back, "You are going to let plain hatred of the personality dictate to you to do something that you realize is very harmful to the interest of the country."[70]

A crisis arose when some soldiers received and sent mail-in postcards printed by the America First Committee opposing the draft extension. When Stimson learned of the campaign he said, "this comes very near the line of subversive activities against the United States – if not treason." Marshall called the actions "sabotage" and said, "We cannot have a political club and call it an army."[71] Stimson later became convinced that soldiers got the postcards inadvertently and apologized to the isolationists, but the incident demonstrated the politicization of the issue.

The Senate approved the draft extension bill by 45–30 on August 7 after including some restrictive amendments. In the House, Rayburn predicted a close vote, at most for a one-year extension. He then lobbied members personally and relentlessly. "I need your vote. I wish you'd stand by me because it means a lot to me", he pleaded. When the final roll call came on August 12, Rayburn quickly announced the results – 203 in favor, 202 against – and gaveled down efforts by several arm-waving members to change their votes. On this vote, 21 Republicans joined with 181 Democrats in favor, while 65 Democrats and 133 Republicans – plus four from other parties – were opposed. To assure a strong Senate vote on the House-passed version of the bill, supporters stalled the debate until the army could fly absentees back to Washington.[72] The final version still barred the use of draftees beyond the Western Hemisphere. The only other major legislative fight before Pearl Harbor was in November, when Congress voted to repeal key remaining sections of the neutrality act.

Back door to war

Although Roosevelt never admitted sharing the view of his senior advisers that war was inevitable, he acted throughout 1941 as if he agreed. Yet he was cautious, telling Marshall in mid-January that "the Army should not be committed to any aggressive action until it was fully prepared to undertake it; that our military course must be very conservative until our strength had developed."[73] Nevertheless, Roosevelt was also quite willing to order naval actions that put US forces in direct conflict with Germany. Openly he expanded America's defense zones and secretly he collaborated with Britain against Germany.

He also put in place military officers more willing to follow his strategy. Although he respected General Marshall's honest disagreement on occasion, he could not tolerate the brash behavior of his Pacific Fleet commander,

Admiral James Richardson. When Richardson visited Washington and lunched with Roosevelt on October 8, 1940, he warned that the fleet was unprepared for war. But he went further and brazenly told the commander-in-chief, "Mr. President, I feel I must tell you that the senior officers of the navy do not have the trust and confidence in the civilian leadership of this country that is essential for a successful prosecution of the war in the Pacific." Less than three months later, Richardson was abruptly relieved of command and replaced by Admiral Husband Kimmel. Roosevelt also installed Admiral Ernest King – considered by his daughter to be "the most even-tempered man in the navy: he is always in a rage" – as commander of the upgraded Atlantic Fleet – and later as successor CNO. Roosevelt took his personal interest in commanding the navy to the point that he had a direct phone line to the director of the Ship Movements Division and plotted fleet movements with a wall chart in his office.[74]

In February, Roosevelt extended his designation of the Western Hemisphere neutrality zone to the twenty-sixth west longitude, just west of Iceland and east of the Azores. He said that belligerent ships or aircraft in that area should be viewed as "possibly actuated by unfriendly interests." Positions of hostile ships were then to be passed on to the British. In April he sent US troops to occupy Greenland pursuant to an agreement with the Danish ambassador in Washington, whose home country was now controlled by the Nazis. In late May he ordered about a quarter of the Pacific Fleet to be moved to the Atlantic.[75] In July, troops were sent to Iceland, Trinidad, and British Guiana.

US military leaders opposed these new garrisons and the convoy operations – as well as the July decision to impose an oil embargo on Japan. But Roosevelt overruled them, determined to press ahead in accordance with his own vision. That strategy, as described by his chief speechwriter, was "to keep one step ahead of public opinion, not to be stampeded into one direction or the other, and to encourage full debate before taking too drastic action."[76]

In fact, as early as January, 1941, the American people agreed – 48 percent to 42 percent – that we were already in the war. By June the figures on that question were 79.1 percent to 10.9 percent. By July, they supported convoying ships as far as Iceland, 75 percent to 15 percent. By September they were ready to have US ships shoot on sight – 62 percent – rather than waiting until they were first attacked – 28 percent. By early October, they favored 72 percent to 21 percent arming US merchant ships – a change in the law approved by Congress a few weeks later. Perhaps most significantly, by mid-September, the American people overwhelmingly – 71 percent to 22 percent – agreed that if the United States is to be free, the Nazi government must be destroyed.[77]

What the American public did not realize, however, is how provocative the United States forces became. They were outraged at the German attacks on American ships but ignorant of the secret orders to the navy to follow

German submarines and report their locations to the British. When a US flag ship *Robin Moor* was sunk by a German submarine in the South Atlantic on May 21 and its passengers left adrift in lifeboats for over two weeks, Roosevelt sent a strident message to Congress, calling the attack "outrageous and indefensible" and a violation of freedom of navigation. He declared that the United States would not yield "to world domination at the hands of the present leaders of the German Reich."[78]

Roosevelt took these steps because the Germans were winning the battle of the Atlantic. By May 1941, the Nazis were sinking three times as many merchant ships as the British capacity to replace them, and more than double the combined US and British ship production. Roosevelt decided to make a radio address from the White House on May 27 pointing out those sober facts and declaring an "unlimited national emergency." He said, "We are placing our armed forces in strategic military position. We will not hesitate to use our armed forces to repel attack." And he said cryptically, "Our patrols are helping now to insure the delivery of the needed supplies to Britain. All additional measures necessary to deliver the goods will be taken." Roosevelt also declared a preemptive policy. "Our Bunker Hill of tomorrow may be several thousand miles from Boston, Massachusetts .... Old-fashioned common sense calls for the use of a strategy that will prevent such an enemy from gaining a foothold in the first place."[79]

The very next day, however, Roosevelt tried to calm public opinion by telling his press conference that he had no plans to ask Congress to repeal the neutrality act and no plans to introduce convoys. He also wasn't sure what orders he might issue pursuant to the unlimited national emergency declaration. Stimson felt that the press conference was "one of the worst and almost undid the effect of the speech." Harry Hopkins saw it as a reversal "from a position of strength tone of apparently insouciant weakness." Yet that was Roosevelt's puzzling but irritating style, as explained in his comment, "I am a juggler. I never let my right hand know what my left hand does."[80]

Even General Marshall was sometimes uncertain of the president's policies. In late September he inferred from a newspaper article that Roosevelt favored a reduction in the size of the army in order to free more production and shipping for aid to Britain. His staff labored for several days on point papers opposing any reductions, but the army eventually proposed placing the best National Guard divisions in inactive status and organizing new divisions in their place. The plan, slated to start in February 1942, was overtaken by the events of December 7.[81]

On September 4, the US destroyer *Greer*, while trailing a German submarine for three and a half hours and dropping depth charges along with a British bomber, had at least two torpedoes fired at it, without suffering damage. Roosevelt responded to this first direct German–American exchange of fire by issuing a shoot on sight order and giving a radio address on September 11 with a carefully edited version of events. After first briefing congressional leaders of his planned text, he said the *Greer* was in "waters of self-defense" and that the German submarine had fired first. He did not mention the trailing of the sub or the collaboration with the British bomber. He listed earlier incidents – including the *Robin Moor*, the August 17 sinking of an American-owned, Panamanian-flagged ship, the *Sessa,* and the sinking of a US merchant vessel, *Steel Seafarer,* in the Red Sea on September 6 – which he said demonstrated a Nazi design to abolish freedom of the seas. He then accused the Germans of "unrestricted submarine warfare" – the code words for what triggered US entry into the First World War – and declared "our patrolling vessels and planes will protect all merchant ships." Comparing the German ships to rattlesnakes, he said, "when you see a rattlesnake poised to strike, you do not wait until he has struck before you crush him."[82]

That same day, General Marshall and Admiral Stark submitted their Joint Board military estimate of the overall situation, a comprehensive strategic document. While listing preserving the security of the United States and the Western Hemisphere as primary, they also said major US objectives were to prevent the disruption of the British Empire, prevent the further extension of the Japanese empire, and to establish regional balances of power in Europe and Asia to ensure US security. Significantly, they noted that "These national policies can be effectuated in their entirety only through military victories outside this hemisphere." The strategy paper declared, "if our European enemies are to be defeated, it will be necessary for the United States to enter the war and to employ a part of its armed forces offensively in the Eastern Atlantic and in Europe or Africa." Finally, the military document recommended fighting Germany first, "while holding Japan in check."[83] This became the template for the ensuing war.

On October 9, Roosevelt formally asked Congress to repeal most of the remaining restrictions of the neutrality act and allow the arming of US merchant vessels. He argued that keeping US ships out of combat zones "was inviting [Nazi] control of the seas .... It is time for this country to stop playing into Hitler's hands and to unshackle our own." Support for the legislation was further stimulated by the October 17 attack on the US destroyer *Kearny* with 11 killed, and the October 31 sinking of the US destroyer *Reuben James,* with the loss of 115 men. On November 7 the Senate passed the bill repealing key sections of the Neutrality Act and allowing the arming of US merchant ships by a 50–37 vote. A week later, the House passed the measure by another close margin, 212–194.[84]

Despite the public acceptance of naval clashes, Roosevelt escalated his rhetoric but still refused to call for a declaration of war. Even a former leader of the America First Committee, General Robert E. Wood, endorsed such action. The president did tell a Navy Day audience on October 27, "America has been attacked." And he said, "we do not propose to take this lying down." The orders to shoot on sight still stood. Yet he asked only for repeal of the neutrality act, nothing more decisive. Admiral Stark confided to a friend, "The Navy is already in the war in the Atlantic, but the country doesn't seem to realize it. ... whether the country knows it or not, *we are at war.*"[85]

Figure 6.1   Franklin Roosevelt signing the declaration of war against Japan in the presence of congressional leaders, 1941 (Library of Congress)

Meanwhile, the crisis with Japan was worsening. In response to an unacceptable Japanese note on November 20, Marshall and Stark urged diplomatic maneuvering to allow more time to deploy forces to the Pacific. Roosevelt overruled them, as he had the previous summer when he imposed the oil embargo, and instead sent an ultimatum on November 26 that the Japanese were sure to reject. As Stimson recorded in his diary, "The question was how we should maneuver them into the position of firing the first shot without allowing too much danger to ourselves."[86] With diplomacy failing and with the Japanese task force secretly headed toward Hawaii, the die was cast for war with Japan.

Interplay of civil–military relations

The rearmament fight revealed the extensive powers of the president – to act on his own at times as well as to persuade the public and the Congress. Roosevelt skirted the boundaries of his legal authority by his actions to aid Britain and police the North Atlantic. He also used his communication skills to inform, educate, and lead a reluctant citizenry along the path of military expansion and probable war. But he was always acutely sensitive to public opinion and on numerous occasions retreated from his declared positions when they met hostile responses.

For its part, Congress followed Roosevelt's lead, while asserting its own special prerogatives, such as controlling the direction and expenditure of funds. On occasion it added money for favored projects, as has always been usual. When Roosevelt declined to push for a draft or a draft extension, Congress assumed the responsibility for acting on the politically charged issues. After trying to tie the president's hands with the neutrality legislation, the legislators slowly, but with public support at each stage, undid their restraints. While some members fought the drift toward war loudly and vigorously until December 7, the Senate and House as institutions deferred substantially to the president throughout the buildup. They did not even conduct embarrassing or revelatory hearings, which might have undercut support for US policies.

US military leaders accepted civilian control without question or open dissent. They accepted presidential decisions, even when Roosevelt overruled them. They followed the weak leadership of some service secretaries while welcoming their more skilled replacements. Marshall and Stark spoke truth to power in the White House and on Capitol Hill and gained respect and support in return. Marshall also discovered that he could get out in front of the president, as on the draft issue, without damaging his relationship.

Together, the civilian and military leaders fashioned an amazingly large and successful rearmament program. More by luck than by design, they began building the armed forces and weaponry to fight a global war and adjusted foreign policies to make use of America's strengths. They developed the outlines of a grand strategy which, despite surprises and setbacks, they were able to pursue after Pearl Harbor. This is a story of prudence and success.

7 Harry Truman and the politics of rearmament

I will not buy a pig in a poke.

Harry Truman on the NSC 68 rearmament policy paper[1]

A military establishment is not a political democracy. Integrity of command is indispensable at all times. There can be no twilight zone in the measure of loyalty to superiors and respect for authority existing between various official ranks.

Navy Secretary Matthews on the firing of CNO Admiral Denfeld[2]

The removal of Admiral Denfeld was a reprisal against him for giving testimony to the House Armed Services Committee. This act is a blow against effective representative government in that it tends to intimidate witnesses and hence discourages the rendering of free and honest testimony to the Congress ....

House Armed Services Committee report, March 1, 1950[3]

Harry Truman didn't want to rearm America in 1949. He wanted to fight communism, but with other weapons – abroad with foreign aid and at home with tough new laws and a vigorous FBI. He preferred to focus on domestic issues, including national health insurance and civil rights.

His feisty 1948 campaign returned him to the White House with a surprising victory and helped replace the "do nothing" Republican-controlled eightieth Congress with strong Democratic majorities in the eighty-first. He sent the new Congress his proposed budget for fiscal year 1950, starting July 1, 1949, with a level $14.3 billion requested for defense – less than half what the military services had originally sought.

He fired his first secretary of defense, James Forrestal, in March and replaced him with a politically ambitious lawyer, Louis Johnson, who proved eager to limit military spending. Truman strengthened Johnson's hand by forcing Congress to pass a new law giving the secretary of defense much greater control over the Pentagon and its budgets. The president also quelled the "revolt of the admirals" by replacing the Navy Secretary and the Chief of Naval Operations.

Abroad, Truman strengthened Europe against Stalin's probes with the creation of NATO and continued aid through the Marshall Plan. The Soviet leader ended his eleven-month blockade of West Berlin and acquiesced in the establishment of a West German government. In Asia, however, the United States washed its hands of the failing Kuomintang government in China as its leaders retreated offshore to Formosa (Taiwan). American forces also withdrew from South Korea, since that peninsula was deemed outside the redrawn US "defense perimeter" in Asia.

And then, in September 1949, things fell apart. The comfortable assumptions driving US policy proved faulty and the political challenges became significant. Even so, it would take another 14 months – and shocking, border-crossing aggression in Korea – before Truman fully embraced and fought for the full-scale rearmament that allowed America to reach a standoff in Asia and more broadly in the Cold War with the Soviet Union.

New team, new priorities

Harry Truman believed that presidents should be decisive, truly in charge of their administrations, and willing to accept responsibility. The sign on his desk echoed his view: "the buck stops here." He was respectful of senior military officers, but not intimidated by them. Even during his tough reelection fight in 1948, he did not hesitate to impose racial integration on the armed forces or tough budget limits. In a May 13, 1948 meeting with Defense Secretary James Forrestal and the Joint Chiefs of Staff, he insisted that the fiscal year 1950 defense budget be kept within $15 billion, despite their pleas for more. The president also handed his military leaders a formal memo, concluding:

> As Commander in Chief I expect these orders to be carried out whole-heartedly, in good spirit and without mental reservation. If anyone present has any questions or misgivings concerning the program I have outlined, make your views known now – for once this program goes forward officially, it will be the administration program, and I expect every member of the administration to support it fully, both in public and in private.[4]

After his surprising election victory, he was even more determined to maintain fiscal discipline on the armed forces. Despite the ongoing Berlin blockade and the communist military successes in China, Truman insisted on further cuts. He met with the JCS and their civilian bosses on December 9, 1948 and listened politely, but refused to relent. After an hour's discussion, he changed the subject. "Thanks, boys", he said. "I used to be a judge in Kansas City and found a couple of bottles of bourbon. Let's have a drink."[5]

Harry Truman was direct and unpretentious, self-confident while recognizing his limitations. He had military experience as an artillery captain in the First World War and remained active in the army reserve. He retained a soldier's prejudice against the other services, however, noting in 1948 that "The air boys are for glamour and the navy as always is the greatest of propaganda machines." In 1950 he had to apologize publicly for saying, in a letter to a Republican congressman, that the Marine Corps was only "the Navy's police force" and that he intended to keep it that way, despite the fact that it had "a propaganda machine that is almost equal to Stalin's."[6]

It's important to remember that there was no Defense Department in early 1949. There was a Pentagon and a Secretary of Defense with a small staff of about 150 professionals.[7] The Secretary presided over – but didn't really control – the strangely named National Military Establishment – NME – and the real powers in the Pentagon were the Service Secretaries, who had large staffs, established traditions, cabinet rank, and statutory membership on the National Security Council. In one of the ironies of history, the first Secretary of Defense, James Forrestal, had fought efforts to create a strong position and then suffered the consequences of its weakness. By 1949 he was ready to support much greater power for the post.

Truman's 1950 fiscal year budget, sent to Congress on January 10, allowed only $14.3 billion for defense. And he said that figure would stay level for "the foreseeable future." He held several meetings with the military leaders in subsequent months in order to remind them of the need for a united front in support of his program. To help enforce discipline on the unhappy Chiefs, the president brought in General Dwight D. Eisenhower to be the "presiding officer" over the JCS, and he replaced Forrestal with the more compliant Louis Johnson. Eisenhower shared Truman's concerns about the budget. He confided to his diary that the president should be tough on the Chiefs. The general began his new duties on January 24 by giving the Chiefs a pep talk, urging them to be tough on themselves as well as on the other services. He got them to agree to work within the proposed budget.[8]

Louis Johnson had been a vigorous advocate of rearmament when he was Assistant Secretary of War during 1937–40. By 1948, he was politically active and ambitious, raising $2 million for Truman's reelection campaign. Rewarded with the Pentagon post, he joined in preaching fiscal discipline. In a speech to the National War College, he said that the armed forces had "to provide honest value for the dollars" they received, since those funds competed with "revenues for measures dedicated to the health, progress and social welfare of the American people." The challenge, he said, was to find a balance that deterred aggression "without militarizing the nation or bankrupting it in the ordeal."[9]

The new defense secretary practiced what he preached by canceling the Navy's new aircraft carrier and insisting on further cuts in military spending. This provoked what was dubbed "the revolt of the admirals", but what in fact was a deeper debate over US military strategy.

America's armed forces were demobilized and cut back following the Second World War. The 1945 force of 12 million men and women had shrunk to 1.4 million in 1948, an 88 percent cut. Defense spending had fallen 89 percent, from $83.3 billion in 1945 to $9.1 billion in 1948.[10] The army and the navy were locked into what they viewed as a life or death struggle with the newly established air force, the service which offered the glamour of new technology and the promise of military victory through strategic bombing.

The navy pinned its hopes on carrier-based aircraft and had already laid the keel on its 65,000-ton super carrier, *United States,* just five days before Secretary Johnson cancelled the program on April 23, 1949. The Navy Secretary resigned in protest, while the admirals stayed and started a counterattack. They complained openly of inadequate budgets and low morale. They orchestrated an attack on the air force and its B-36 program, which led to the dramatic congressional hearings described below. And they challenged the emerging US strategy of nuclear deterrence.

Lacking a capability to launch atom-bomb-carrying aircraft, navy leaders began arguing that such weapons were immoral as well as indecisive. Admiral Arthur Radford, later to become JCS Chairman under President Eisenhower and a defender of Ike's "massive retaliation" strategy, in 1949 argued, "I do not believe that the threat of atomic blitz will be an effective deterrent to a war, or that it will win a war." He went on to say that "the threat of instant atomic retaliation will not prevent [war], and it may even invite it." Rear Admiral Ralph A. Ofstie went further, calling the bombing of urban areas "contrary to our fundamental ideals", and declaring strategic bombing "contradictory ... to fundamental ideals, policies, and commitments of the United States."[11]

The air force defended its programs and its strategy to enthusiastic audiences. A month before the super carrier was cancelled, the air force dramatically revealed its new in-flight refueling technique by flying a B-50 bomber around the world non-stop. The medium range B-50 was a modernized version of the B-29 of the Second World War. The air force also announced that one of its new, top priority long-range bombers, the B-36, had made a successful 9,600 mile nonstop flight, carrying a load equivalent to an atomic bomb for 5,000 miles, thus demonstrating an ability to strike distant targets and return to base. A few days later the press carried leaked reports of an air force presentation pinpointing seventy strategic targets in the Soviet Union that could be hit by B-36s on non-stop return flights from North America.[12] These events helped to solidify US public and congressional opinion in support of the air force and its capabilities.

Truman and Johnson tried to restrain the inter-service rivalry and to maintain a balanced military force. The president impounded funds added to his budget by Congress to build more planes for the air force. He also acted to preserve his options regarding nuclear strategy by keeping both the physical custody as well as the operational control of atomic weapons in civilian hands until after the start of the Korean War. The new defense secretary tried to muzzle the military with his Consolidation Directive No. 1, centralizing security review procedures in his office. He also slashed service public information staffs by 90 percent, transferring many of the people to his own departmental staff. He even maintained leverage over the civilian service secretaries by keeping their pro forma letters of resignation, submitted when he assumed office, on file for possible later use.[13]

In the spring of 1949, with the super carrier cancelled and the Berlin blockade lifted, Johnson demanded additional cuts in budget plans for fiscal year 1951. He bragged publicly that he was cutting another billion dollars in waste and duplication from the Pentagon budget and insisted internally that the Chiefs cut another $1.4 billion from their programs to bring the new budget to $13 billion. The Chiefs reluctantly complied.[14] A few months later, when the Chief of Naval Operations, Admiral Louis E. Denfeld, was insufficiently supportive of the administration in congressional testimony, Johnson relieved him of his command. The Navy Secretary admonished the CNO with sharp words: "A military establishment is not a political democracy. Integrity of command is indispensable at all times. There can be no twilight zone in the measure of loyalty to superiors and respect for authority existing between various official ranks."[15]

The impact of these actions, Mark Perry has written, was that "the JCS was stunned into paralysis."[16] For good or ill, civilian control was complete. In fact, Harry Truman had a strategy which was far more comprehensive than the Chiefs, or the public, seemed to realize. His goal was to contain communism, "to support free peoples who are resisting attempted subjugation by armed minorities or by outside pressures." He first announced this Truman Doctrine in his message to Congress proposing aid to Greece and Turkey in March 1947. But the means he chose were military and economic aid to threatened nations rather than an increase in US military capabilities. He followed this narrowly focused military assistance program with the comprehensive economic aid program named after the enormously popular former general and then secretary of state, George C. Marshall.

Under these programs, the State Department budget surged to levels never achieved before or since. In 1949 the United States spent 53 cents on foreign aid for every dollar spent on defense, and together defense and foreign aid accounted for one half of the federal budget. In 1950, before the Korean War, nonmilitary programs were equal to one-third of the Pentagon budget. In 2006, by contrast, even before counting the costs of war in Iraq, the Pentagon gets 12 times as much as the United States spends on international programs for security and development.[17]

Geographically, Truman's strategy put Europe first. That was where US leaders feared Soviet probes, where local communist parties still had large followings. China was seen as lost to the communists despite the best American efforts to shore up the crumbling Kuomintang government under Chiang Kai-shek. America's defense perimeter in Asia ran through Japan and the Philippines, and excluded Korea until it was actually attacked. The keystone in the strategy was the treaty establishing the North Atlantic Treaty Organization, NATO, pledging each member to defend all the others, signed on April 4, 1949 and ratified by the US Senate on July 21. This strategy reflected and sustained an unusual level of bipartisan support.

Congress and national security strategy

Although the legislative branch shared Truman's antipathy to communism and his desire for fiscal discipline, it asserted independent views on many aspects of policy. Congress was slow to enact the Marshall Plan, delaying final action until just after the communist coup in Czechoslovakia in February 1948. Legislators remained uneasy about supporting what could be labeled foreign aid, since such programs ranked low in public opinion. Even today, Americans seem to believe that US aid programs amount to 10 percent to 15 percent of the federal budget, instead of the one percent actual figure. And public opinion remains hostile to "foreign aid."[18]

Congress was unified over the defense of Europe but divided over Asia policy. There was a large "China lobby" that supported Chiang Kai-shek and demanded substantial US diplomatic and material assistance to his crumbling anticommunist government. The House of Representatives defeated, however, a modest aid program for Korea, requested as US troops were withdrawing from the peninsula.

Like the public it represented, Congress was enthusiastic about air power, seeing atomic weapons as the ultimate defense. Air power advocates favored a minimum of 70 groups for nuclear deterrence and war-fighting, compared to the 45 groups then in existence. In 1948, Truman had approved 55 "limited strength" groups and another 15 "skeleton" units. Later that year the then-Republican Congress overwhelmingly approved a 66-group force and added $1 billion for additional aircraft. Truman refused to spend the extra money.[19]

Democrats regained control of Congress after the 1948 elections. They went from a 45–51 vote minority status in the Senate to a 54–42 majority. In the House, they surged from a 188–246 minority to a 263–171 majority. The eighty-first Congress got along well with the president, who held weekly meetings with the leaders and engaged in frequent phone calls.[20] Although Truman had strong views on presidential prerogatives, he was otherwise solicitous of and deferential to legislative sensitivities. Both parties had conservative and liberal wings, facilitating bipartisan majorities on defense and foreign policy as well as domestic programs.

Some members championed particular services and took sides in the rivalries raging in the Pentagon, but the most vocal were usually the ones trying to protect the most beleaguered, especially the navy and Marine Corps. Despite press reports that Truman had slashed the Chiefs' budget requests in half and had even cut his defense secretary's program by 15 percent, Secretary Forrestal was asked no questions during his 1949 budget testimony about what the higher figures would provide in added capabilities. Congress seemed content with the notion and the level of restraint. Even longtime shipbuilding advocate Carl Vinson (D-Ga) supported cancellation of the super carrier because of the budget limitations.[21]

During consideration of the 1950 fiscal year budget, the House cut the navy request by three percent and army by five percent while adding 17 percent for the air force. The Senate restored a small portion of the cuts and rejected the air force add-ons. In conference, the two sides agreed to most of the air force increases within a modest three percent boost overall. Truman's advisors said that the president could not refuse to spend the extra money, but he overruled them and impounded the funds.[22]

Where the Congress was most influential, however, was in investigating military programs and in enacting significant new legislation strengthening the secretary of defense. Rep. James Van Zandt (R-Pa), a naval reservist who had served in both world wars, made good use of his minority status to defend the navy and criticize the air force. Senior naval officers fed him materials which he used to expert advantage, gaining press coverage and forcing action by the Democrats. Claiming that the B-36 was vulnerable to enemy fighters, Van Zandt won House approval of a nonbinding resolution asking the Pentagon to conduct mock battles between the new bomber and navy fighters. He then introduced a resolution calling for a select committee to investigate charges of deception and mismanagement in the B-36 program. To deal with the firestorm sparked by Van Zandt, House Armed Services Committee Chairman Carl Vinson announced detailed hearings into the matter.[23]

Those hearings in August, 1949 exposed the navy's propaganda campaign and solidified support for the B-36. The navy civilian who had authored a widely reported document alleging scandalous charges about the bomber program and its management, concluding it was a "billion dollar blunder", was summoned to testify and recanted his allegations. So complete was the air force victory in the hearings that the House committee unanimously approved a statement that there was no "one iota, not one scintilla of evidence … that would support charges or insinuations [of] collusion, fraud, corruption, influence or favoritism" in the B36 program.[24]

On the question of reorganizing the Pentagon, Congress also asserted its powers over the military and against the wishes of the president. It recognized the problems caused by inter-service rivalries and the weak secretary of defense. In the National Security Act of 1947, the eightieth Congress had rejected Truman's proposal for a strong secretary, siding instead with the navy's idea of loose coordination and service autonomy. In 1949, however, Truman had new reorganization authority as a result of recommendations from the Hoover Commission, which had been established to find ways to make government more efficient. The president pressured Congress to enact new legislation by confronting them with an executive order unifying the services which would otherwise take effect.

In May 1949, the Senate passed a measure, supported by the administration, establishing a formal Department of Defense and giving its secretary specific power over the services. The bill empowered the secretary to reorganize the new department without further action by Congress. The bill also created the new post of Chairman of the JCS and named him the principal military advisor to the president and NSC. The measure also dropped the service secretaries from membership on the NSC.

Chairman Vinson opposed the new legislation but responded by offering amendments strengthening the legislature's role in defense policymaking. He proposed language forbidding the creation of a general staff or of an overall chief of staff of the armed forces. His bill required the secretary to consult with the Senate and House Armed Services Committees before exercising transfer or consolidation authority and repealed the Hoover Commission reorganization authority for the new Department of Defense. Finally, Vinson insisted on language authorizing the service secretaries and chiefs of staff to present to Congress "after first so informing the Secretary of Defense, any recommendation relating to the Department of Defense that he may deem proper."[25] Dwight Eisenhower later complained that this amounted to "legalized insubordination." But the lawmakers wanted to avoid any muzzling of military officers.

Vinson won most of his provisions, but the secretary of defense won direct control over a consolidated department. Congress had asserted itself and preserved its ultimate authority over DOD structure and organization, and its shared control over military officers. Truman signed the new bill into law on August 10, 1949. That month was the high water mark in Truman's effort to shrink the military establishment and avoid the costs of rearmament.

Bleak September

Events during the next month shattered many of the assumptions on which Truman's national security policy had been based. In Asia, the Chiang Kai-shek forces retreated offshore to the island of Formosa, now known as Taiwan. The Chinese communists, led by Mao Tse-tung, proclaimed their new government on October 1. The US government had foreseen the collapse of anti-communist forces, despite strong US support over many years. Secretary of State Dean Acheson sent a report to the NSC on February 28, 1949, declaring,

> it is now beyond question of doubt that any further military program for the Chinese mainland will in the foreseeable future (a) be ineffectual, (b) eventually contribute to the military strength of the Communists and (c) perhaps most important of all, solidify the Chinese people in support of the Communists ....[26]

On June 16, the CIA predicted that "before the year is out, the Communists will have formed a central government which will seek international recognition." The intelligence estimate argued that "The US cannot reverse or significantly check this course of events ...."[27] Nevertheless, the establishment of a communist government under Stalin's tutelage was an enormous defeat for US policy. It also sparked a "Who lost China?" debate in which the Republicans charged US officials with sympathy for and actions supporting the victorious communists.

Even within the Truman administration there were differing approaches to the new circumstances, Defense Secretary Johnson called for an NSC effort to develop a "carefully considered and comprehensive plan" to contain communism in that region, thus creating a paper trail of internal doubt over Truman's policy.[28] This was only one of several disputes between the secretary of defense and the secretary of state. The Joint Chiefs of Staff, according to JCS Chairman, General Omar N. Bradley, sided with the China lobby in terms of providing limited military assistance to buy time.[29] But in a formal memorandum of August 17, the Chiefs declared that "the strategic importance of Formosa does not justify overt military action ... to prevent Communist domination ...."[30]

All officials concurred in the decision to withdraw US troops from Korea by June 30, 1949, thereby leaving only diplomatic and military assistance missions and exemplifying the decision to exclude Korea from America's defense perimeter in Asia. Meanwhile, the United States continued to occupy Japan pending the conclusion of a formal peace treaty, not achieved until 1951, and to maintain major bases in the Philippines, a former colony granted independence in 1946.

The most surprising and alarming event in September was the discovery that the Soviet Union had tested a nuclear weapon. On September 3, an air force weather reconnaissance plane on routine patrol picked up signs of abnormal radioactivity.[31] Subsequent flights led to a determination that the Russians had exploded a bomb.

In March 1948, the Joint Intelligence Committee had concluded that "The earliest date by which the Soviets may have exploded their first test bomb is mid-1950" and that "The probable date ... is mid-1953." By 1955, the estimate concluded, the Soviets might have a stockpile of 50 atomic weapons.[32] An intelligence assessment the previous May had concluded that a "deliberate Soviet resort to direct military action against the West during 1949 is improbable."[33] There was no mention of the prospect of a Soviet A-bomb. Press reports in the fall of 1948 said that the JCS did not expect a Soviet test before 1952. [34]

The Soviet bomb shattered the belief in American invulnerability. It meant that the United States had lost its nuclear monopoly, thus denying it leverage over others and giving Stalin a check on US action against him. It also meant that the time of genuine US vulnerability, when the Russians might have the capability for a devastating surprise attack on America, was only a few years away, in 1955. The Soviet Union was on the verge of becoming the world's premier military force, combining massive ground forces with enough nuclear weapons to defend itself and to threaten others.

The Cold War had many traumatic moments, when the dangers of direct conflict were palpable or when the reassuring assumptions of the past were shattered by new realities. One such moment came in March 1947, when the United States realized that it had to act vigorously to prevent the further spread of communism in western Europe. Another came in February 1948, when the communist coup in Czechoslovakia convinced American policymakers that the Kremlin was on the march and had to be stopped. Still another came when the Berlin blockade demonstrated the collapse of the Soviet–American agreement on the control of Germany and when the Berlin airlift proved that American air power could sustain a people struggling to remain free. Those were moments of anxiety rescued by years of hope. What happened in September, 1949, however, were changes in the geopolitical landscape – tectonic shifts in fact – that forced Americans to reassess basic policies.

The events that month also changed the domestic political environment, forcing Truman and his fellow Democrats onto the defensive. Critics charged that they had "lost" China – by trusting the communists and by failing to give enough support to the nationalists. They failed to prevent the Russians from getting the bomb and failed to know that the Soviet program was so far along. And they had failed to recognize the threat posed by communist agents and sympathizers inside America. The public's surprise and sense of loss and fears of approaching dangers were seized upon by the administration's political opponents. The bipartisanship which had bolstered policy toward Europe collapsed into recriminations over policy toward Asia. Conservative Democrats joined their Republican colleagues in demanding tougher measures against communists and fellow travelers. The political atmosphere had turned poisonous and would stay that way at least until Senator Joseph McCarthy's fall from grace in 1954.

In the immediate aftermath of the September developments, however, Harry Truman held fast. The NSC repeated its commitment to a defense budget within the previously established $13 billion ceiling on September 29.[35] Truman repeated his action in 1948 by refusing to spend congressional add-ons for airplanes. The administration continued to distance itself from the Chinese nationalists on Formosa.

The only military reaction to the Soviet detonation was a review of plans to develop a new more powerful bomb, "the super", the hydrogen bomb, a weapon perhaps a thousand times more powerful than those that destroyed Hiroshima and Nagasaki. And despite the events of September, there was substantial opposition. The Atomic Energy Commission voted against the program. The nuclear scientists at Los Alamos, who built the first atomic weapons, recommended against it on surprising moral grounds: they argued that true city-busters, killing orders of magnitude more civilians than the original A-bombs, would be immoral.

Sentiment in Congress was in favor of the new weapon. Truman also recognized the military and psychological benefits of the program. But what made a go-ahead decision unavoidable was the concern that the Russians were likely to build their own super weapon as soon as they could. That concern was coupled with growing domestic fear of communist spies. On January 13, 1950 Klaus Fuchs, a German-born naturalized Briton who had worked on the weapons program at Los Alamos during and after the war, confessed to having provided the Russians with information on how to build an atomic bomb.[36] On January 30, 1950, Harry Truman approved the program to develop the H-bomb. He also ordered a fundamental policy review, launching the process that would produce the seminal US strategy document, NSC 68.

NSC 68 Cabal

Most of the literature on NSC 68, the policy paper which laid out America's Cold War strategy of rearmament and containment, treats it as a far-sighted, consensus document which laid the foundation for decades to come. I think that the evidence points, instead, to an effort by a small group of rearmament zealots who were repeatedly rebuffed by the president and even the Congress until the Korean War made a military buildup unavoidable – and then their plan was the least worst of the alternatives.

Truman's top secret directive to his secretaries of state and defense ordered them "to undertake a re-examination of our objectives in peace and war and of the effect of these objectives on our strategic plans, in the light of the probable fission bomb capacity and possible thermonuclear bomb capacity of the Soviet Union."[37] In fact, the new director of the State Department's Policy Planning Staff, Paul Nitze, had been pushing for such a review since the previous summer. He was concerned that the United States was not doing enough to build up its defenses, either for large-scale war or more limited war. He was especially troubled by a Joint Staff briefing that suggested US air forces were not expected to control the air in a third world war.[38]

The Pentagon had resisted any reexamination of policy because it threatened its budget plans. Louis Johnson feared that the lid would come off his economy program. The defense secretary had also gone to great lengths to limit contacts with the state department by directing that all communications to that department be channeled through one of his deputies, Major General James H. Burns. For their own reasons, the JCS also ruled against having a JCS representative on the study group. They did allow three officers on the Joint Strategic Survey Committee to participate, but the men had no real authority to speak for the Chiefs.[39]

The group worked hard over the next several weeks, developing the rationale for comprehensive rearmament to deal with the growing Soviet threat. Its initial report was a 66-page declaration of alarm, arguing that the USSR sought world domination, that it was developing the military capacity to achieve that goal, that even in 1950 it could attack and overrun Western

Europe and strike selected US targets with atomic weapons. The study group endorsed containment but questioned whether the United States was doing enough to be successful. Its report noted "a sharp disparity between our actual military strength and our commitments" and said that "our military strength is becoming dangerously inadequate." It warned that the USSR could achieve the ability for a "decisive initial attack" by 1954 unless the United States greatly increased its military strength. The study group said that a continuation of current policies would force the United States "to shift to the defensive, or to follow a dangerous policy of bluff." It ruled out isolation as ineffective and preventive war as immoral, then settled on the preferred course of action: "a rapid build-up of political, economic, and military strength in the free world." To do this, the report acknowledged, would probably require substantial increases in military spending, reduction of domestic spending programs, and increased taxes.[40]

The study group included no price tag in its report because the members could not agree on one and feared rejection of its views if the costs seemed unacceptable. The military participants thought in terms of a $5 billion increase in current levels, to $17 or $18 billion per year. But Nitze and his colleagues envisioned budgets at $35 billion or perhaps even $50 billion per year, compared to the current $13 billion ceiling.[41] Also, no one from the Budget Bureau had been included in the deliberations.

On March 22, 1950, Acheson convened a meeting with Johnson and the study group at the State Department. Nitze outlined the paper and its conclusions while Johnson listened, tilting back in his chair. "Suddenly he lunged forward", Acheson later wrote, "with a crash of chair legs on the floor and fist on the table, scaring me out of my shoes. No one, he shouted, was going to make arrangements for him to meet with another Cabinet office and a roomful of people and be told what he was going to report to the President." He gathered his people and stalked out of the room. An NSC representative told the President, who immediately called Acheson to express his outrage and tell him to carry on with the project.[42]

Johnson was angry that such extensive interagency meetings had been conducted contrary to his instructions. He was also upset that the paper conflicted with established policies. He believed that the State Department was out to undermine his programs at Defense. But while Johnson was away for nearly a week at a NATO meeting, the report was circulated widely in the Pentagon and given unanimous approval by the JCS and the three service secretaries. When Johnson returned, confronted by the widespread support for the report, he joined in signing it to send to the President on April 7. Since the paper was only rhetoric, he could fight the budget fights another day.[43]

Nitze briefed the president's staff with mixed results. The special counsel was alarmed by the Soviet threat while the budget director held fast to his conviction that the economy could not tolerate huge defense increases. He also briefed Senator Walter George (D-Ga), chairman of the Finance

Committee and a senior Democrat on the Foreign Relations Committee, but the senator remained unconvinced of the need for radical change.[44]

The president temporized. He was not ready to endorse full-scale rearmament, saying "I will not buy a pig in a poke." Instead, on April 12 he sent the report to his economic advisors in the Budget Bureau, Council of Economic Advisors, and Secretary of the Treasury for cost estimates.[45] Further evidence of Truman's thinking came in a May 4 news conference, when he was asked about the need for increasing military spending. "The defense budget next year will be smaller than it is this year", he responded, "and we are continually cutting it by economies. And we are not alarmed in any sense of the word. We are simply maintaining a defense program that is adequate for the defense of this country."[46]

Four days later the president's Council of Economic Advisors reported to the NSC that "substantial new programs could be undertaken without serious threat to our standards of living, and without risking a transformation of the free character of our economy. Yet the adoption of such programs would create major problems of economic and social policy."[47] Meanwhile, Johnson permitted his military planners to develop cost figures without regard to any particular ceiling. They were given a July 1 deadline for their first flash estimates. To meet that deadline, the JCS packaged each service's programs into a $50 billion first-year estimate.[48] By then, however, the United States faced a hot war in Korea.

Korea shock

As late as June 1, 1950, Truman discounted fears of a growing Soviet threat and the danger of war. When asked at a news conference about public opinion polls saying that a majority of Americans expected a war within five years, the president replied, "I don't agree with that at all. I am doing everything I possibly can to prevent any war of any kind and to make the United Nations operate for a permanent peace in the world. I think we are closer to that now than we have been in the last 5 years."[49]

Three weeks later, North Korean forces charged across the thirty-eighth parallel, challenging Truman's assumptions and confronting the US government with difficult decisions about its regional and global policies. American officials had not expected war in Korea. The US ambassador had warned that the North Koreans had "undeniable materiel superiority" that would provide the "margin of victory" in the case of an invasion. But the head of the US military assistance mission reported that the South Korean troops were better trained and equipped than those in the North – and Washington policymakers preferred to believe the optimistic assessments.[50]

US officials also shared a general consensus that Korea was not important to the United States. The decision to withdraw US troops had been made two years earlier, and the JCS had reaffirmed that policy, concluding that Korea was of "little strategic value to the United States" and that any military commitment there would be "ill advised."[51] But once troops crossed the line dividing communist from noncommunist regions, American leaders believed they had to respond to the new aggression as they had failed to do in the 1930s. The attack was a challenge to the international order established in 1945 and based on the United Nations and its Charter.

Acheson's first action after consulting with Truman was to call for a UN Security Council meeting on the crisis. And within 27 hours of the start of the invasion, the Security Council passed a resolution urging a cessation of hostilities and North Korean withdrawal to the thirty-eighth parallel. Most significantly, the resolution determined that a breach of the peace had occurred and called upon UN members "to render every assistance to the United Nations in the execution of this resolution." This was the legal trigger for international use of force. The council avoided a Soviet veto because the Soviet delegate was boycotting the UN in protest of its refusal to seat the new Chinese communist government in place of the Chinese nationalists.[52]

Despite American concern about aggression, its policy toward the Korean conflict was tempered by other considerations. Many US officials doubted the reliability of the South Korean government under Syngman Rhee and had limited US military aid so as not to give Rhee a capability to attack the North. And most US policymakers still believed that the greatest and most likely threat to US interests would come from the Soviet Union and into Western Europe. Some feared that the Korean attacks were a diversionary effort, intended by Moscow to get so committed to a land war in Asia that it could not respond to Soviet probes in Europe.[53]

As JCS Chairman General Bradley said in Truman's first meeting with his advisors on June 25, "We must draw the line somewhere." He believed Korea "offered as good [an] occasion for action in drawing the line as anywhere else."[54] The president asked for a review of where the Soviet Union might next strike – for the Soviets were believed to be behind the North Korean attack.

Truman made clear his own assessment in his first meeting with congressional leaders on June 27. "This act was very obviously inspired by the Soviet Union", he said. "If we let Korea down, the Soviets will keep right on going and swallow up one piece of Asia after another. We had to make a stand some time, or else let all of Asia go by the board. If we were to let Asia go, the Near East would collapse and no telling what would happen in Europe."[55]

At first, despite the president's initial reaction that aggression had to be resisted, the Joint Chiefs of Staff resisted the idea of ground force support to the South Koreans. Air and naval support yes, but not ground troops. General Bradley and his colleagues argued that such action would require a large-scale mobilization. As late as June 28, the Chiefs still opposed the commitment of ground troops. On June 29 they agreed to a limited use of ground troops, but only to secure a defense perimeter around the southern port of Pusan, either to funnel aid to the South Koreans or, as they more likely felt, to ensure the safe evacuation of Americans. They did not envision using soldiers along the front in the north. But when MacArthur, in a 3am teleconference with Army Chief Collins on June 30, demanded permission to move one regimental combat team into Korea as a prelude to a two division force, Collins called the Army Secretary, who called the President at 5am and secured a favorable decision.[56] The military situation had deteriorated too quickly, and there was no other alternative to prevent a communist victory.

Later that day, Truman met with his advisors and later with congressional leaders to tell them of his decision to send US forces to repel the invaders and restore peace on the peninsula. He also ordered a blockade of the Korean coast. The president linked his actions to the UN Security Council's request for support to Korea in a resolution passed on June 27, the second measure on the conflict approved in the absence of the Soviet delegate.

Meeting with congressional leaders, the president found broad support for his actions. In his first session on the crisis, on June 27, Truman indicated that he did not expect to commit ground troops. He also explained his decisions to send the seventh fleet to defend Formosa and to increase military aid to the Philippines and the French in Indochina. In answer to a question about the possible need to expand the navy, Secretary Johnson said the Chiefs were already at work on a balanced expansion plan for the armed services if that became necessary.[57]

On June 30, when he told the legislators of his decision on combat troops, he received questions and suggestions about getting other nations involved under the UN umbrella. Sen. Kenneth Wherry (R-Neb), the minority floor leader, complained that Congress ought to be consulted before moves like this. "I just had to act as Commander-in-chief", Truman said, "and I did." Wherry repeated his concern that Congress ought to be consulted before any large scale actions. Truman said, "If there is any necessity for congressional action, I will come to you. But I hope we can get those bandits in Korea suppressed without that."[58]

Those exchanges triggered a series of administration meetings on the question of asking for congressional action. Pentagon officials drew up drafts declaring support for the US actions taken but not containing words like "authorize" or "declare war." In a July 3 meeting, joined by the Senate majority leader, Scott McLucas of Illinois, Acheson urged Truman to make an address to Congress and accept, but not propose, a resolution of support. McLucas saw no need to call the Congress back from its short July 4 recess and noted that things were going well on the Hill regarding Korea. He was also concerned that a presidential appearance would seem to be asking for a declaration of war, and that other issues – like Formosa and Indochina – might lead to a prolonged debate.[59]

Truman decided to send a written message to Congress on July 19, followed by an evening speech to the nation. The president labeled the attack in Korea as "naked, deliberate, unprovoked aggression." He noted that his actions to defend Korea were based "on the unanimous advice of our civil and military authorities." He acknowledged, "Under all the circumstances, it is apparent that the United States is required to increase its military strength and preparedness" both in Korea and elsewhere. He also said "it will be necessary for a number of years to support continuing defense expenditures, including assistance to other nations, at a higher level than we had previously planned." He called for increased taxes and authority to prioritize domestic production.[60]

Despite these words, Truman delayed until December actually endorsing the full-scale, long-term rearmament plans envisioned by NSC 68. In July and August, he sent Congress supplemental appropriations requests for $11.6 billion for defense and $4 billion in foreign military assistance, 87 percent of which was earmarked for NATO. But Truman told his new budget director in July that he didn't want to be "putting any more money than necessary at this time in the hands of the Military." And even George Marshall, recalled to be Secretary of Defense after Truman fired Louis Johnson in September, wanted to keep pressure on Pentagon expenditures because he was concerned that "these great expenditures will not be supported over the five-year program by the American people."[61]

On September 30, at a meeting with the NSC, Truman approved the conclusions of the NSC 68 paper "as a statement of policy to be followed over the next four or five years" but deferred action on the rest of the report, including a table of expenditures suggesting $44 billion to $54 billion defense budgets for the next four years. The president wanted cost estimates to be more firmly developed.[62] As late as November 22, Marshall argued for a slower buildup than Acheson proposed, saying that a steady pace was better "than building up a mountain and then sliding off."[63]

Congress approved the July and August supplemental requests speedily and without cuts. Just after the start of the war it had completed action on a two year extension of the draft, dropping a previously approved provision permitting callups only if Congress had declared a national emergency. On September 1, the legislators approved the Defense Production Act, giving the president authority to allocate materials and facilities for defense production and to impose wage and price controls if necessary.[64]

From the start of the conflict, there was strong bipartisan support for aiding South Korea. Republicans tried to score points, however, by suggesting that failure to oppose communists in China had invited this latest attack. Senate Republicans caucused on June 26 and announced their support for maximum aid to South Korea in terms of equipment but said the United States had no obligation to go to war itself. They were highly supportive of Truman's statement about defending Formosa. When Truman decided to commit ground troops, he received additional support, with Sen. Wherry applauding that "at long last" the president had taken a "strong stand" against the "Red tide."[65]

Congress was also eager to fight the Red tide at home. Hearings had exposed communist party members and Soviet spies. High level officials were accused of helping the communists in China and the Soviet Union.

Alger Hiss had been convicted of perjury in an espionage case in January 1950, the same month that Klaus Fuchs confessed giving the Russians atomic bomb secrets and that ten officials of the US Communist Party went on trial for advocating the overthrow of the government. On February 9, Sen. Joseph McCarthy (R-Wisc.) claimed to have a list of 205 communists still working in the State Department, thereby sparking a four-year campaign of smears and accusations.

The biggest domestic policy debate in the summer of 1950 was over the proposed Internal Security Act, which Truman felt compelled to veto on September 22 because of vague yet far-reaching language. The president called the law "unnecessary, ineffective and dangerous." The legislation authorized the emergency detention of people thought to be likely to conspire with others for espionage or sabotage and barred members of communist-front organizations from jobs in defense facilities or with the Federal Government.[66]

Republican leader Senator Robert Taft (R-Ohio) had declared even before the Korean War that the 1950 congressional elections would be fought on the three issues of "socialism, spending, and softness toward communism."[67] By the time of the November balloting, communism topped the list and led to the defeat of several prominent Democrats, including Senate majority leader McLucas. The Democrats lost five seats in the Senate, leaving them with a nominal 2-seat majority. They lost 28 seats in the House, cutting their majority from 95 to 35. And this was before the war turned from near victory into a stunning setback.

Command, control, and MacArthur

There were surprisingly few disputes between the president and his military leaders in the first six months of the war. The Chiefs had been disappointed in the earlier budget cutbacks by Secretary Johnson, but they worked cooperatively with him in responding to the military situation and in developing the budget supplementals. The Chiefs also felt that they could approach the president directly and did so several times, end-running the secretary of defense. Once Marshall succeeded Johnson, the senior civilian leaders had a very close and cooperative relationship, and this made it easier on the Chiefs.[68] The Chiefs also had few if any split papers or disagreements among themselves as the conflict proceeded.[69]

"President Truman never interfered with military operations", Army Chief of Staff General Collins said, "but in the Korean war … he was deeply committed personally and wished to be kept constantly informed."[70] The president had approved a directive giving the Chiefs "general direction of all combat operations."[71] They were the point of contact with MacArthur, the source of precise orders to the theater commander and the channel for requests for decision by the president. Only after the massive intervention by Chinese troops in November did the President insist on personal and prior clearance, by himself and the secretary of defense, of all messages from the JCS to MacArthur.[72]

Truman asked and depended on the Chiefs for military advice. That advice became somewhat easier to provide after General Bradley became the first formal Chairman of the JCS and during the war met with Truman almost every morning. The Chiefs consulted regularly with State Department officials once Johnson was gone and the firewall between departments removed, but they provided the key military advice in Washington. As Paul Hammond concluded, "Although the difference between a civil and a military viewpoint was thus sometime drawn, it did not divide the Defense Department; and it was a difference without contentious disputes, at least among the civil and the military in the executive branch in Washington. The disagreements ... involved Washington-field relations rather than inter-service conflict."[73]

In the field was the imposing presence of General Douglas MacArthur, hero of the war in the Pacific, pacifier of Japan, and former Army Chief of Staff in the 1930s. MacArthur, as a five-star General of the Army, outranked all of his nominal superiors in Washington until Truman and Congress rewarded Bradley with a fifth star on September 18, 1950. MacArthur knew how to orchestrate favorable press coverage, and he ignored presidential orders intended to muzzle him. He maintained close contacts with Republican political figures, who became a conduit for many of his criticisms of administration policy. And he knew how to force favorable decisions from his chain of command by sending urgent cables predicting dire consequences if his requests were not immediately granted. His June 30 request for the introduction of ground combat troops, for example, claimed that that was "the only assurance of holding the present line, and the ability to regain later lost ground." When General Collins said he would have to ask the president, MacArthur responded, "Time is of the essence. And a clear-cut decision without delay is imperative."[74] That led to the 5am call to Truman.

In November, when the president cancelled an unauthorized air strike planned against Yalu River bridges, MacArthur fired back that enemy forces were "pouring" across those bridges. "This movement not only jeopardizes but threatens the ultimate destruction of the forces under my command." MacArthur went on to tell the Chiefs that "your instructions may well result in a calamity of major proportions for which I cannot accept the responsibility."[75] Truman backed down.

That incident and several others where MacArthur disregarded orders or spoke out publicly in contravention of official policy ultimately led Truman to relieve the popular general of command in April 1951. But in the final months of 1950, MacArthur was untouchable. He planned and carried out the risky Inchon landing, the surprisingly successful amphibious attack in September behind North Korean lines, despite strong doubts on the part of the Chiefs. He objected to constraints on his operations near or over the Chinese border and dismissed the likelihood of massive Chinese intervention. The Chiefs deferred to MacArthur both because of his seniority and experience and

Figure 7.1   Harry Truman meeting General Douglas MacArthur, 1950 (Truman Library)

because they believed that commanders in the field usually knew best. As General Bradley said, "General MacArthur is a man of long distinguished service, and experience, and I think it would be quite improper to try to tell him from here how exactly to dispose his divisions, and so we did not do so."[76]

The politicians in Washington were more suspicious of the famous general. In the very first cabinet-level meeting of the war, Secretary Johnson recommended that any instructions to MacArthur "should be detailed so as not to give him much discretion."[77] Truman was always suspicious of MacArthur's political ambitions and disdainful of the general's pomposity. On his flight to his one and only meeting with MacArthur, on Wake Island on October 15, he wrote to his cousin, "I've a whale of a job before me. Have to talk to God's right-hand man tomorrow ...."[78] That was the meeting where the general reassured the president that "formal resistance will end throughout North and South Korea by Thanksgiving." And he hoped "to be able to withdraw the Eighth Army to Japan by Christmas." Truman asked, "What are the chances for Chinese or Soviet interference?" MacArthur replied, "Very little .... We are no longer fearful of their intervention."[79]

"An entirely new war"

In late November, just after MacArthur launched what he called his final offensive, the Americans discovered that tens of thousands of Chinese troops had infiltrated Korea and were launching powerful attacks against allied forces. The general seemed to panic, cabling Washington that this was "an entirely new war." He said that his command had "done everything humanly possible within its capabilities but is now faced with conditions beyond its control and strength." He said he would have to switch to defensive operations.[80]

The Chinese intervention shocked policymakers in Washington as well. On November 28, Truman told his staff, "We've got a terrific situation on our hands." While they sat in stunned silence, he told them of MacArthur's message. "The Chinese have come in with both feet." He decided to meet with the cabinet and ordered planning for another budget supplemental and a message declaring a national emergency.[81] That afternoon, Marshall warned against getting "sewed up" in Korea or into a war with China. "To do this would be to fall into a carefully laid Russian trap. We should use all available political, economic, and psychological action to limit the war." Acheson agreed. "We can't defeat the Chinese in Korea. They can put in more than we can."[82] General Bradley believed that at this meeting the consensus finally developed that the long-pending recommendations of NSC 68 would have to be implemented, that rearmament would have to proceed even if Americans "had to give up such things as refrigerators and television", in the words of NSC member Stuart Symington.[83]

Troubled by the turn of events in Korea but decisive as always, Truman held a news conference on November 30 and spoke grimly of the prospects in Korea. "The battlefield situation is uncertain at this time", he said. "We may suffer reverses as we have suffered them before." He announced a three-fold plan of UN action in Korea, strengthening allies around the world, and rapidly increasing America's military strength. At the end of the session with the press, Truman made a general statement that "We will take whatever steps are necessary to meet the military situation, just as we always have." A reporter asked if that included the atomic bomb. "That includes every weapons that we have", Truman responded, thereby setting off a trans-Atlantic firestorm that prompted an emergency visit by the British Prime Minister.[84]

In fact, Truman had always maintained tight presidential control over nuclear weapons. They were in civilian custody until after the start of the Korean War. Even then, on July 30, Truman allowed the dispersal of non-nuclear components for the bombs for storage in Guam. But General Bradley's message to MacArthur noted that it would take a presidential decision, and 72 hours for shipment of nuclear components, before such weapons could be employed.[85]

On December 1, Truman sent Congress a special message requesting $16.8 billion in additional military funds, bringing the total for the year to $41.8 billion. He listed the improvements in US defense capabilities already achieved and said the new funds were for military improvements world-wide. This "is not a war budget", he said. "That would obviously require far more money." It merely provided the basis for possible mobilization if that became necessary.[86] Congress approved the extra funds before adjourning on January 2, 1951, following a delay over funds for 50 cargo ships favored by the Senate and opposed by the House.[87]

Two weeks later, the president declared a national emergency and spoke gravely to the nation. "Our homes, our Nation, all the things we believe in, are in great danger", he said. "This danger has been created by the rulers of the Soviet Union." He went on to note that "The danger we face exists not only in Korea … but Europe and the rest of the world are also in very great danger." Truman detailed the increased figures of military personnel and weapons production, then warned of higher taxes, credit controls, and reduced nonmilitary expenditures.[88]

On December 14, the day before his nationwide address, the president formally approved the top secret policy paper, NSC 68/4, setting forth "an effort to achieve, under the shield of a military build-up, an integrated political, economic, and psychological offensive designed to counter the current threat to the national security posed by the Soviet Union."[89] This was the final blueprint for the policy of containment and the programs of military rearmament to fight the Cold War.

Although the Korean War provided the occasion for rearmament, the policy had been advocated long before that conflict because of the belief that the Soviet Union had aggressive intentions. An August 25, 1950 NSC report warned that the attack in Korea "could be interpreted as the first phase of a general Soviet plan for global war." The document noted that the Kremlin would likely wait "until such time as the United States had reached the point of maximum diversion and attrition of its forces-in-being …." The report suggested that the USSR might consider action in such places as "Finland, Korea, the Near and Middle East, and the Balkans."[90] On December 5, a National Intelligence Estimate concluded, "The Soviet rulers have resolved to pursue aggressively their world-wide attack on the power position of the United States regardless of the possibility that global war might result …. Further direct or indirect Soviet aggression in Europe and Asia is likely, regardless of the outcome of the Korean situation."[91] The next day, the JCS were sufficiently concerned that they sent a personal "war warning" message to all theater commanders. "The JCS consider that the current situation in Korea has greatly increased the possibility of general war."[92]

Since Europe had, all along, been the area of greatest concern to US policymakers – except MacArthur – it is significant that the decisions on rearmament included greater forces for the defense of Europe – and the actual deployment of troops to that continent. On September 9, Truman had announced plans to substantially increase the number of US forces stationed in Europe. The JCS had wanted to shift two divisions from Asia to Europe as soon as Korea stabilized. And on December 19, after several weeks of delay, Truman announced the appointment of General Dwight Eisenhower as the new Supreme Allied Commander in Europe, the head of all the NATO troops.[93] The war hero who shared Truman's vision of strategy and who had long practiced deference to civilian control was going back to Europe, while the other war hero, prickly and insubordinate, remained in Korea.

That war stalemated. MacArthur was fired and returned to ticker tape parades in America and standing ovations in Congress. Truman's popularity plummeted, but it was Eisenhower, not MacArthur, who succeeded him in the White House. Meanwhile, the military buildup envisioned by Nitze and the Chiefs continued. By the end of Truman's term, US military manpower had more than doubled, from the pre-war level of 1.5 million men and women to 3.6 million, and military spending as a share of GDP had nearly tripled, from 5 percent to 14.2 percent. America had rearmed.

Part III

The challenge of transformation

8 Theodore Roosevelt and military modernization

I will have no criticism of my Administration from you, or any other officer in the Army.

President Roosevelt to the Commanding General of the Army, 1901[1]

If, during the years to come, any disaster should befall our arms, afloat or ashore ... the blame will lie upon the men whose names appear upon the roll-calls of Congress on the wrong side of these great questions."

Governor Roosevelt in 1899 speech[2]

Moderate in stature but brimming with radical ideas and outsized ambition for himself and his country, Theodore Roosevelt entered the White House with firm views on how to strengthen the American military. He brought to the presidency a breadth of understanding and experience rare for a 42-year-old. As a student of history who wrote a well-regarded book on the naval aspects of the War of 1812, he appreciated the value of sea power and the advantages of technology. As the Assistant Secretary of the Navy in the year before the Spanish–American War, he understood the ways of Washington bureaucracy. As a member of the National Guard and later a Colonel in combat in Cuba, he knew the frustrations of logistics and the terror and exhilaration of battle.

The story of civil–military relations under Theodore Roosevelt is a tale of bold ideas, experimentation, foot-dragging, and partial success. The new president was determined to modernize and strengthen the US armed forces so that they could bolster his expansionist foreign policy. He wanted to take full advantage of the emerging technologies which American industrial might was providing. As an exemplar of a younger generation, the first post-Civil War political leaders, he insisted on reshaping US military institutions and elevating bright, if iconoclastic, younger officers. These laudable goals, however, met powerful opponents: senior officers resistant to change and a Congress comfortable with its role and reluctant to cede power to the upstart president.

A sickly child, embarrassed that his own father had avoided combat in the Civil War by hiring a substitute, young Theodore seemed fascinated by military things and ranked warlike qualities high in his table of virtues. He romanticized war, wished for war, and viewed peace "dull and effeminate", as one biographer put it.[3] Throughout his public service, he was a frequent commentator and vigorous advocate of US military strength and assertiveness.

One of the clearest expositions of his philosophy was in a speech at the Naval War College soon after becoming the Assistant Secretary of the Navy in 1897. In it he set forth a detailed agenda for the armed forces and propounded themes that echoed throughout his life. He saw military strength as the means to achieve national greatness.

- "In this country there is not the slightest danger of an over-development of warlike spirit, and there never has been any such danger."[4]
- "This nation cannot stand still if it is to retain its self-respect."[5]
- "[W]e need a first-class navy" that "should not be merely a navy for defense."[6]
- "It is necessary to have a fleet of great battleships if we intended to live up to the Monroe Doctrine ...."[7]
- "No master of the prize ring ever fought his way to supremacy by mere dexterity in avoiding punishment. He had to win by inflicting punishment."[8]
- "Diplomacy is utterly useless where there is no force behind it; the diplomat is the servant, not the master, of the soldier."[9]

In subsequent speeches, Roosevelt embraced the imperialism of the European powers and urged Americans to follow those examples. "We are a great nation and we are compelled, whether we will or not, to face the responsibilities that must be faced by all great nations", he declared. "Where we have won entrance by the prowess of our soldiers we must deserve to continue by the righteousness, the wisdom, and the even-handed justice of our rule."[10]

He gathered around him men of ideas and accomplishment, often authors like himself. By 1890 he was in regular correspondence with other advocates of expansive nationalism and military preparedness like Alfred Thayer Mahan and Henry Cabot Lodge. They echoed and reinforced each other's views, for they shared a common vision of America as a great power equal to the nations of Europe.[11] They also succeeded in the political dialogue with the anti-imperialists and progressives who wanted America's great national energies directed toward domestic reform.

Perhaps the most explicit articulation of his plans came, while he was still Governor of New York, in an April 10, 1899 speech to the Hamilton Club of Chicago, where he declared

> that our country calls not for the life of ease but for the life of strenuous endeavor. The twentieth century looms before us big with the fate of many nations. If we stand idly by, if we seek merely swollen, slothful

ease and ignoble peace, if we shrink from the hard contests where men must win at hazard of their lives and at the risk of all they hold dear, then the bolder and stronger peoples will pass us by, and will win for themselves the domination of the world.

In this speech, he also said "Our army needs complete reorganization – not merely enlarging – and the reorganization can only come as the result of legislation. A proper general staff should be established, and the positions of ordnance, commissary and quartermaster officers should be filled by detail from the line."[12]

Roosevelt anticipated that such changes would meet opposition in Congress, which he said "has shown a queer inability to learn some of the lessons of the [Spanish–American] war." He warned that "If, during the years to come, any disaster should befall our arms, afloat or ashore ... the blame will lie upon the men whose names appear upon the roll-calls of Congress on the wrong side of these great questions."[13]

The accidental president never doubted his abilities or his authority. "I believe in a strong executive; I believe in power", he said.[14] While he saw the necessity of working closely with the Legislative Branch on domestic issues, he felt differently about foreign policy. As he once told William Howard Taft, "You know as well as I do that it is for the enormous interest of this government to strengthen and give independence to the executive in dealing with foreign powers."[15] Never having served in a legislative body, he saw little need for compromise, particularly of his strongly held convictions. Yet he was a professional politician, who understood the necessity of building and maintaining, through consultation and patronage, a strong party organization.

Congress was comfortably in Republican control, but divided by sectional and substantive differences over Roosevelt's programs. The House of Representatives during much of his presidency was under the iron rule of "Uncle Joe" Cannon, a domineering Speaker who ran a tight ship throughout the Roosevelt administrations. The president met frequently with Speaker Cannon, who used his office as a clearing house to vet White House ideas. The Senate was controlled by "The Senate Four", the powerful quartet of rich men – Aldrich of Rhode Island, Spooner of Wisconsin, Platt of Connecticut, and Allison of Iowa.[16] They, too, met informally and worked collegially with the young president.

Reduced tariffs for products from Cuba and other newly acquired territories met the strongest congressional opposition, since tariffs were viewed as a domestic rather than foreign policy issue. When William Howard Taft, then governor of the Philippines, complained about Republican protectionists, the president strongly defended them. "With every one of these men I at times differ radically on important questions; but they are the leaders, and their great intelligence and power and their desire to do what is best for the government, make them not only essential to work with but desirable to work with. Several of the leaders have special friends whom they desire to favor, or special interests with which they are connected and which they hope to serve. But, taken as a body, they are broad-minded and patriotic, as well as sagacious, skillful and resolute."[17]

This was a time when congressional committees fashioned budgets through direct consultations with the executive departments, without much involvement of the White House. While presidents might, as Roosevelt did, recommend revised laws and new battleships, the key initiatives and follow-through came from the cabinet members. The Legislative Branch took seriously its responsibilities to raise and support armies and provide and maintain a navy. And the Senate expected to give advice as well as consent to international agreements.

The Senate's Military Affairs Committee was chaired by Joseph Hawley of Connecticut, who was close to Secretary of War Root since both had graduated from Hamilton College. Every member of that committee had served in the Civil War, eight Republicans who had fought for the Union and four Democrats who served in the Confederate army.[18]

US armed forces were rebuilding after decades of neglect and trying to adjust to the new strategic situation following the Spanish–American War, which left the United States in charge of overseas territories and confronting competitive military powers in Europe and Asia. The army in 1898 had been a dispersed and malcoordinated force of about 28,000 men. After surging above 200,000 to fight in Cuba, it was still an enlarged force of 85,000 when Roosevelt took the oath of office. The navy, even smaller than that of Austria–Hungary or Turkey a decade earlier, was gaining new, modern warships each year, provided by a generous Congress. The 3,600-man Marine Corps was seen as the navy's onboard gunnery managers and offshore police force. It would soon grow into the navy's army and be used repeatedly in military interventions in support of the Roosevelt Corollary to the Monroe Doctrine. It doubled in size by 1904 and was over 9,000 when Roosevelt left office.

Power struggle

Senior officials waged nonviolent but vicious guerrilla war against each other in the early years of the twentieth century. The Commanding General of the Army, Nelson A. Miles, was a celebrated officer who was much-wounded and decorated during the Civil War and later led forces to triumph over such Indian leaders as Chief Joseph, Geronimo, and Sitting Bull. As the senior serving officer, he became Commanding General on the mandatory retirement of his predecessor in 1895. Despite its title, that post had little real power. The Secretary of War ran the quasi-independent bureaus of the army in peacetime, and the president named field commanders in wartime – as McKinley did in 1898, sidetracking Miles and letting Major General William R. Shafter command troops fighting in Cuba.

Tensions between the senior general and the Secretary of War had been so high, and so persistent, that two previous Commanding Generals had moved their headquarters away from Washington. Winfield Scott went to New York in the 1840s and William T. Sherman moved to St. Louis in 1874.[19] Those absences, of course, only strengthened the civilian leader's power over the rest of the army. The various bureaus were headed by permanently detailed staff officers, who were usually happy to escape the rigors of frontier life and relax in the comforts of the capital city.

Miles himself had strongly differed with Secretary of War Russell Alger over how to fight Spain. Miles vigorously opposed any attack on Havana, or any invasion of Cuba during the rainy season, and instead badgered his boss with his own plan for invading Puerto Rico first. He also objected to the Administration's policy of accepting large numbers of volunteers for the war, fearing that the resources for training and equipping them would siphon away officers and supplies needed for immediate combat.[20]

Within days of the end of the fighting, Miles was giving interviews to the press with sharp criticisms of the War Department's handling of the campaign. He complained that the Department had "mutilated and garbled" reports about the command issue and that it had suppressed his recommendation that US troops in Cuba be moved to healthy camps or evacuated to avoid disease. Back in the United States, he repeated his criticisms to a welcoming press corps. Despite speculation that he would likely be court-martialed for insubordination, Miles solidified his standing in public esteem by testifying, before the official Board of Inquiry investigating the war, about feeding the troops large quantities of what he labeled "embalmed beef."[21]

Miles had political ambitions, hoping to be nominated – by either major party – for president. He even approached Roosevelt to suggest that the New York Governor be his Vice Presidential running mate in 1900. When Elihu Root succeeded Alger at the War Department, the new Secretary, though warned Miles would be difficult to work with, nevertheless tried to cooperate with him, at least at first. Root asked the general's advice on officers to head volunteer regiments in the Philippines. Root wanted young and energetic officers but Miles recommended selection based strictly on seniority. The very next day, despite Root's plea for secrecy in order to forestall an avalanche of applications, the matter surfaced in the press, and Root suspected Miles of the leak.[22]

Two days before McKinley was shot in Buffalo, Root wrote to the president complaining that Miles was trying "to promote his own views and undo my plans." As McKinley's successor, Roosevelt also had strong antipathies toward Miles, whom he had derided as "merely a brave peacock" in 1898. The commanding general later suggested in a public speech in 1901 that the then vice president had not even been at San Juan Hill.[23] This further poisoned Miles' relationship with Roosevelt.

The feuding pair had a shouting match at a White House reception in December 1901, after Miles had publicly criticized a navy board of inquiry's finding in a dispute between two admirals. The general came to a White House reception to explain, and the president bellowed at him: "I will have no criticism of my Administration from you, or any other officer in the Army. Your conduct is worthy of censure, sir." Responding "You are my host and superior officer", Miles bowed and departed, but the resulting publicity was sympathetic to the general.[24]

Miles had cultivated good relations with members of Congress, and they came to his defense whenever Roosevelt contemplated ridding himself of the commanding general. One reason for Miles' popularity on Capitol Hill was that he had resisted Root's efforts to consolidate army posts throughout the country.[25]

In the subsequent months the president and Root compiled a record of Miles' misbehavior. In one such memorandum from the White House in March 1902, Roosevelt wrote:

> During the six months that I have been President, General Miles has made it abundantly evident by his actions that he has not the slightest desire to improve or benefit the army, and to my mind his action can bear only the construction that his desire is purely to gratify his selfish ambition, his vanity, or his spite.[26]

When Root advanced his proposal for a General Staff headed by a Chief of Staff early in 1902, Miles led the opposition. He believed he could administer the army without a staff and bragged that he had done that during the recent war without having to "get around a dozen or more majors."[27] Testifying before the Senate Military Affairs Committee, the commanding general noted that every member, like himself, was a veteran of the Civil War and then trashed Root's plan as a revolutionary scheme that would abandon the lessons of history and "Germanize and Russianize the small Army of the United States."[28] He also doubted the wisdom of civilian control.

> In fact, the general's authority for initiative is taken away, and he can make no move without the direction or sanction of the all powerful General Staff, which, under the bill is subject to the control of the Secretary of War, whose knowledge of military affairs may be meager or nil.[29]

Miles' comments on military inexperience were especially pointed, for Root, as a frail 17-year-old, had been rejected when he tried to enlist in 1865.[30]

The immediate impact of Miles' testimony was so powerful that the committee chairman announced that no favorable action could be expected on the general staff bill that year. Miles continued his campaign against the administration by disclosing information about US atrocities in the pacification campaign in the Philippines. Roosevelt was tempted to remind the world that Miles' troops at Wounded Knee had "killed squaws and children as well as unarmed Indians", but reconsidered and pigeonholed his letter.[31]

Roosevelt was so incensed by Miles' actions that he prepared papers to force the general to resign. "General Miles' usefulness is at and end and he must go", he wrote to a friend. But he also acknowledged: "It is a great question, upon which I must consult two or three of the leading members of the Senate and House, as to whether it will not be well to avoid complicating passage of the Army bill ... by refraining from acting ... until that is out of the way." Several Senators defended Miles and urged the president not to oust the general, saying that it would cause another bitter controversy, stir up bad feeling in Congress, and be injurious to the Republican party in the coming Congressional campaign. Roosevelt relented, but later complained that "the only matter of importance in which I have sacrificed principle to policy has been that of Miles."[32]

To assuage supporters of Miles, Root modified his proposal to provide that the serving Commanding General would become the first Chief of Staff, though in the end the law took effect only after Miles turned 64 in August 1903 and was legally required to retire. Root also got Miles away from Washington for several months, including the next winter session of the Congress, by sending him on an information-gathering trip to the Philippines, Asia and Europe.[33]

Meanwhile, Root launched a public relations campaign "to start a backfire." He urged that several thousand letters be sent to members of Congress supporting army reorganization. He circulated articles to editors making the case for reform. He also arranged for supporting testimony before Congress from other retired generals, including Miles' immediate predecessor as commanding general. Root even planted questions with key Senators to guarantee that the best arguments were aired.[34]

Early in 1903, with Miles circling the globe and public opinion more sympathetic, Congress passed the General Staff bill. The measure was the first of the four major modernization initiatives by the Roosevelt Administration, and it fulfilled the vision the New York Governor had articulated in 1899. But it came only after a severe challenge to civil–military relations from the nation's senior military officer.

Reorganization

Secretary of War Elihu Root was already developing radical plans to reorganize the US Army when Roosevelt took office. The former New York lawyer had been named by President McKinley to fix the numerous problems evident in 1898 – such as sending the expeditionary force to Cuba clad in winter woolen uniforms – but he and Roosevelt had a longstanding friendship and a close convergence on ideas for the army. The commander of the Rough Riders called for "a thorough shaking up" of the War Department during the conflict in Cuba and later stressed to Root his belief in the need for substantial army reorganization.[35]

Root's plan ultimately had four major features: (1) Creation of a General Staff for the army; (2) Abolition of the post of Commanding General, replacing it with a Chief of Staff directly under the Secretary of War; (3) Centralizing control of the various army bureaus under the Secretary and Chief of Staff; (4) Creation of an Army War College. All of these measures required legislation, and only the last met little resistance.

Knowing that he faced strong opposition from "officers who had become entrenched in Washington armchairs", Root initially proposed only the elimination of future permanent details to staff bureaus and cutting such assignments to four years. After Congress accepted this change in 1901, Root began pushing the idea of a General Staff to do war plans and a War College to do studies and education. He also recommended making the senior general the Chief of Staff and abolishing the post of Commanding General.[36]

The navy went through a similar reorganization struggle, though it was less visible because there was no counterpart to the commanding general. Even more than the army, the navy was organized into fiefdoms – eight bureaus – run by long-serving officials. No one was tasked with planning for war. Finally, Secretary John Long, by a March 13, 1900 directive, took a partial step in the same direction as the army was taking by creating the General Board to advise him on strategy, war plans, and ship designs. He named the popular Admiral George Dewey as the first Board president.[37] The US Navy did not acquire a senior officer and slightly less decentralized organization until the post of Chief of Naval Operations was created in 1915.

Long had wanted to have a general staff, but he ran into fierce opposition from inside and from Congress. The Chairman of the Senate Naval Affairs Committee, Eugene Hale of Maine, denounced the idea, as did Long's own deputy and most of the bureau chiefs. When Long's successor, William Moody, decided to press ahead with a very modest general staff proposal, for what he described as a purely advisory body, he was defeated by overwhelming opposition. His own Assistant Secretary, Charles Darling, testified against the measure, saying "it savors too much of militarism."[38]

Meanwhile, the Secretaries of the Army and the Navy moved to improve coordination between the Services by creating, in July 1903, the Joint Board. The new mechanism was born weak, however, lacking staff and prestige. It also fell into disfavor – and was sharply criticized by Roosevelt – when it failed to agree on the defensibility of Subic Bay in the Philippines in 1907. Nevertheless, it was a sign of the managerial revolution in American planning for war.

One effort at reorganization was particularly unsuccessful. Roosevelt, like many in the army, had little enthusiasm for the Marine Corps. Before becoming president, he had urged the amalgamation of the Corps into the Navy. He witnessed the service's close ties to Congress and public opinion

Figure 8.1 Theodore Roosevelt reviewing naval parade off Long Island, 1903 (Library of Congress)

and later admitted privately that "no vestige of their organization should be allowed to remain. They cannot get along with the navy, and as a separate command with the army the conditions would be intolerable."[39] In his final year in office, Roosevelt ordered marines off ships, purportedly to free up men to form units to seize advance bases, but Congress, persuaded intellectually and politically, passed a rider countermanding the president's order.[40]

Rejuvenation

Although the senior leadership in the military and in the Congress had wartime experience, it was dated. As late as 1901, every general officer in the army, line and staff, had first been commissioned before or during the

Civil War.[41] Roosevelt himself had complained that the navy began that war with 70-year-old captains, a fact he blamed on "the shortsightedness and supine indifference" of politicians who opposed reorganization efforts a half century earlier.[42] Both services promoted by seniority rather than merit, and those long-serving officers had more reverence for the past than excitement about the future.

The youngest president preached – and practiced – "the strenuous life." He wanted to elevate vigorous young men to positions of responsibility and authority. Not just in the military: he wanted the new territories to be administered by "only good and able men, chosen for their fitness, and not because of their partisan service."[43]

Just as he had embraced civil service reform and merit promotions in his first Washington job, as one of three Civil Service Commissioners, Roosevelt sought to rejuvenate the armed forces by promoting bright young officers faster than their more pedestrian comrades. He said "our men come too old, and stay too short a time, in the high-command positions."[44] He also tried to reduce the line-staff distinction by trying to give talented staff officers line commands. This also generated opposition from those who stood to lose from such changes.

His military aides served as conduits for new ideas from the lower ranks, notably William Sims, who persuaded the president to overrule navy officials and impose a new means of continuous aim firing.[45] He repeatedly asked Congress to allow merit promotions in the services but met with fierce opposition, in part because he elevated a disproportionate number of men from the cavalry compared to the other branches of the army. Eventually he allowed officers nearing retirement with 40 years of service to advance in rank upon retirement. He also began promoting promising young officers directly to brigadier general, nominating some 39 officers ahead of their seniors. In 1906, for example, he named Army Capt. John J. Pershing a one-star general. By 1907, however, congressional opposition had become so strong that Roosevelt stopped the practice.[46]

Roosevelt had a low opinion of old and overweight officers. Looking at his 300-pound commander in Cuba, Major General Shafter, Roosevelt told a friend that "men should be appointed as Generals of Divisions and Brigades who are physically fit." Later as president, he tried to weed out the unfit by imposing tough new physical standards on the armed forces, ordering that each year navy officers walk 50 miles over three days and that army officers walk and ride horses for 90 miles over three days. When tired and blistered officers publicized their complaints, the president himself, with the press in tow, completed the army test in a single day![47]

Technological innovation

Roosevelt was an activist president, always in motion, filled with ideas, often impetuous. When it came to things military, he was often, in Matthew Oyos' phrase, the "Chief Dilettante." Soon after becoming president, he urged the army to switch from its traditional dark blue shirt to a more neutral gray or brown, which he argued would make a less obvious target. Later on, the president suggested that cavalry officers switch to a smaller spur, to make walking easier. In 1905 he launched campaigns to get the army to develop new, more efficient entrenching tools and to design improved bayonets for troops and swords for officers.[48]

Organizational innovation also captured the president's interest. Advised by a friend from 1898 that the army was resisting a proposal to develop a separate machine-gun corps, Roosevelt intervened and ordered a pilot project in one cavalry regiment and recommended an increase in officers to command machine-gun units. Congress never approved the added slots, however, and the army itself resisted setting up a separate branch.[49]

Roosevelt's most far-sighted efforts at technological innovation were focused on aircraft, submarines, and battleships. While in the Navy Department, he endorsed support for Samuel Langley's experiments with heavier-than-air machines, which had broad political support in Washington but which crashed ignominiously into the Potomac River shortly before the Wright Brothers' success. As president, he pushed the War Department to use discretionary money previously approved by Congress to fund three prototypes. Only the Wright Brothers delivered a usable aircraft, but its initial successes ended with a fatal crash in 1908.[50]

The US Navy also had been slow to embrace new technology. In 1869 it had unceremoniously decommissioned the fastest warship in the world, the *Wampanoag*, with a record not equaled until the 1890s, and the sea service continued to resist building ships without sails and with steel hulls and steam engines until the 1880s. As the officers who recommended scrapping the *Wampanoag* declared:

> Lounging through the watches of a steamer, or acting as firemen and coal heavers, will not produce in a seaman that combination of boldness, strength and skill which characterized the American sailor of an elder day; and the habitual exercise by an officer, of a command, the execution of which is not under his eye, is a poor substitute for the school of observation, promptness and command found only on the deck of a sailing vessel.[51]

Eventually, however, the navy was forced to accept ironclad, steam-driven warships. There was also enthusiasm in Congress for submarines, both from representatives from shipbuilding districts and from those who viewed them as an alternative to expensive battleships. Roosevelt was so excited by the prospect of these new boats that in 1905 he secretly boarded one for a tour and nearly an hour of underwater operations. Having survived, he told the press of his adventures, which the *New York Times* trumpeted as "President Takes Plunge in Submarine." He went on, as with the machine gun corps idea, to recommend more favorable pay and promotion treatment for submariners, who tended to be disparaged and discriminated against by the rest of the navy.[52]

Besides seeking more and bigger battleships, Roosevelt endorsed the idea of an all big-gun ship even before the British *Dreadnought* demonstrated the value of such a design and, in a single stroke, rendered all existing warships obsolete. In this case, the president sided with his naval aide, then commander William Sims, and against his friend and naval sage, Captain Alfred Thayer Mahan. When Sims and others later criticized the design of the new *North Dakota* class battleships, Roosevelt largely ignored their views in order not to delay construction.[53]

Expansion

The military program with Roosevelt's most ardent and consistent support, and the most ultimate success, was increasing the size of the armed forces, especially the fleet. A large modern navy was essential to his vision of great power America, particularly since the nation now had to defend overseas territories in the Pacific and the sea lanes to the forthcoming Panama Canal.

When Roosevelt was Assistant Secretary of the Navy, the fleet was rapidly growing and had reached sixth in overall strength compared with other nations, with its first generation battleships, the *Maine* and *Texas*, and three fully modern ones. By the time he entered the White House, the US Navy ranked fourth in the world, with nine battleships at sea and eight more authorized or at some stage of construction. When he left office, there were 25 battleships and ten heavy cruisers in commission and two more battleships finishing construction. Only Britain had more capital ships, though Germany had more tonnage.[54]

He did not get all he asked for, or when he asked for it, because Congress had its own ideas about timing and affordability. The biggest fight was in 1907, when Congress cut the president's request for four additional battleships in half, with even the naval affairs committee chairman lukewarm to the idea.[55] Some legislators still resisted the costs of the military buildup, but few questioned Roosevelt's standard – to have a fleet as large as any competitor other than Britain.

Navy personnel also increased dramatically during Roosevelt's presidency, rising from 20,900 in 1901 to 47,533 in 1909. But even these numbers fell short of the manning needs of the larger, more complex steamships.

Despite Roosevelt's antipathy toward the Marine Corps, it also grew by 65 percent while he was in the White House, from 5,865 to 9,696. The army was about 84,000 at the beginning and end of his term, but it declined during his presidency to a low point of 64,000 in 1907.[56]

Resistance to modernization

Roosevelt had an agenda for change for the US military, for change in organization, size, technology, and personnel. His motives were many – the goal of national greatness, the measure of merit in military power, a projection of ideas of manly virtue onto the global stage. He was strikingly successful in much of what he tried, but only after surmounting the predictable and recurring roadblocks to military transformation.

Innovation is particularly difficult for military organizations. A successful, war-winning force has no incentives to change, or even to risk unforeseen problems by altering its existing ways. Advocates of the status quo feel threatened, either directly by the loss of position or prestige, or indirectly by the prospect of uncertainty and adjustment. To impose change on reluctant military services, therefore, requires a strong advocate, supportive allies, adequate resources, and patience.

In most but not all of his efforts, Theodore Roosevelt served as that strong, steady advocate. Sometimes he lost interest or became preoccupied with other ventures, as one would expect of a hyperactive president who faced numerous domestic and international crises.

The opposition was predictable – from the officers "entrenched in their armchairs" and from Members of Congress who believed they had a preeminent Constitutional role in shaping the US armed forces and who had political incentives to support particular programs, whether or not they were consistent with the president's proposals.

Where funds were required – or new laws – the Legislative Branch had the ultimate power. But where executive discretion was available, Roosevelt acted forcefully – such as in ordering tougher physical fitness tests and in sending the Great White Fleet halfway around the world, and daring Congress to fund its return.

Civil–military relations under Theodore Roosevelt were no more strained than usual, for many in uniform welcomed his efforts to remove deadwood from on top and embrace new technology, despite the griping of those uncomfortable with the changes. Congress was also more often than not an ally of the president, funding his expansion of the fleet, even if not as fast as the president wished, and sharing his views on the need for a stronger military to play a global role.

9 The McNamara revolution

> To this day, I see quantification as a language to add precision to reasoning about the world.
>
> Robert McNamara[1]

> [The Whiz Kids were] the most egotistical people that I ever saw in my life. They had no faith in the military; they had no respect for the military at all. They felt that the Harvard Business School method of solving problems would solve any problem in the world...
>
> General Curtis LeMay[2]

In 1961 the Pentagon was not quite two decades old; the Defense Department housed within it was only a dozen years old; but many of the management and budget practices dated back to the nineteenth century. Robert McNamara, not yet 45 years old, arrived to change things. McNamara knew a lot about business but only a little about the military. He had served in the Second World War as an Army Air Corps statistician, analyzing how to improve US bombing missions in the Pacific. After the war, he became a rising star at the Ford Motor Company, which made him president just before John F. Kennedy recruited him to come to Washington. When McNamara claimed a lack of qualifications for the Pentagon job, Kennedy replied that there were no schools for secretaries of defense, or for presidents.

The Pentagon was ripe for change, and under strong political pressure to change. President Eisenhower had succeeded in 1958 in getting Congress to strengthen the powers of the secretary of defense, allowing him to transfer, reassign, abolish or consolidate functions "for more effective, efficient, and economical administration and operation and to eliminate duplication." The separate armed services were put clearly under the "direction, authority and control" of the Secretary of Defense.[3]

Many members of Congress wanted to increase military spending to respond to the growing Soviet threat, including what was seen as an emerging "missile gap." But even the proponents of higher budgets complained about the inter-service rivalry and wasteful duplication in weapons programs. They wanted, in the phrase of that era, a "bigger bang for the buck." In 1959

Figure 9.1 Defense Secretary Robert McNamara (LBJ Library)

the Chairman of the House Defense Appropriations Subcommittee wrote to the then Defense Secretary, Neil McElroy, seeking budget information for particular military commands and missions. The secretary's staff responded that it was too difficult to get reliable figures – and that even if some numbers were developed, "there does not appear to be any agreed strategy against which the adequacy of the figures could be measured." In fact, the staff admitted, "everyone has his own individual strategy."[4]

McNamara set out to change that, to bring everyone into a single, common method of determining needs and costs. The tools were available in the defense research community, such as the air force-sponsored think tank, the RAND Corporation. Economists such as Charles Hitch had refined the statistical methods of operations research into tools of systems analysis that could be applied to narrow issues of program management and to broad questions of military strategy. Anyone could learn the techniques, but the only ones who were already masters were the bright, eager, quite young civilian analysts who soon became dubbed McNamara's "whiz kids." They became the soldiers of McNamara's revolution and they overpowered the senior generals and admirals who thought that their military experience should prevail over any civilian's numerical calculations.

Before 1961, the separate services decided the main outlines of most military programs and their associated budgets. The president set overall ceilings for defense and other activities, and the secretary of defense allocated the funds. Each service's share, however, tended to stay about the same. Each service jealously protected its most favored programs and gave low priority to activities that related to the other services and contributed to joint warfare. The air force cared most about strategic bombers, not tactical fighters. The navy preferred aircraft carriers over submarines. The army was determined to maintain a full 14-division force structure even if many units were under strength and ill-equipped. Meanwhile, airlift and sealift were orphan programs, since the navy and air force were not especially interested in spending their limited dollars to buy ships and planes that would only be used to carry army soldiers and their equipment.

The typical military answer to the basic question, how much is enough? was invariably "more." Throughout the 1950s the services declared their force requirements were at least 25 percent above the levels budgeted for them. They also tended to discount the capabilities of their sister services. The air force planned as if it alone had to win a nuclear war with the Soviet Union. The army and air force each thought it needed enough tanks and close air support planes, respectively, to destroy Warsaw Pact tank forces that might invade western Europe. And in the anxiety provoked by the first Soviet space satellites, each service was eager to push duplicative programs to see which would pay off quickest.

John F. Kennedy had pledged a "defense second to none" during his campaign and promised "arms … sufficient beyond doubt" in his stirring inaugural address. He told McNamara to: "1. Develop the force structure necessary to meet our military requirements without regard to arbitrary budget ceilings. 2. Procure and operate this force at the lowest possible cost."[5] He could never avoid setting ceilings, at least for planning purposes, but he worked overtime to define those military requirements and to make it efficient as well as effective.

McNamara's first task as secretary was to craft a budget request to jump start the military buildup the president had promised. To help him, he recruited his own army of analysts. From RAND, he brought Hitch and Alain Enthoven to crunch the numbers. To manage various components, he recruited such later cabinet officers as Harold Brown, Joe Califano, John Connally, Paul Nitze, and Cyrus Vance.[6] Later on, another future secretary of defense, Les Aspin, served as one of the "whiz kids." McNamara had secured Kennedy's promise of a free hand in picking Pentagon officials, and he used his authority rapidly and aggressively.

Processes of control

The new defense secretary sought military advice, but found it deficient. Shortly before Kennedy's inauguration, he asked the Chiefs for any changes they might suggest in the existing Eisenhower budget. Their answers were a rehash of previously submitted requests for increases. "Do they think I'm a fool?" McNamara cried. "Don't they have ideas?"[7] He reacted by setting up civilian-run task forces.

Ultimately he ordered nearly 100 special studies of defense issues, large and small. He immersed himself in briefings on defense programs and capabilities and was sometimes surprised – or appalled – by what he learned. One of his early discoveries was that the "missile gap" that Kennedy campaigned about did not exist, but in fact was a gap favoring the United States. Naïve in the ways of Washington, McNamara told some journalists about this, thereby embarrassing the president. He was also troubled to learn of the large number of nuclear weapons being programmed for minor targets behind the Iron Curtain.[8]

Just two months after taking office, McNamara was ready with a comprehensive revision to the budget that President Eisenhower had submitted in January. His new plan called for over $1.5 billion in additional funds, compared to the original request for $41.8 billion for defense. About half the increase was slated for strategic nuclear programs, the other half for conventional force capabilities and personnel. The actual request to Congress sought only $650 million in new money, however, with the balance offset by program cuts and transfers from other accounts.[9]

McNamara asked for increases in the Polaris submarine program, more than doubling the rate of construction from five to 12 submarines per year, as well as for a doubling of production capacity for solid-fuel Minuteman inter-continental ballistic missiles. He also sought to strengthen the bomber force by putting one-eighth of the force constantly in the air and half the fleet on 15-minute alert. But he cancelled production of the last two squadrons of Titan missiles, which were liquid-fueled and more vulnerable to surprise attack. Preferring survivable missiles to slow-flying bombers, he cut one-third of the funds requested for the new B-70 bomber and turned the program into a technology development effort. He also cancelled the costly and unsuccessful effort to build a nuclear-powered airplane.[10]

The March 1961 budget amendments revealed the new administration's quite different defense priorities. In addition to the less vulnerable strategic systems, Kennedy poured money into airlift and sealift and into additional weapons for limited wars and counter-insurgency efforts. He also sought an immediate increase of 13,000 personnel for the various services. The president's message to Congress set forth strategic principles which would remain the touchstones of policy throughout McNamara's long tenure in the Pentagon. Kennedy said that defense would not be "bound by arbitrary budget ceilings"; that future budgets might have to be increased further; that civilian control should be strong; that the United States needs increased capacity to fight limited and guerrilla wars; and that "Our arms will never be used to strike the first blow in any attack."[11] When a crisis arose over Berlin in the summer of 1961, Kennedy sought further increases: another $3 billion for defense, two more army divisions, and the call-up of 150,000 reservists.

One important reason why McNamara succeeded in imposing tighter controls and even program terminations on the Pentagon was that he was simultaneously increasing the overall budget. Extra spending also helped him win support on Capitol Hill.

After seizing power with demands for information, McNamara moved decisively to consolidate control over the Pentagon with new bureaucratic processes and new ways of thinking about defense issues. When the new DOD Comptroller, Charles Hitch, briefed him on ways to gather information and structure the review process and suggested some pilot efforts, McNamara ordered him to apply the new system DOD-wide in less than a year. He knew that delay could be deadly and that prompt action would catch the foot-draggers off guard. He believed in decisiveness: "I would rather have a wrong decision than no decision at all."[12]

Later he explained his approach.

> I was determined to subordinate the powerful institutional interests of the various armed services and the defense contractors to a broad conception of the national interest. I wanted to challenge the Pentagon's resistance to change, and I intended that the big decisions would be made on the basis of study and analysis and not simply by perpetuating the practice of allocating blocs of funds to the various services and letting them use the money as they saw fit.[13]

He forced the military leadership to speak a new language, the language of numbers, of systems analysis, of cost-effectiveness. As he told his biographer, "Numbers, as you know, are a language to me."[14] Until then, the only numbers given much attention were the "us versus them" tables of weapons and forces and the bottom-line figures in dollars for defense. "This lack of quantitative standards of adequacy", his whiz kids argued, "meant that, in many cases, 'minimum' military requirements were 30 percent more than what we had, whatever we had."[15] McNamara insisted that his subordinates speak to him in his language and make their case for their recommended policies in terms of costs and trade-offs. He wanted to know precise answers to the question, how much is enough?

Those who could speak in numbers were listened to; those who could not were ignored. That gave prominence and power to the whiz kids – the brash, young, civilian analysts – and reduced the influence of the career military whose experience was impressionistic rather than analytical. While McNamara acknowledged that assumptions drove results, he seemed to believe that numbers based on transparent assumptions were somehow dispassionate and truthful. As he later told Congress, "The basic objective of the management system we are introducing and trying to operate, is to establish a rational foundation as opposed to an emotional foundation for the decisions as to what size force and what type of force this country will maintain."[16]

Disputes over numbers, however, often became quite emotional. When the 34-year old Air Force Secretary, Harold Brown, slashed funds for a new manned bomber, General Curtis Lemay exploded, "Why, that son of a bitch was in junior high school when I was out bombing Japan."[17] Another air force general was shocked when Alain Enthoven, McNamara's leading systems analyst, tried to end an argument over nuclear war plans by saying, "General, I have fought just as many nuclear wars as you have."[18]

McNamara restructured the budget process to capture and control all of the major decisions on force structure and strategy. Centralization was extensive and deliberate.[19] Instead of the annual review to develop the next year's requests, he created a five year defense program (FYDP), forcing the services to project their spending and acquisition into the future – and then forced them to live within their plans by requiring his approval for any major program change proposals (PCP). He created a whole Planning, Programming, and Budget System (PPBS) for reviewing budgets and programs – one which is still essentially the same in DOD and now widely followed throughout the Federal Government.

As Alain Enthoven, one of the most important whiz kids, explained, "The main purpose of PPBS was to develop explicit criteria, openly and thoroughly debated by all interested parties, that could be used by the Secretary of Defense, the President, and the Congress as measures of the need for and adequacy of defense programs."[20] But those measures ultimately had to be quantifiable – hard numbers to evaluate intellectual notions. While McNamara formally disavowed being a prisoner of numbers – "I am sure that no significant military problem will ever be *wholly* susceptible to quantitative analysis"[21] – the practical effect of his new processes was to relegate arguments without numbers to the realm of opinions, not facts.

The PPBS process followed a strict timetable of paperwork, from initial guidance by OSD to service comments to decisions by the secretary to submissions to the White House and eventual inclusion in the president's budget. Instead of following standard bureaucratic lines, however, McNamara created new categories for analysis that covered more than one service. Air force and navy strategic nuclear weapons programs were lumped in one mission category for strategic forces, and that meant that bombers competed against missiles and navy missiles against air force missiles for extra funds. In conventional forces as well, programs were judged by their cost-effectiveness in achieving similar missions – such as how best to kill Soviet tanks, whether by aircraft or American tanks.

McNamara understood the "golden rule" of budgeting: "he who has the gold rules." And his process guaranteed that he would make the final decisions, regardless of the advice and recommendations provided along the line. The PPBS process changed the power balance in the Pentagon by reducing the influence of the services and the uniformed military and strengthening the role of the civilians within the Office of the Secretary of Defense, which grew 50 percent while he was in charge.[22] The new process shifted the competition for resources from an emotional fight among the services, each linking past victories to promised future ones, to bloodless combat between number-crunchers, each claiming the mantle of truth.

The new mission categories also changed the balance of power within the services, giving new standing and leverage to the less glamorous conventional warfare communities, who no longer were the neglected stepchildren dominated by their nuclear-armed siblings. Until McNamara's time, the services regularly took cuts imposed from above and protected their flagship programs while slashing the less-favored forces. There had been alternative budgets, with tiers of decreasing priority, so that officials could see what would be gained or lost by different funding levels – but the priorities were developed by each service, not by the Secretary of Defense.[23] McNamara changed that.

Angry officers

Senior military leaders resented McNamara's imperious style and the undisguised arrogance of many of his civilian aides. Fueled by frustrations over McNamara's handling of the Vietnam War, their views became such a strong consensus among the officer corps that the Nixon Administration chose to dismantle the office of system analysis and otherwise to downgrade the role of civilian analysts.

Two years after General Thomas D. White retired as Air Force Chief of Staff in 1961, he echoed the feelings of many officers in an article in a popular magazine. "I am profoundly apprehensive of the pipe-smoking, tree-full-of-owls type of so-called professional 'defense intellectuals' who have been brought into this nation's capital", he wrote in 1963. He called them "amateurs", "temporary experts", "termites at work", and doubted that they "have sufficient worldliness to stand up to the kind of enemy we face."[24]

General Curtis LeMay, picked by Kennedy as White's successor in June, 1961, had a similar reaction. He later said, "The Kennedy Administration came in and right from the start we got the back of the hand. Get out of our way. We think nothing of you and your opinions. We don't like you as people. We have no respect for you. Don't bother us."[25]

Kennedy downgraded the role of the Joint Chiefs of Staff quite openly in July 1961 by naming retired Army Chief of Staff, General Maxwell Taylor, as his personal "military representative" to the JCS. The president had long admired Taylor – an outspoken critic of Eisenhower's defense policy – and he had lost confidence in the existing Chiefs because of their muddled advice at the time of the failed Bay of Pigs invasion of Cuba. A year later, he named Taylor as JCS Chairman, thus formalizing his authority as Kennedy's principal military adviser. Despite the awkwardness of the initial bureaucratic arrangement, Taylor's relations with McNamara were "remarkably harmonious."[26] Their styles and policy preferences were quite similar.

The president and McNamara retained the other Chiefs until the end of their designated terms and then replaced them with men who remained loyal and supportive of the administration. Even the irascible LeMay was given another year as Air Force Chief of Staff despite his anger over cancellation of the B-70 bomber. He was viewed by the administration as an effective leader of the air force. The Chief of Naval Operations, however, was denied another term because he had greatly angered McNamara by his conduct during the Cuban missile crisis. Admiral George Anderson had resisted the secretary's detailed and insistent questioning of naval blockade procedures, telling McNamara, "Now, Mr. Secretary, if you and your deputy will go back to your offices, the Navy will run the blockade."[27]

The civilians disagreed with the military over style and substance. McNamara and his people were intrusive, insistent, and not always respectful of the officers and their traditions. One incident reveals his pettiness in pursuit of greater commonality of equipment among the services. "Early on, McNamara held a 'fashion show' in his conference room attended by his civilian and military deputies. The different services' belts and butchers' smocks and women's bloomers were modeled, as were jackets, caps, boots, and other things. As each item was shown, McNamara decided on the spot which of the versions would henceforth by used by all the services."[28]

Disputes were more serious and consequential on issues of nuclear strategy and ways to fight conventional wars more effectively. In these matters, McNamara dominated but did not always prevail.

Nuclear strategy

McNamara reflected the growing consensus of civilian defense intellectuals who were applying new concepts to the new kind of war – concepts of game theory, and different types of deterrence, and escalation ladders. They were "thinking about the unthinkable" and coming up with interesting concepts and strategies. Men like LeMay had long believed that nuclear wars could be won – by striking first with overwhelming power. But the new president had ruled that out in his first defense message to Congress.[29] Instead, the civilian war planners emphasized secure second-strike forces, weapons that could survive a surprise attack and still destroy the enemy as a functioning society. Since only a fraction of land-based bombers could be airborne in time to escape a sneak attack, they argued for quick-reaction solid-fuel missiles in hardened silos and missiles aboard submarines hiding in the depths of the broad ocean. They also believed in moving up the escalation ladder slowly, sending signals by not attacking certain targets or areas rather than retaliating with everything available. In time, these ideas became the new orthodoxy, embraced by military leaders and civilians alike. But in the early 1960s, they were points of contention.

Soon after taking office, McNamara began hearing briefings on US nuclear capabilities and war-fighting plans. One of the landmark achievements of his predecessor, Thomas Gates, was the development of the first SIOP, the Single, Integrated Operational Plan for the use of nuclear weapons, the first time the navy and air force had to work together to plan which weapons would be used on which Soviet bloc targets. This avoided wasteful "overkill" as well as exaggerated "requirements" when each service planned to fight the war alone.

The briefings did not reassure McNamara, however. He concluded that the US military still hoped to launch a full-scale first strike, targeting millions of people who contributed little if anything to the Soviet war effort. He was determined to devise rational ways of calculating military requirements and war plans that gave the civilians control of the conflict as long as possible.

By the end of March 1961, he was able to codify several of the administration's new ideas in the president message on defense. Kennedy told Congress that nuclear weapons had to be under "civilian control and command at all times." The president rejected the idea that the number of strategic weapons in each arsenal were the way to figure the balance of power. Instead, he said deterrence depended on having "sufficient retaliatory forces … able to survive a first strike and penetrate [enemy] defenses in order to inflict unacceptable losses upon him." In addition to increases in missile and submarine production, Kennedy sought added funds for warning system and command and control.[30]

In the following months, McNamara elaborated the concept of "assured destruction" and said the Soviet Union would be deterred from attacking the United States if surviving US forces could destroy 20 percent to 25 percent of the Soviet population and 50 percent of industrial capacity. The systems analysts later put a ceiling of 400 megaton-equivalent delivered warheads as an adequate minimum deterrent force because their calculations showed little increased damage from significant additional warheads. Their charts showed a knee-bend of sharply diminishing returns at higher force levels.[31]

Throughout his subsequent years in office, McNamara refined his thinking and oversaw revisions in the SIOP. As he became more concerned about the civilian casualties in a nuclear exchange, he shifted actual targeting toward "counterforce" capabilities – that is, Soviet military sites. But he moved away from the "no cities" doctrine he announced in a 1962 speech. He also wrestled with the question of defenses against nuclear attack – from the civil defense preparations strongly favored by the president to an anti-ballistic missile (ABM) system that emerging technology seemed to promise – and came to the conclusion that it would always be easier and cheaper for an aggressor to overwhelm any system than for the United States to upgrade it.[32] These defensive measures were linked to his criterion of "damage limitation", in contrast to the surviving offensive forces for "assured destruction." Here as elsewhere, his choice of words tilted the argument in his favor: "damage limitation" is more tentative than "active defense;" "assured destruction" is more confident than "retaliatory capability."

McNamara succeeded in bringing nuclear strategy under his control through the SIOP and through his program decisions. Although he used very conservative force planning assumptions – even to the point of assuming that each leg of what came to be called the "Triad" of bombers, land-based and sea-based missiles had to be large enough to perform the assured destruction mission in case of war – he was able to cap those forces and reduce the share of the defense budget going for strategic forces. Between 1961 and 1965, the share of defense spending going for strategic forces dropped by more than half, from 27 percent to 12 percent.[33] He also won the battle of ideas by installing his vocabulary as the language for analyzing and discussing nuclear war. For the rest of the Cold War, US policy stayed within the framework he established in the 1960s.

Counter-insurgency forces

President Kennedy himself took the lead in pushing another revolutionary change in US military capabilities – the endorsement and expansion of special forces, the Green Berets. Indeed, the second national security action memorandum issued in his presidency, NSAM 2, ordered the Secretary of Defense to "examine means for placing more emphasis on the development of counter-guerrilla forces." The president had concluded that the most likely future conflicts would be those peripheral wars between clients of the superpowers, or between friendly governments and their communist-supported insurgents, and he wanted usable military power in the form of highly trained, culturally attuned warriors.[34]

The army already had some special forces units at Fort Bragg, NC, but there were fewer than a thousand men, and they were not given prestige or much resources until the president got personally involved and visited the base in 1961. Then they became – at least for a while – a favored, elite force. Kennedy went to surprising lengths to demonstrate his personal interest in the special forces and his strong support for them. He even summoned all of the major army commanders to the White House in November 1961 and ordered them to develop new counter-insurgency capabilities. He set up a special cabinet group, including his brother Robert, to oversee the army's progress.[35]

Despite the president's direct and personal involvement, the innovation had limited success. Additional units were created and given the right to wear the distinctive green beret, but the rest of the army was slow to develop doctrine for those forces and reluctant to include them in their war plans. One analyst of innovation concludes that the effort fell short because the army did not set up a special promotion path for officers in the special forces, and promotion boards gave little credit for "advisory" assignments rather than commanding US soldiers. Another explanation is that the army preferred to fight the escalating Vietnam War with its own regular forces, and the special talents of the Green Berets were insufficiently exploited. In fact, there were never more than about 2200 special forces personnel in Vietnam at any time during the war.[36]

Air mobility

A third major innovation under McNamara was the development of helicopters and the creation of new army divisions to exploit their capabilities. Here McNamara took ideas from within the army that had been resisted by higher authorities. His actions also challenged the air force, which tended to resist army efforts to acquire aircraft rather than relying on blue-suiters for close air support and transport.

Staffers from the Office of Systems Analysis linked up with the army's aviation mafia and developed a concept paper with specific questions for the army leadership to answer. McNamara sent the paper to the Secretary of the Army in April 1962, along with a biting personal message. "I have not been satisfied with army program submissions for tactical mobility", he wrote. "I do not believe that the Army has fully explored the opportunities offered by aeronautical technology for making a revolutionary break with traditional surface mobility means." McNamara demanded "a bold 'new look' at land warfare mobility" and said that "bold new ideas … [should] be protected from veto or dilution by conservative staff review." He even went so far as to name particular people, already known to be sympathetic to these ideas, as potential members of the review panel.[37]

The army group met the secretary's expectations and recommended the creation of an airmobile division built around 450 helicopters. New air mobility concepts were also simultaneously being tested in combat in Vietnam, so the recommendations were practical and they fell on friendly ears. The army also helped assure the success of the new approach by creating attractive career paths for aviators.[38] Nowadays, helicopters and air mobility are essential parts of both the army and Marine Corps.

Showdown in Congress

McNamara succeeded in carrying out his revolution because he maintained strong support from the president and from the key leaders on Capitol Hill.

Members of Congress were surprised and pleased to see a secretary of defense so knowledgeable and responsive. He had answers for every question, precise answers because he had numbers to back up his conclusions. This was rare in defense hearings. He brought fewer backup staff to demonstrate his own mastery of the subjects that might be raised. He deluged Congress with data. He expanded the secretary's annual report from the 33 pages of his predecessor to 166 pages his first year and to 280 pages by his last year.[39] He also included large sections on US foreign policy, though he claimed that he had shown them to Secretary of State Dean Rusk.

He also cultivated some of the most powerful members of Congress. Before Kennedy's inauguration he met with the longtime Chairman of the House Armed Services Committee, Rep. Carl Vinson (D-Ga), who had been in Congress since before McNamara was even born. Although the new administration had been leaning toward a further, radical defense reorganization – abolishing the service departments and creating a single chief of staff, as recommended by a panel of Democratic defense experts – Vinson argued strongly against the idea and McNamara publicly pledged, "I will undertake no major reorganization of the Defense Department in the near future."[40]

Vinson in turn lavished praise on the incoming official, saying "he'll make the best Defense Secretary the country has had." Later in 1961, McNamara spoke at a special dinner in Atlanta honoring Vinson and his Senate counterpart, Senator Richard Russell (D-Ga), calling himself "the newest pupil in the Russell–Vinson school for secretaries of defense."[41]

It helped, of course, that McNamara was proposing increases in defense spending. He met his greatest resistance on those programs he tried to cancel or cut back. The biggest fight came over his decision to kill the B-70 manned bomber, the planned successor to the B-52. With Vinson's strong support, Congress in 1961 had added $400 million to the budget for the B-70. But the administration refused to spend the money because it saw no need for such aircraft because of the promise of ICBMs and missile-carrying submarines. Vinson's committee retaliated in 1962 by adopting a new bill, adding $491 million for the aircraft program, and "directed" that it be spent.[42]

Fearing a Constitutional impasse as well as a political problem, McNamara met privately with Vinson and helped arrange a "walk in the Rose Garden" for the chairman with the president. Kennedy said, "Uncle Carl, this kind of language and my ignoring it will only hurt us and the country. Let me write you a letter that will get us both off this limb." They exchanged letters and Vinson got his committee to drop the "directed" language while still authorizing added funds. Vinson's biographer called this one of the few times in his long career when the Georgia congressman backed down from a big fight.[43]

Despite the fight over the B-70, Vinson remained an admirer of McNamara. "Anyone who makes decisions is bound to have people disagree with him", he told reporters.[44] Congress accepted most of McNamara's budget proposals in the early years. His only other major confrontation with Congress came in 1967, when he overrode subordinate recommendations on the contract for a new multi-service tactical fighter, the TFX. Supporters of the losing contractor raised procedural and substantive arguments against the decision and subjected McNamara to weeks of well-publicized criticism.

By then, however, McNamara was busy as the secretary of war, and domestic opposition to his policies in Vietnam tarnished his reputation as the revolutionary manager of the Pentagon.

McNamara's legacy

Before the Vietnam War diverted him, McNamara had succeeded in imposing far-reaching changes on the US military. He brought the armed forces until strong civilian control, control extending to the minutia of weapons development and to the targeting of nuclear weapons. He created a budget process and management techniques which have spread government-wide and are still in place, barely changed from his original designs. He forced civilians and the military to learn and think in and speak a new language of analysis, rooted in the economics of cost-effectiveness. He created the presumption, beneficial to all his successors, that the Secretary of Defense was the ultimate authority for defense policy decisions and that military leaders were only advisers, whose advice could be rejected with cause.

He set a new standard for secretaries of defense in dealing with Congress by providing vast amounts of information, exuding expertise and self-confidence, and challenging contractors and other parochial interests. In one significant area, however, he failed to persuade the lawmakers to follow his lead. Despite the presentation of budget materials in terms of military missions, Congress still appropriates funds by traditional line items for each service and its historical spending categories.

By 1965, the managerial revolution had been accomplished. New challenges, particularly a war in Southeast Asia, consumed McNamara's energies and ultimately his power and person. As the ancient Greeks warned, men can be brought low by an excess of their virtues, by too much of their otherwise commendable qualities. McNamara became another tragic figure because of the Vietnam War. He stumbled there, but the revolution he had wrought in the Pentagon outlasted him.

10 The Goldwater–Nichols revolution from above

> You know, this piece of legislation is so bad it's, it's ... in some respects it's just un-American!
>
> Admiral James Watkins to Cong. Bill Nichols[1]

> If the Pentagon is ever going to be straightened out, the only hope is for Congress to do it. The services are so parochial and powerful, there's no way the executive branch will ever get it done.
>
> Sen. Barry Goldwater[2]

> We *are* all screwed up.
>
> General David Jones to Secretary Caspar Weinberger[3]

Barry Goldwater and Bill Nichols didn't plan to criticize the Defense Department, oppose its senior leaders, and impose far-reaching changes on the armed forces. But the momentum of the legislative process and the wounds of legislative-executive combat propelled them into the fight, and once engaged, drove them to seek victory.

Their story is also the story of the ripeness of ideas in Washington – the way some ideas become noticed, and then discussed, and then embraced, and then fiercely contested, before becoming accepted wisdom.

Desert One legacy

On April 25, 1980 the United States armed forces launched a daring raid to rescue Americans held captive in Iran since the US Embassy had been seized the previous November. The plan had been developed over several months within the Joint Staff. It created from scratch a joint task force involving each of the military services, despite the absence of joint operating doctrine or cross-service experience. To maintain the tightest secrecy, units rehearsed separately, under their own commanders and following their regular service procedures. The on-scene commander at the Desert One staging area wrote of "there being four commanders at the scene without visible identification, incompatible radios, and no agreed-upon plan ...."[4] When some of the helicopters got lost in a sandstorm, the mission was canceled, and eight men died when two aircraft collided in the confusion.

The embarrassing failure of the hostage rescue mission underscored organizational problems in the Pentagon and prompted the Chairman of the Joint Chiefs of Staff, General David Jones, to begin to consider significant changes. Jones found an ally in Defense Secretary Harold Brown, but before they could act the 1980 elections brought a new team to Washington, Ronald Reagan and a Republican-controlled Senate.[5]

The victorious Republicans had criticized the Carter Administration for an inadequate defense policy, exemplified by the Desert One fiasco and low unit readiness rates. They promised a revitalized military and greatly increased spending on it. The Republican platform's only mention of Pentagon organization called for less civilian interference with service policies.[6]

General Jones believed that more centralization was needed. Early on, he concluded that the Chairman had to be strengthened, the Joint Staff enlarged and made more independent of the various services, and more emphasis placed on joint operations. In February 1981, he established a study group of retired officers under the leadership of a former DOD official, William K. Brehm, to develop a plan for evaluating JCS organization.[7]

When he approached the new Defense Secretary, however, he met firm resistance. Caspar Weinberger's top priority was increasing the defense budget, and he wanted nothing to interfere with that. He also feared that criticism of Pentagon organization would prevent increases and lead to cuts by the Congress. "If we take on this issue, they'll think we're all screwed up over here", he told Jones. The Chairman replied, "We *are* all screwed up."[8]

Jones was a lame duck in the new administration. Many Republicans had pushed for his ouster even before his term ended in June 1982, because of his acquiescence in Carter Administration's decisions such as cancellation of the B-1 bomber. Jones was allowed to stay, and he responded by keeping quiet and acting deferentially toward his new civilian superiors.

He moved stealthily within the JCS system. His special study group reached some preliminary conclusions in December 1981, and began briefing them to the JCS members. The group favored strengthening the role of the JCS Chairman, giving him a deputy, reducing the need for JCS unanimity, and setting up a personnel process for joint assignments. Army leaders wanted to go further, but only the air force and Marine Corps seemed supportive. The navy leadership rejected both criticism of the current system and the proposed remedies.[9]

Jones decided that he had to go public on his own. At a February 3 appearance before the House Armed Services Committee, he made a brief comment following the opening budget statement by Weinberger. "We do not have an adequate organization structure today [in the Pentagon]", he said, "at least in my judgment." He followed his testimony with an article in the Armed Forces Journal that criticized the JCS as a "patchwork" system that failed to produce good, clear advice. "As would be expected", he wrote, "papers produced by such a multiple committee process are often watered down or well waffled."[10]

The next month, Army Chief of Staff, General Edward "Shy" Meyer, weighed in with his own article, calling for the creation of a full-time advisory body of senior officers, a National Military Advisory Council, separate from the service chiefs. Meyer argued that dual-hatting of the service chiefs divided their loyalties and prevented them from giving "sound, usable and timely military advice."[11]

At first, only a couple of Congressmen took up the cause of JCS reform. Ike Skelton (D-Mo) had been the only House Armed Services Committee member to pick up on Jones' February 3 testimony with a series of questions. Later, Cong. Richard C. White (D-Tex.), chairman of the Investigations Subcommittee, decided to launch a series of hearings on the issue. He had been prodded by a new staff member, retired Air Force Colonel Archie Barrett, who had just finished a study of Pentagon organizational problems. He told White, "Mr. Chairman, when the top military officer says that the JCS system is fatally flawed, Congress can't sit idly by."[12]

Although White planned to retire from Congress at the end of 1982, he seized the issue and held 20 hearings with 43 witnesses between April and the end of July. The sessions built a solid foundation for reform. Ten former high ranking civilians were supportive, as were almost all active and retired army and air force officers and most marine witnesses. Only half of the navy witnesses – those who had significant experience in joint positions – favored reform, however.[13]

By midsummer there had been a major turnover in the JCS. General Jones had been replaced as chairman by Army General John W. Vessey, Jr., and there were new men atop the navy and air force. When they testified before White's subcommittee, they withheld any strong opinions, saying that they had been asked by Secretary Weinberger to review the various proposals and report to him by October 1.[14]

White proceeded with a bill limited to non-controversial provisions, such as allowing the JCS Chairman to provide military advice "in his own right" but not designating him the principal military adviser, as later legislation would. The bill was approved unanimously by the full Armed Services Committee and passed the House a few days later by voice vote. Weinberger reported to Reagan that the measure was done "primarily as a courtesy" to the retiring subcommittee chairman and that it was "a much watered down version" of earlier proposals.[15]

The apparent death knell for reform came on November 22, when the JCS reported to Weinberger just what he wanted to hear – that "sweeping changes to title 10 USC [U.S. Code] are unnecessary."[16] It would take another year and more military disasters before Congress moved against the entrenched Pentagon leaders.

Beirut and Grenada

Secretary Weinberger was fully occupied in 1983 defending his request for a 10 percent hike in the Pentagon budget and in securing support for the controversial MX missile and basing system. There was also considerable pressure for a "freeze" in nuclear weapons programs.[17] When reorganization issues were raised in congressional hearings, he sidestepped them, arguing that no major changes were needed but that some modest changes were being reviewed.

House members pushed a minor revision of the 1982 bill, adding the legislative tweaks endorsed by Weinberger. They held a meeting with the defense secretary and JCS chairman on May 18, when the Pentagon leaders reiterated their opposition to major changes. Weinberger declared that "[the present] system works and is satisfactory." General Vessey said, "The JCS agreed that the law should not be changed with respect to the duties given to the JCS." Nevertheless, the House committee made a few additional changes, and the full House passed the new measure by voice vote on October 17.[18]

Events a week later gave new impetus to reform. On October 23, a suicide truck bomber drove to the front of the building housing US Marines sent to Beirut on a peacekeeping mission, killing 241 servicemen. Subsequent investigations revealed a dysfunctional command arrangement with 31 different "stovepipes" reporting to the Pentagon as well as insufficient regard for the local threat of terrorism.[19]

Two days later, when US forces were sent into the Caribbean island of Grenada to rescue American medical students threatened following a leftist coup, the operation revealed numerous organizational and operational problems. The army and Marine Corps had separate chains of command, incompatible radios, and outdated tourist maps. A few weeks later, Senator Sam Nunn (D-Ga.) met some returning soldiers who told him that the only way one army officer could get naval gunfire support was to go to a public telephone booth and call Fort Bragg using his AT&T calling card. Colin Powell, who was Weinberger's senior military assistant at the time, later called Grenada "a sloppy success." He said, "Relations between the services were marred by poor communications, fractured command and control, interservice parochialism, and micromanagement from Washington."[20]

Beirut and Grenada strengthened the resolve of those in Congress who had been pressing reform. Instead of a hypothetical intellectual exercise, it became an urgent practical military necessity. Congressman Bill Nichols (D-Ala.), who had succeeded Dick White as chairman of the Investigations Subcommittee, had met with marines in Beirut only a few weeks before the barracks bombing. His subcommittee was charged with investigating the tragedy, and it discovered and reported a flawed chain of command as well as serious errors of judgment. The events made Nichols a more committed reformer, who soon found new allies and entrenched adversaries.[21]

Organized resistance

Caspar Weinberger opposed anything that would detract from his budget plans. As he later told Jim Locher, "Reorganization was put forth frequently by many people as a substitute for defense spending. They'd say, 'If we just had reorganization, we wouldn't need so much money,' which was quite absurd."[22] That was certainly the motivation for some members of Congress, who seized upon management scandals – such as grossly overpriced hammers, coffee pots, and toilet seats – to discredit Weinberger's budget requests.

But there were many others, particularly on the defense committees of Congress, who wanted to improve the war-fighting capabilities of the armed forces by reducing service parochialism and increasing inter-service coordination. They were fighting a less visible inside game to correct the flaws identified by General Jones and others, flaws that had been part of the US military system at least since 1947.

Leading the fight against reform in the 1980s, as in the 1940s, was the leadership of the US Navy. After the Second World War, Navy Secretary James Forrestal and a host of admirals successfully blocked centralization of the armed forces. When Forrestal was then named the first Secretary of Defense, he soon discovered that the post lacked the power to do bring the services into line under a common budget. Nor could General Dwight Eisenhower, as President in the 1950s, persuade Congress to take more than baby steps toward reducing service autonomy.

In the 1980s, the navy was led by John Lehman, a strong-willed, politically connected, seapower advocate. Even Admiral William Crowe, who became JCS Chairman in 1985, viewed Lehman as ambitious and ruthless, calling him "the ultimate bureaucrat. He was unscrupulous. Didn't hesitate to lie."[23] Colin Powell called him "probably the best infighter in the building …. To him, the Navy position was always the Alamo."[24]

Lehman ran the navy as a very tight ship, often telling his officers, "Loyalty is agreeing with me." He promoted those who shared his views and followed his orders. He ignored outside pressures, even from Weinberger, and single-mindedly maneuvered to increase the navy's budget and guard against interference. To win friends on Capitol Hill, he launched a Strategic Homeport Initiative, seeking to disperse the fleet into a dozen new bases. Ostensibly, this was to prevent any Pearl Harbor-like concentration of ships. In fact, it worked to increase political support for navy programs as numerous cities vied for the jobs and spending the homeports promised.[25]

His arguments against strengthening the JCS Chairman and the Joint Staff were the same ones made over the years by other naval officials. He claimed there was too much centralization already. He warned against a "Prussian general staff." And he blamed Congress for causing these problems and failing to fix them by halting its micromanagement of the services.[26] He repeated these points in a series of speeches and articles while legislation worked its way through Congress.

Lehman also worked behind the scenes to set up roadblocks to reform. A retired marine brigadier general fed him insider reports on the Jones study group as it developed its recommendations. He pressured the Hudson Institute to establish a study group of anti-reform retired officers which ultimately issued a report echoing Lehman's own criticisms of the reform proposals. And when the conservative Heritage Foundation was on the verge of releasing its own report that urged eliminating the service secretariats and other measures, Lehman succeeded in having the report's release delayed for eight months.[27]

The navy also had a friend in the Senate, the chairman of the Armed Services Committee, John Tower (R-Tex.) He was proud of his service as an enlisted seaman and otherwise supportive of Lehman and the navy. He also hoped to succeed Weinberger as secretary of defense and thus was careful about causing problems for the administration. In May 1982, he headed off an amendment by Sen. Nunn requiring a DOD report on JCS reforms by promising "hearings at the earliest possible date."[28] Nunn withdrew his amendment, but the hearing was not scheduled until December 16, shortly before Congress adjourned for the year.

In June 1983, to counter the House action on reform legislation, he announced a comprehensive series of hearings on DOD organization. His preference was for even less centralization, including dismantling the office of the secretary of defense, but the staff went to work on its study with a more open mind. Hearings later on demonstrated Weinberger's defensiveness and the growing chorus of critics. Former defense secretary James Schlesinger testified on November 2 that the JCS structure was the "central weakness" of the system. "The unavoidable outcome is a structure in which log-rolling, back-scratching, marriage arrangements, and the like flourish. It is important not to rock the boat."[29]

In 1984, with politicians distracted by the presidential and congressional elections, little progress was made on defense reform legislation. When Tower had done nothing to get Senate action, the House committee added the previously passed Nichols bill to its broad DOD authorization bill, the principal annual vehicle for defense policy and budget legislation. When the Senate considered its version of the bill, Sen. Thomas Eagleton (D-Mo.) offered an amendment to replace the JCS with an advisory council. Tower deflected the proposal with a promise of later committee action. Joining the debate and pressing for some kind of action were Sam Nunn, who became the committee's senior Democrat in September 1983 with the death of Sen. Henry M. "Scoop" Jackson (D-Wash.) and Barry Goldwater (R-Ariz.) who was expected to succeed the retiring Tower after the 1984 elections.[30]

In the House–Senate conference on the authorization bill in September, Tower repeatedly blocked Nichols' efforts to discuss the House-passed language. The Texan postponed action until 1a.m., following 15 hours of marathon negotiations on other issues. Angry and discouraged, Nichols agreed to back down with report language promising action in 1985. But Nunn laid the groundwork for the next year with language requiring a DOD report answering detailed questions about organizational issues.[31]

Goldwater's legacy

Ronald Reagan was overwhelmingly reelected and kept Weinberger as secretary of defense. Goldwater became Senate Armed Services Committee chairman, with Nunn as ranking Democrat. In the House, Les Aspin became chairman of the House Armed Services Committee after Democrats ousted the aging and ailing former chairman. The stage was set for serious consideration of reform issues.

Joining the chorus for change was a distinguished panel brought together by the Center for Strategic and International Studies (CSIS), which released a report on January 25, 1985, blaming inter-service rivalries for most of the problems in the Pentagon and recommending a stronger JCS chairman and joint staff. Hill members of the panel included Nunn, Aspin, Senator Bill Cohen (R-Me.) and Congressman Newt Gingrich (R-Ga.). The group's report eventually won the endorsement of six of seven living former secretaries of defense – all except Don Rumsfeld.[32]

Criticism of Pentagon organization coincided with new horror stories about weapons program costs and mismanagement. Investigators uncovered $180 flashlights, $400 hammers, $7,000 coffee pots, $74,000 folding ladders – and the infamous $600 toilet seat. Officials on the National Security Council staff were concerned about Weinberger's reduced credibility on Capitol Hill and the risks of punitive legislation. They decided to try to "seize the initiative from Congress" and develop a presidential proposal.[33]

What the NSC staff proposed, and the president endorsed, was a "blue ribbon commission" headed by former business and Pentagon executive, David Packard. Administration officials hoped to buy time pending the report by the new panel. As things turned out, the commission's interim report, in February 1986, was supportive of the reforms then moving through the Congress.[34]

Meanwhile, both House and Senate committees pressed ahead with their investigations and hearings. Prodded by Les Aspin, his committee approved a tougher JCS reorganization bill on October 24, 1985. It designated the JCS Chairman as the principal military adviser to the president and made changes in the personnel system to encourage joint experience. The House passed the bill 383-27 on November 20. The administration opposed the measure, pleading with Congress to wait for the Packard Commission's report.[35]

In the Senate, Goldwater and Nunn teamed up to build a committee consensus in favor of reform. In typical fashion, Nunn had accepted minor victories, such as Tower's promise of hearings, in return for not pressing for formal legislation. He also sought DOD reports that might help build

Figure 10.1   Senators Barry Goldwater and Sam Nunn (US Senate photo)

his case. For his part, Goldwater saw this subject as a fitting one to embrace in his final two years in the Senate and his first as chairman of the Armed Services Committee. He came to reform instinctively, not bureaucratically, but his standing as an unabashed military hawk made his support all the more persuasive.

Goldwater established a nine-member task force in the committee to review the staff study being prepared by Jim Locher and others. The group met about once a week during June–October 1985 to review and discuss the staff's findings. The effort was serious, but Senators remained unsure how far to go. As late as September, one thoughtful senator, Jeff Bingaman (D-N.Mex.), told Locher, "your arguments and proposals appear sound, but all the generals and admirals across the river in the Pentagon are against this."[36]

Soon after Labor Day, Goldwater and Nunn devised a careful rollout strategy for the reform ideas. They planned to start October 1 with a series of hard-hitting Senate floor speeches spelling out the problems found in the current DOD organization and processes. They scheduled a weekend retreat for the task force, joined by a number of defense luminaries, most but not all of whom were on record favoring reforms. They decided to release Locher's study as a "staff report" *to* the committee rather than a report *by* the committee, thus preserving their distance and flexibility. And they planned hearings with administration and other officials following release of the report. Actual legislation was postponed until 1986.

The plan went smoothly and garnered significant and favorable media attention. In the first of six paired floor speeches, Goldwater warned, "If we have to fight tomorrow, these problems will cause Americans to die unnecessarily. Even more, they may cause us to lose the fight." The conservative icon went on, "You will hear over and over again the old maxim: 'If it ain't broke, don't fix it.' Well, I say to my colleagues: It is broke, and we need to fix it." Nunn listed numerous Pentagon problems, but also acknowledged congressional trivialization and micromanagement. "We have found the enemy and it is us."[37]

Taking the task force to a weekend retreat at a Virginia military base also served to reenforce the criticisms of current law and build consensus for change. Most of the former officials and other experts in attendance echoed the findings of the staff study. When Goldwater called on the senators for their views, many seemed emboldened by the company and for the first time enunciated positions in favor of various reforms.[38]

In preparing to release the staff study, Nunn urged Locher to include some controversial recommendations that were no longer favored – so that the proposals could be dropped as a gesture of compromise. "We need staff recommendations that scare them so badly that when we do what we really intend to do, they will take out their handkerchiefs and wipe their brows and say, 'Boy, we sure are lucky'", Nunn advised. These measures also served as what one journalist called "bullet traps" that drew the fire of opponents away from more fundamental changes. Locher says he kept seven such provisions in the final report, including General Meyer's idea of disestablishing the JCS and replacing it with a joint military advisory council and another proposal to make the unified commanders senior in rank to the service chiefs.[39]

Just before releasing the staff study, Goldwater and Nunn went to the Pentagon to brief Weinberger and the Chiefs. The meeting started politely but quickly deteriorated into a shouting match. Deputy Secretary Will Taft, whose nomination Goldwater had openly opposed the previous year, calling the lawyer unqualified to manage the Pentagon, objected to the level of criticism of the Department. Goldwater fired back, "Your operational performance has been so piss poor, you guys would have trouble defending the River Entrance [to the Pentagon] from an attack by a troop of Boy Scouts."[40]

The 645-page staff report received the expected favorable media coverage and led to a series of committee hearings with a range of witnesses. Weinberger continued to deny there were any serious problems affecting his department and rejected any suggestions for reform. John Lehman's complaint that OSD had too much bureaucracy was rebutted by Nunn, who pointed out that the navy listings took up 52 pages in the Pentagon phone book, almost as many as OSD, JCS, and all the other services combined.[41]

New to the ranks of reformers but unwilling to be outspoken, was Admiral William Crowe, who became JCS Chairman in October, 1985. Crowe earned a PhD at Princeton in addition to serving in a variety of naval assignments as he moved up in rank. By the time he was the Pacific Commander, he had come to appreciate the need for greater inter-service jointness – and he recognized his own service's opposition to collaboration.[42]

Once he became Chairman, Crowe said he had to "tread carefully." The Chiefs felt unjustly maligned by so much criticism. But Crowe knew he needed a good working relationship with them, so he tried to stay out of the public debate, working behind the scenes to get the Chiefs to come up with things they could support instead of fighting all change.[43] Most of the Chiefs remained adamant in their opposition.

Early in 1986, Goldwater and Nunn drafted a revised bill, still leaving in some lightning rod provisions they could drop when necessary. On February 3, the day before the committee markup of their bill, they went again to the Pentagon for a meeting with the Chiefs. As before, the Senators met strong objections from Marine Corps Commandant, the Chief of Naval Operations, and the Army Chief of Staff. Army General John Wickham said bluntly, "This legislation would cripple the Joint Chiefs of Staff."[44]

The Senators tried to answer objections but ultimately realized the effort was futile. As they returned to the Capitol, Goldwater told Nunn, "If the Pentagon is ever going to be straightened out, the only hope is for Congress to do it. The services are so parochial and powerful, there's no way the executive branch will ever get it done."[45]

A month-long drama began the next day with the start of markup. Of the 10 Republicans and nine Democrats on the committee, only nine Senators seemed fully supportive of the reform legislation. Goldwater assured Nunn that he could bring Sen. Strom Thurmond (R-SoCar.) along, to provide a 10–9 majority. When Sen. John Warner (R-Va.) took the mantle of leader of the opposition and offered a package of 13 amendments on the first day, Goldwater announced that the committee would conduct no other business until it had completed the markup of the reorganization bill.[46]

On the first substantive vote, Goldwater phoned the absent Sen. Dan Quayle (R-Ind.) and threatened to take his subcommittee chairmanship away from him if he supported Warner. Quayle complied, but the threat increased tension among the members. Over time, the committee debated 53 amendments by Sen. Warner and defeated the only three brought to rollcall votes. Some 60 percent of his proposals were adopted – including the Virginia senator's far-sighted proposal requiring an annual national security strategy report by the president.[47] Goldwater and Nunn used the amendment process to make revisions, garner support, and smooth ruffled feathers.

Outside, the navy was running a crisis management center to help block the legislation. Alerted by a journalist, Goldwater called the navy office and spoke to an unsuspecting staffer, who acknowledged their purpose. This incident of executive branch interference with the legislature also helped build unity in the committee.[48]

On March 6, following the lengthy debates and votes on amendments, the committee voted on reporting the bill to the Senate. To the surprise of all, the vote was unanimous. Even Warner and other navy stalwarts voted for the bill. The legislative process had turned them from staunch opponents to at least lukewarm and grudging supporters.

Administration opposition crumbled further when the president embraced the cause of reform – though he did it by offering his own proposals, without mention of the work already done on Capitol Hill. Reagan endorsed the Packard Commission recommendations on April 5. The Office of Management and Budget announced support of the Senate bill, provided only that wording on the expiration of the JCS chairman's term be deleted. The change was made and the bill went before the Senate on May 7.[49]

Despite a last-minute attempt to kill the bill – Lehman asked Warner to offer an amendment exempting the navy from having to comply with its provisions – debate proceeded swiftly. Just before final passage, Nunn offered an amendment to name the measure the "Barry Goldwater Defense Reorganization Act of 1986." Stunned into silence by the tribute, Goldwater was visibly moved. A few moments later, the Senate voted unanimously, 95–0, to pass the bill. The opposition had vanished, driven away by the desire to honor the retiring chairman and the sense that the time for reform had come.

In the House, there was a similar drama. The day before markup on June 25, Nichols and others met with the Chiefs in the Pentagon. Despite the changed administration position, some of the military leaders continued to object. The CNO, Admiral James Watkins, got red in the face and shouted at Nichols, "You know, this piece of legislation is so bad it's, it's … in some respects it's just un-American!"[50]

When markup started, Chairman Aspin offered the first amendment – to name their measure the "Bill Nichols Defense Reorganization Act of 1986." Once again, the opposition vanished as the committee rallied around its member and his landmark bill. Few amendments were raised; most were withdrawn before a vote. The committee reported the bill by an overwhelming 39–4 vote.[51]

Nichols added his bill to the overall DOD authorization bill in August, and the two versions went to conference in September. The final version tracked closely the original ideas of General Jones, but it had been vetted and massaged and modified to answer the concerns raised over the years. Strangely, despite the White House's earlier endorsement of reform legislation, Reagan signed the bill only at the last minute and without a formal ceremony with the chief sponsors.[52]

Impact

Admiral Crowe moved gingerly to take advantage of his increased powers. The full impact of the legislation strengthening the JCS Chairman did not occur until Colin Powell was appointed in September 1989. Almost overnight, however, the Joint Staff became a power center in the Pentagon. Service in a joint position like the Joint Staff became, under the new law, a prerequisite for becoming a general or admiral, and the best and brightest young officers clamored for a chance to serve in such posts. Another lasting impact has been the increased influence of the regional combatant commanders, who now can offer their own budget and policy recommendations directly to their civilian leaders. The military operations conducted by the United States since 1986 have been significantly better planned and organized – and more effective – as a direct consequence of Goldwater–Nichols.

An important lesson from this story is that Congress can transform the Pentagon, just as powerful secretaries of defense can. Congress in league with some senior military officers can prevail over the most determined opposition of the executive branch – and even over objecting military leaders.

11 The Bush–Rumsfeld wars and transformation

> I will give the [Defense] Secretary a broad mandate – to challenge the status quo and envision a new architecture of American defense for decades to come.
>
> Gov. George W. Bush, September, 1999[1]

> The Constitution calls for civilian control of this department, And I'm a civilian.
>
> Don Rumsfeld[2]

> JCS had a lot less of a voice in this administration. The Pentagon in previous administrations really had two voices. Not in this administration. It was just Rumsfeld.
>
> Richard Haass, State Department, 2001–3[3]

Texas Governor George W. Bush needed a national security speech for his campaign for the presidency. He knew what he didn't like – the Clinton administration's policies – and he asked his growing circle of advisors for their suggestions for alternatives.

Condoleezza Rice, his closest advisor on national security issues, headed a group of eight experienced Republican policy hands who wound up calling themselves the Vulcans, after the Roman god of the forge and metalwork, whose statue loomed over Rice's hometown of Birmingham, Alabama. Among this group were Paul Wolfowitz, Rich Armitage, Richard Perle, Steve Hadley and Robert Zoellick, all of whom had served in the Reagan or G.H.W. Bush administrations.[4]

With Armitage writing the first draft, the Vulcans produced a sharp critique of Clinton's policies as well as a vision of a greatly changed US military. This appealed to Bush, who didn't want the typical Republican rhetoric of "more is better and the generals know best." He wanted to be the outsider with outside ideas.[5] What Armitage offered were the ideas of a new group of defense intellectuals who had been developing the concept of a "revolution in military affairs" – which was immediately turned into a Pentagon-friendly acronym, RMA. Few disagreed with the promising vision of an RMA; fewer still knew how to achieve it.

As the speech went through successive drafts, it was shown to a wider circle of advisors, including the older, cabinet-level types like Dick Cheney, Don Rumsfeld, and Colin Powell. Several criticized its specificity on some points, such as a call for spending fully 20 percent of procurement dollars on transformational programs. But Bush kept pushing for innovative ideas and insisted that that pledge be left in.[6]

On September 23, 1999, the Texas Governor spoke at The Citadel, South Carolina's military college. In his speech, he criticized the Clinton administration for over-stretched resources and lower morale. For himself as future President, he set three goals: to "renew the bond of trust between the American president and the American military"; to "defend the American people against missiles and terror"; and to "begin creating the military of the next century." He also pledged "an immediate, comprehensive review of our military" with the goal of moving "beyond marginal improvements – to replace existing programs with new technologies and strategies. To use this window of opportunity to skip a generation of technology." He also promised to his Secretary of Defense "a broad mandate – to challenge the status quo and envision a new architecture of American defense for decades to come."[7]

This approach appealed to Bush. It took advantage of America's technological strengths. It promised a much better defense capability for little or no extra spending. It allowed him to support a strong defense and major tax cuts without greatly increasing the federal deficit. It even let him outflank Vice President Al Gore, who prided himself on his futurism but who advocated only a conventional, evolutionary approach to defense.

Advocates of revolution

The Citadel speech served its campaign purpose as a set of themes on defense, and as a set of marching orders once the governor became president. Probably Bush's most consequential decision before his election was his choice of Dick Cheney as his running mate. The former defense secretary and former House Republican whip had instant credibility as a Washington power player. Once in office, Cheney built an enlarged and activist Vice Presidential staff, with 13–15 people working on NSC matters, or as many as 35 counting consultants and secondments, thus allowing him to monitor and be represented on a full range of issues.[8] Even before 9/11, Cheney was often seen as Bush's prime minister, not merely his potential successor.

Bush chose Don Rumsfeld as defense secretary not only because of his long experience in security matters but also because he would be a counterweight to Colin Powell at the State Department. Bush had been expected to name Senator Dan Coats (R-Ind), one of the leading congressional sponsors of measures to push military transformation, but Coats failed to impress Bush.

Figure 11.1 President George W. Bush and Defense Secretary Donald Rumsfeld (Defense Department photo)

Rumsfeld had prior Pentagon experience and long ties to Cheney. He was an advocate of missile defense and space programs, although not at first a zealot for transformation. He seemed to accept RMA as an assignment. As he told the president, "If you want me to change the building [the Pentagon], I'll change the building."[9]

The blueprint for transformation was taken from a 1997 report by the National Defense Panel (NDP), a group commissioned by Congress to give an outside, second opinion to place alongside the administration's required Quadrennial Defense Review (QDR). Armitage had been a member of the elite, nine-member NDP, as had retired Army Colonel Andrew Krepinevich, a leading contributor to the RMA literature. The NDP was prescient in many respects. It forecast threats to American "domestic communities and key infrastructures" and urged greater attention to homeland defense. It dismissed as a "low probability scenario" the two major war planning assumption which Rumsfeld eventually discarded in 2001. "We are on the cusp of a military revolution", the NDP said, because of rapid advances in information technologies. Those who would exploit those technologies could "dissipate the 'fog of war'" and "gain significant advantages." The panel disparaged "legacy systems" which would increasingly be at risk and questioned the procurement plans of the services. Instead, the NDP urged a dedicated "transformation strategy" with at least $5 billion to $10 billion more per year devoted to new systems.

These ideas appealed to the new president more than to his new defense secretary.[10] Rumsfeld's tentative embrace of transformation was evident in his confirmation hearing before the Senate Armed Services Committee. He described his goal of transforming the defense establishment chiefly in terms of a faster weapons acquisition process. He also hedged on skipping a generation of weapons by saying, "We cannot allow the effectiveness of our military forces to degrade while we are modernizing and transforming." And his example of great technological change was merely the switch from diesel to turbine engines in the M-1 tank, something most observers considered evolutionary.[11]

After a few months on the job, Rumsfeld further tried to dispel notions that he had come to the Pentagon with fixed ideas for radical change. "Some people think I arrived in this job from the pharmaceutical business with a head full of plans, ready to bring it out, unwrap the cellophane package, and hand them over to the Pentagon", he told reporters. "I didn't. I am very sincerely trying to figure out what I ought to think about these things."[12]

Civilian in charge

What the new defense secretary did have firm, fixed views on, however, was the need for strong civilian control of the military. As he later told reporters, "The Constitution calls for civilian control of this department, And I'm a civilian."[13] At his first meeting with the Joint Chiefs, he ordered a halt to efforts to brief Congress on the military's wish list for $8 billion in extra spending. A few weeks later he went further and ordered senior offices to notify his office a week in advance of all meeting with lawmakers.[14]

Many in the new administration thought that Clinton and his cabinet had not exerted tight enough control over the military, and that the senior officers were not in step with the new leadership. The holdover JCS Chairman, General Hugh Shelton, later said, "I think he [Rumsfeld] felt like we were part of the old administration, that we were part of the problem, not looking for solutions. I don't know why he thought that."[15]

Rumsfeld set about to find a new generation of senior officers. He made a point of personally interviewing all candidates for three- and four-star posts, and rejecting those he considered unqualified. He even interviewed several dozen officers in order to fill each of the most important positions of JCS members and combatant commanders. In addition to vetting senior officers, he sought to increase the time in position of those selected so that they could better learn and fulfill their assignments. Rumsfeld and his people began a "silent purge" of other officers and civilians and seized control over senior appointments from the services.[16]

His style was provocative, even intimidating. Early in 2003, a *New York Times* reporter called his management style "equal parts debating club and wrestling match." A senior official said the secretary welcomed challenges to his views. "But those who challenge the secretary must be prepared for withering cross-examination in a style that some, especially military commanders who are used to a more respectful hearing, find so abrasive that one senior officer has dubbed it 'the wire brush treatment'."[17]

His actions were also assertive and controlling. The new secretary angered the Chiefs early on by excluding them and the Joint Staff from the more than 50 studies he launched when he took office. Following the pattern set by Robert McNamara four decades before, Rumsfeld commissioned reports from different groups of mostly outsiders, retired officers and former officials. "We've been kept out of the loop", complained a senior general to the *Washington Post*. Rumsfeld retorted, "The people it [change] shakes up may very well be people who don't have enough to do." By May, 2001, the griping reached Capitol Hill and the press, and Rumsfeld made a point of meeting with the Chiefs and with members of Congress, so that they could present their views.[18]

Rumsfeld also disappointed the senior military by the way he handled the budget. Having heard the Republican campaign rhetoric "help is on the way", senior officers developed information for an $8 billion increase prior to Bush's inauguration. Rumsfeld silenced that idea, and the President decided against any immediate supplemental request, staying with the final Clinton defense budget. The White House press secretary bragged that the new team would not "throw money in the direction of defense" until it had completed a full strategic review.[19] The administration later relented and in June proposed an extra $5.6 billion, mainly for higher pay, readiness, and program cost growth.

In the summer, Rumsfeld requested an extra $35 billion for the coming year, but accepted a reduction by Bush's budget office to an $18 billion increase. His failure to fight harder and get more money led leading conservatives to call for Rumsfeld's resignation.[20] In August, the president also dashed cold water on military spending hopes when he told reporters, "There is no question that we probably cannot afford every weapons system that is now … being designed or thought of." He said the administration would take the ideas and "winnow them down."[21]

Meanwhile, Rumsfeld encountered pushback from the Chiefs and the services. Several planners suggested cutting two-divisions from the army, which prompted a letter from 82 congressmen opposing any such reduction. Rumsfeld openly rejected and sent back for revision one group's call for a 34-carrier navy, compared to the 12 in the fleet, and a doubling of production of the advanced but expensive F-22 fighter for the air force. By August 2001, he gave up on the idea of dictating the organization and weaponry of the forces and agreed to let the services make those decisions within his broad guidelines. He defended his setbacks by repeating to the press, "Change is hard."[22]

By early September 2001, the Rumsfeld revolution in defense appeared to be a failure. There was press speculation that the defense secretary would be the first to leave the cabinet. On September 6, a reporter asked, "Do you feel a little beat-up? Kind of a punching bag, you know, being hit from all sides?" The embattled secretary replied, "No ... there's a kind of rhythm to this whole thing. The new group comes in, everyone's kind of nice for five minutes, and then ... they start throwing them in the barrel and beating them up a little bit, and life goes on ...."[23]

On September 10, 2001, Rumsfeld spoke to Defense Department employees, ostensibly to urge them to support management reforms. But his words had an edge, for he called "the Pentagon bureaucracy" – his very audience – "an adversary that poses a threat, a serious threat, to the security of the United States", an enemy that "stifles free thought and crushes new ideas."[24]

A few hours later, hijacked airplanes crashed into the World Trade Center and the Pentagon itself, and Don Rumsfeld was transformed from a beleaguered Secretary of Defense into a commanding, admired secretary of war.

War on terror

After September 11, George W. Bush also was transformed, from a minority president, elected with fewer popular votes than his opponent, to the popular commander-in-chief, rallying the nation and ordering US troops into combat against the terrorists and their allies. As soon as he learned of the second plane striking the World Trade Center, he concluded that America was at war and had to fight. In his first call to Rumsfeld, the president said, "we'll clean up the mess and then the ball will be in your court and [General] Dick Myers's court."[25]

The commander-in-chief had very definite ideas about how he should act. His overall management style, derived in part from his Harvard MBA training, was to give guidance and then delegate operational responsibilities. But when Cheney suggested himself as head of a war cabinet that would develop options for the president, Bush rejected the idea. He wanted to run the meetings himself, wanted to show that he was in charge. He also wanted to avoid what he considered the errors during the Vietnam War. He did not want to micromanage operations or set tactics, but he wanted to guarantee that there was a "sense of purpose and forward movement."[26]

The secretary of defense was also determined to assert tight civilian control over any military operations. Time and again in meetings, he would answer questions directed at General Myers or General Tommy Franks, the combatant commander for the Middle East (Centcom). After one such exchange, Bush asked Franks directly, "Tommy, what do you think?" The general responded, "Sir, I think exactly what my secretary thinks, what he's ever thought, what he will ever think, or whatever he thought he might think."[27]

Rumsfeld refused to give subordinates negotiating authority for interagency meetings, thus clogging the process and forcing even minor issues to the senior leaders' meetings. If DOD had a position, department officials had to defend it; if DOD had not yet developed a firm position, they were under orders not to preclude one by agreeing to anything else. As Richard Haass, Powell's director of policy planning later said, "JCS had a lot less of a voice in this administration. The Pentagon in previous administrations really had two voices. Not in this administration. It was just Rumsfeld."[28]

On September 12, the day after the attacks, the NSC convened and debated whether to go only after al Qaeda, or to pursue other terrorists as well. Rumsfeld even raised the question of going after Iraq. At Camp David on September 15, Rumsfeld and especially his deputy, Paul Wolfowitz, again suggested attacks on Iraq. Such operations seemed more doable, more likely to succeed, while US troops could be bogged down in mountain fighting in Afghanistan. Bush listened, but decided to put a stop to such discussions. He wanted to avoid losing focus by trying too many things. He also turned down routine retaliatory strikes inside Iraq by the aircraft that had been patrolling since 1991. "We have to be patient about Iraq", he said.[29]

It was much harder to be patient about Afghanistan, but the US military did not have any ready options. At Camp David, outgoing JCS Chairman, General Hugh Shelton, presented three options: 1. A cruise missile attack on al Qaeda training camps. 2. Up to 10 days of cruise missile and bomber attacks on the camps and some Taliban targets. 3. The air strikes plus some "boots on the ground." While the first two seemed inadequate, the third would require at least 10–12 days to get initial forces in and to obtain necessary basing and overflight rights. Rumsfeld had earlier warned Bush that major operations could take up to 60 days to arrange. Now he disparaged the available military plans, "The military options look like five or ten years ago", he grumbled. He said he favored unconventional approaches using special forces.[30]

CIA Director George Tenet, however, was ready with a bold plan using CIA personnel. His plan called for Agency-run paramilitary forces to aid and invigorate the Afghan opposition called the Northern Alliance. He also sought the president's authorization for "exceptional authorities" to pursue and destroy al Qaeda cells throughout the world. To Rumsfeld's dismay, Bush eagerly endorsed Tenet's plans for immediate action.[31] The defense secretary then pressed Franks to come up with good plans quickly. He also insisted that the plans be creative to deal with the distinctive nature of the enemy. "The Taliban and Al Qaeda do not have armies, navies, and air forces", he said.[32]

Legally, the US chain of command runs from the president to the secretary of defense and then directly to the combatant commander, with the JCS

Chairman in the loop only to transmit communications. Rumsfeld and Franks quickly developed direct links and held frequent conferences, both in Washington and by video teleconference (VTC). As planning continued, the Centcom commander repeatedly complained of interference and unsolicited advice from the Chiefs. At one point, Franks called General Myers. "Dick, we're gonna have to unscrew the Service contributions to this fight .... I'll provide the command, you work on the Service Chiefs to get the unity of effort." He later wrote that "a number of officers on the Joint Staff were on their own tactical wave length, and it was these officers who were the focus of my strategic 'push'."[33]

The civilian leaders wanted action faster than the military could deliver. The warriors needed to build up staging bases, needed on-the-ground intelligence to plan targets, needed to have Combat Search and Rescue (CSAR) units in place before launching air strikes, needed overflight rights from nearby countries. All this took time.[34] Rumsfeld went to the region in early October to secure cooperation, notably from Uzbekistan.

General Franks developed an initial plan and briefed the president on September 21, just 10 days after the terror attacks. The first phase involved completing the basing and staging arrangements. Phase II involved air strikes and the deployment of special forces teams to work with the Northern alliance against the ruling Taliban. The "decisive combat operations" of Phase III would involve local and coalition forces "to seek out and eliminate pockets of resistance." Only about 200 special forces personnel were planned for phase II, and only 10,000–12,000 US troops in Phase III. The final phase, a three–five year effort in Franks' estimation, was for strengthening the new government and helping its people – nation building.[35]

Neither the president nor his defense secretary had much interest in the idea of nation-building. Bush had criticized the Clinton Administration for the practice during the 2000 campaign. Rumsfeld told the press on October 9, "I don't think [defeat of the Taliban] leaves us with a responsibility to try to figure out what kind of government that country ought to have." A week later the president interrupted an NSC meeting with the comment, "There's been too much discussion of post-conflict Afghanistan."[36] The low priority given to Phase IV was repeated again in Iraq, with painful consequences. For the combat operations, however, Bush was quite involved and supportive. "Tommy, are you getting what you need?" he asked Franks in early November. "I'm happy. I'm getting what I need", the general replied. The president also reassured his commander, "We will be patient. This will take as long as it takes."[37]

Air strikes began October 7. In mid-October, after repeated delays in infiltrating special forces, Franks came under heavy pressure to get boots on the ground. "This isn't working", Rumsfeld told him. "I want you to build options that *will* work." These comments so upset the Centcom commander that he called the defense secretary and offered to resign. "It appears that you no longer have confidence in me", he told Rumsfeld. "If you have lost confidence ... you should select another commander." After a long pause, Rumsfeld replied, "General Franks, you have my complete confidence. This operation will succeed."[38]

In mid-October, the defense secretary succeeded in taking over control of the CIA forces as well as the military ones. This had been a point of contention in the early weeks of the operation.[39] And after another period of frustration, and press reports hinting at a "quagmire" – the code word for "another Vietnam" – Operation Enduring Freedom was successful. The first major victory was the capture of Mazar a-sharif on November 9. The Taliban evacuated the capital of Kabul three days later. The last major city to be captured, Kandahar, was taken on December 6. The war then shifted to the mountains and caves of Tora Bora. On December 16, Rumsfeld flew to Afghanistan to proclaim the victory. "The President of the United States, the commander-in-chief, is determined to let the world know that our country cannot be attacked without consequences", he told soldiers from the 10th Mountain Division, "and you are bringing the consequences."

The Iraq option

On November 27, with much of Afghanistan in friendly hands, Rumsfeld called his commander with a surprising request. "The president wants us to look at options for Iraq. What is the status of your planning?"

"We have a plan, of course. OPLAN 1003", Franks replied. "It's out of date, under revision because conditions have changed."

"Please dust it off and get back to me next week", Rumsfeld ordered.[40]

Over the next 15 months, Franks and his Centcom planners developed three revised war plans: first, a large scale, "generated" buildup; second, a "running start" operation in case fighting began before the buildup had been completed, and finally a "hybrid", with a quick start of combined air and ground operations and follow-on forces. The first draft plan called for a US force of 400,000. By February 2002, under pressure from Rumsfeld to be creative and make do with fewer troops, Franks cut the figure for the start of the war to 160,000 – but he still envisioned a buildup to 300,000 before the end of major combat operations. On at least six occasions during the course of the planning, the defense secretary insisted on further cuts in ground troops. The multinational coalition force assembled on D-Day, March 21, 2003, numbered 290,000, and two weeks after the war began on March 21, 2003, there were 310,000 US military personnel in the region involved in Operation Iraqi Freedom.[41]

Throughout the planning process, the defense secretary was "like a dentist's drill that never ceased", according to Franks. The Centcom staff faced a "daily barrage of tasks and questions [that] was beginning to border on harassment." The Joint Chiefs, by contrast, were kept at arm's length from the planning process. They were not formally briefed until September 2002, nine months after Franks had been ordered to start revising the Iraq

War plan. While the Chiefs raised some service-specific concerns with Franks, and later with the president, they were supportive of the operation. In a final warning shot to his civilian superiors and the Chiefs, Franks sent a formal "letter of concern" to the Pentagon leadership two days before the start of the war. Among other things, he objected to the presence of the service Chiefs at any of his video teleconferences (VTCs). Though politely phrased, the point of his message was "Leave me the hell alone to run the war."[42]

Bush told Franks directly that he didn't want to be picking targets – one of his lessons from what he had been told about Vietnam. But he showed a strong interest in many operational details, as did Rumsfeld and his staff. Although the civilians considered starting the war earlier, the combatant commander convinced them in February 2002 that his forces could not be ready before October and that the best period for fighting in Iraq would be December through March. "We can go earlier", he told the president. "What it would mean is it would be ugly."[43]

Franks also received Bush's approval of his regional deployment and deception plans. The Pentagon transferred several hundred millions of dollars from other accounts in order to prepare airfields and bases for the deploying troops. Centcom planners scheduled exercises and spikes in troop presence to confuse the Iraqis about the number of American forces in the region and the actual timing of any combat. Rumsfeld himself interfered with the planned notification of units required for activation by spreading out the deployment orders over several weeks, thus minimizing press coverage and public reactions.[44]

While Franks dealt directly with the civilian leadership during the planning for the war, the Chiefs reportedly weighed in with some significant advice. When pressure grew for an early attack during 2002, they sided with Franks in recommending a delay until a more formidable force could be built up. Military leaders also reportedly urged that congressional approval be sought for the attack – a position consistent with the US military's post-Vietnam conditions for the use of major force.[45]

Congress intimidated

Despite his narrow electoral victory, Bush found Congress to be largely supportive even before September 11. Meeting with congressional leaders on September 12, the president sought endorsement of the use of force, but not a declaration of war as such. The White House draft language, however, was extraordinarily broad, authorizing the president "to use all necessary and appropriate force against those nations, organizations, or persons he determines planned, authorized, harbored, committed or aided" the 9/11 attacks "and to deter and pre-empt any future acts of terrorism or aggression against the United States." Some congressional leaders insisted on removing the blank check to conduct pre-emptive attacks and altered the final language to authorize force only against those responsible for the

9/11 attacks "in order to prevent any future acts of terrorism."[46] Only one person in either chamber, a California congresswoman, voted against the measure. The lawmakers viewed their vote as the functional equivalent of a declaration of war.

Despite the strong support, the president and vice president remained highly suspicious of the Congress. When reporters were told of a classified Hill briefing in which intelligence officials warned of a high probability of another terrorist attack, especially if the US intervened in Afghanistan, Bush decided to fight leaks by cutting off access to information. He signed an order forbidding the sharing of classified information with anyone except eight lawmakers – the party leaders in both houses and the four senior intelligence committee members. After a few days of predictable outrage, Bush cancelled the order. But both sides remained on guard over access to information.[47]

After the defeat of the Taliban in Afghanistan, Bush began building the case for further action. In his State of the Union address in January 2002, he spoke of an "axis of evil" including Iraq, Iran, and North Korea. A few months later, at West Point, he announced that the United States would not wait for terrorist threats to materialize before acting. "The war on terror will not be won on the defensive", he declared. In his first formal National Security Strategy Report two months later, he promulgated a doctrine of preemption – of launching preventive wars in anticipatory self-defense. "To forestall or prevent such hostile acts by our adversaries, the United States will, if necessary, act preemptively", Bush declared. "[T]he United States cannot remain idle while dangers gather."[48] While some in Congress criticized the doctrine, there were no legislative actions taken to try to limit its use.

On the contrary, Bush cleverly maneuvered the Congress into endorsing his planned attack on Iraq by preempting objections and forcing a vote in the heat of mid-term congressional elections. As the evidence grew of planning for war, congressional Democrats demanded that Congress vote on the issue and that the United States, as in 1990 and 2001, go to the United Nations for international legal and political support. In September 2002, Bush did both. He asked Congress for a vote, ostensibly to pressure Saddam Hussein to capitulate and avoid war. And he made an impressive address to the UN General Assembly, warning them to act to enforce UN resolutions or render the international organization impotent and ineffective. The president then indicated that if Congress wanted to fulfill its Constitutional role, it had better act before adjourning for three months in October. Democratic critics had no arguments left: Bush had gone to the UN and had asked Congress to vote – for war, yes, but as the last best chance to preserve peace. Those lawmakers who had argued during the Clinton years that diplomacy should be backed with the threat of force were driven to support the same principle for Bush.

Congress did force the Bush Administration to take one action that later proved controversial and embarrassing: it demanded a formal intelligence community estimate on Iraq's weapons of mass destruction.

The last comprehensive assessment, done in 2000, spoke of Iraq's intent and infrastructure to build such weapons but did not conclude that it had any at that time. By the summer of 2002, the president and vice president were forthright in asserting that Iraq had biological and chemical weapons – and that was the summary judgment of the Special National Intelligence Estimate (SNIE) hurriedly prepared to meet the congressional demand prior to the vote on war. But buried within the 92-page classified document were many qualifications and hedges that came to light only later, after weapons inspectors failed to find the expected arsenal and had to conclude, "We were almost all wrong."[49]

With the threat re-certified, Bush pressed for a vote prior to the elections. White House officials even accepted some changes in its draft resolution to appease Hill Democrats. For example, they agreed to drop language authorizing force to "restore international peace and security to the region", which many viewed as endorsing more widespread military action. They also agreed to include references to the war powers law, which no president has considered controlling on his warmaking authority. When several Senators pressed for further concessions, Republican leaders began moving their version of the legislation in the House, where they had the support of the Democratic leader, Richard Gephardt (D-Mo.), a prospective presidential candidate who regretted his 1991 vote against authorizing the first Gulf War. After defeating all modifying amendments, the House passed the authorization of force 296–133. Ten hours later, the Senate overwhelmingly approved the same language, 77–23, also after defeating all modifying amendments.[50] In the stark language of the joint resolution,

> The President is authorized to use the Armed Forces of the United States as he determines to be necessary and appropriate in order to –
>
> (1) defend the national security of the United States against the continuing threat posed by Iraq; and
> (2) enforce all relevant United Nations Security Council resolutions regarding Iraq.[51]

That measure was clearly seen as the functional equivalent of a declaration of war.

Adding to the political pressure to support action against Iraq was the lingering dispute over creation of a Department of Homeland Security. After opposing such a department for nine months, arguing that an NSC-style committee was sufficient, the Bush Administration announced a secretly drafted plan for a new department in June 2002. The bill got hung up in a dispute over whether to make airport screeners government or private contractor employees and several Democrats were targeted in the elections for failing to enact what the administration by then was calling vital legislation. Some lawmakers feared looking weak on defense if they criticized both the Iraq War and the administration's plan for homeland security. The administration finally accepted government employees as screeners and the basic legislation became law in November 2002.[52]

Having voted for war, Congress had little to do during the final buildup and later invasion. It held informational hearings – but was denied any significant information on actual military plans. Congress later learned that the Pentagon had spent $750 million in operations and maintenance (O&M) funds for military construction supposedly related to the war on terrorism but without providing advance notice to Congress, as required by law and as repeatedly requested by the relevant committees.[53] Only afterward did the lawmakers enact legislation restricting DOD flexibility on construction funds.

Planning failure

The executive branch had free rein in preparing for the war against Iraq, and the whip hand was Rumsfeld's in the Pentagon. The defense secretary, arguing the principle of unity of command, had sought and received full authority over the process. And while Pentagon officials can demonstrate that they held numerous meetings regarding what to do after the expected victory over Saddam Hussein, it soon became clear that insufficient attention and resources were actually devoted to Phase IV of the war plan, Post-Hostility Operations for reconstruction and stabilization.

The decision to concentrate postwar planning authority in the Pentagon was made in October 2002, but not formalized in a presidential directive until NSPD 24 was signed on January 20, 2003, just two months before the war began. That document created the Office of Reconstruction and Human-itarian Assistance (ORHA), and retired Lt. General Jay Garner was promptly recruited to head it. The original plan called for ORHA to move in only about 60 days after the end of the war. The original expectation was that the primary task would be humanitarian relief, especially dealing with a flood of refugees and the consequences of Iraqi use of chemical and biological weapons and destruction of the oil fields.[54]

Rumsfeld and Franks were preoccupied with winning the battles, and the most senior US officials thought that would be enough to win the war. Vice President Cheney and others were explicitly optimistic: "I really do believe that we will be greeted as liberators." That expectation permitted planners to scale down the planned occupation force to 50,000.[55] But it also led to a bitter public dispute between the warriors and the politicians.

Pressed in a Senate hearing at the end of February, Army Chief of Staff General Eric Shinseki ventured the opinion that "a significant ground force presence" would be needed to maintain order in the post-hostilities environment, "on the order of several hundred thousand soldiers." Deputy Secretary Wolfowitz sharply disputed that figure two days later, calling it "wildly off the mark." He said it was "hard to imagine" that more troops would be necessary for stability than to bring down Saddam and his army.[56] This was only the latest in a long-running breach between the civilian leaders and the army, which Rumsfeld considered insufficiently committed to transformation.

The main combat operations went surprisingly quickly and successfully in a three-week war. Despite sandstorms and pockets of resistance, and commentators quick to label delays as an incipient quagmire, the US and British forces seized their objectives easily. The operations were capped by the toppling of Saddam's statues in Baghdad on April 9. The president flew in a jet fighter to an aircraft carrier to proclaim the end of major combat operations on May 1. The baton was passed to those assigned to do reconstruction and stability.

ORHA tried to prepare for its assignment with its limited personnel and resources and then was denied entry into Iraq until after the major fighting was over. What Garner found, when he entered Baghdad on April 21 was that 17 of the 23 ministries he had hoped to restore under new leadership "were gone." The buildings had been looted and the workers had fled. The widespread looting after the fall of Baghdad – which Rumsfeld dismissed as a sign of liberation: "Freedom's untidy", he said – was allowed because US troops had not been given orders to prevent or stop it, and there were probably too few troops to have much success had they tried.[57]

Three days after arriving in the Iraqi capital, Garner was told that he would shortly be replaced by Ambassador L. Paul Bremer, who would head a full-scale occupation government, the Coalition Provisional Authority (CPA). Bremer reported to both Rumsfeld and the White House, and was obviously empowered to make decisions and take actions more broadly than Garner's ORHA. Bremer worked closely with the senior US general in Iraq, but his staff remained largely within the secure "Green Zone" and had few people throughout the country. The CPA created an interim Iraqi Governing Council (IGC), wrote the basic law for Iraq pending the drafting of a new constitution and the election of a new government, the Transitional Administrative Law (TAL), and then declared that there would be a transfer of sovereignty on June 28, 2004.

US officials defended their post-hostilities planning, but few foresaw the rise of insurgent forces and the difficulties widespread violence posed for those who wished to build a new Iraq. The soldiers who had executed the war plan so swiftly and successfully were stymied by the new challenge of counterinsurgency. Early on, General Franks had warned of the possibility of "catastrophic success" – if coalition forces won too quickly[58] – yet that is what happened. The victors in battle were unprepared to secure their victory in the war.

Rumsfeld's transformation

While US ground forces struggled with the Iraqi insurgency, Secretary Rumsfeld turned his attention back to his bigger goal of transforming the armed forces as well as the processes of the Pentagon. The war in Afghanistan had convinced him that military forces could be used in radically new ways, such as soldiers on horseback calling in air strikes. He decided to expand and improve the Special Forces by giving them the lead role in the war on terrorism. The war in Iraq convinced him that speed could be more important than mass, a lesson that made him even less supportive of the heavy-weaponed army. Nothing convinced him that he had made any errors of judgment or performance.

Even as the Defense Department rebuilt the section of the Pentagon damaged in the September 11 attack and sent troops to Afghanistan and Iraq, the bureaucracy slowly maneuvered into line to advance toward Rumsfeld's transformation goals. A special office was set up to promote the new network-centric approach. That office promulgated a fancy transformation strategy, complete with "four pillars" and "six critical operational goals."[59] Each service in turn tried to promote and defend its own modernization programs by slapping on "transformation" labels and rationales.

In dealing with the army, Rumsfeld was particularly harsh. He made the innovative Chief of Staff, General Shinseki, a lame duck by announcing a successor 15 months before his term ended. He cancelled the new artillery program, the Crusader, and pressured the service to make a similar decision against the Commanche helicopter program. He fired the civilian Secretary of the Army. And when it came time to name a new Chief, Rumsfeld rejected all the army's serving generals and recalled from retirement a Special Forces officer, General Peter Schoomaker. The new Chief undertook a radical restructuring of the force from 15,000–20,000 man divisions into brigade units of action with 3500–4000 soldiers. Schoomaker did receive, however, a promise from Rumsfeld that the army would not be cut in size.[60]

While many in the Pentagon saw transformation in terms of hardware and doctrine – promoting inter-service jointness and linking people and equipment with new technologies – Rumsfeld himself, the former CEO, wanted to change the whole way the Defense Department operated. Soon after taking office in 2001, he demanded a briefing on the power centers in the Pentagon. "Where are the levers in the building?" he asked. "Not just where they are, but who pulls them? And what are they connected to?"[61]

The resulting charts reminded him of disconnected factory production lines.

> I looked at all these conveyor belts that seemed like they were loaded six, eight years ago, and they were just chugging along, and you could reach in and take something off, or put something on, but you couldn't

connect the different conveyor belts. Each process had a life of its own and drivers that were disconnected from the others ...[62]

After his initial setbacks in 2001, when he failed to impose his planned cuts and changes on the upcoming budget, Rumsfeld seized control of the processes to which the rest of the Pentagon was programmed to respond. He used the September 2001 Quadrennial Defense Review (QDR) and subsequent Defense Planning Guidance to promote goals and establish criteria that he could use later in evaluating service programs.

In 2003 Rumsfeld began even more far-reaching changes in DOD processes. While many of the actions may seem to be only new labels on old conveyor belts, the unifying principle has been to centralize power in the hands of the Secretary. He dropped the Defense Resources Board, previously used for high level budget review, and instituted a Senior Level Review Group (SLRG) that made all major decisions – and met only when Rumsfeld was in the chair.[63] He renamed the PPBS system PPBE, for Planning Programming, Budgeting and Execution and added new metrics and cost models. He also changed the budget process to link programs and budgets in a single timeline and to require biennial budgets, with only major changes allowed in intervening years.

He also superseded the JCS Chairman's National Military Strategy (NMS) document, which had been the basis for Joint Staff-developed plans, with his own National Defense Strategy (NDS). It took a law by Congress to force Rumsfeld to let the CJCS submit his legally required NMS, and the Secretary followed with his own NDS shortly thereafter. The secretary also dropped the annual Defense Planning Guidance in favor of a biennial Strategic Planning Guidance from his office. When he tried to merge the Joint Staff with the OSD staff, however, he had to back down.

Coupled with his careful vetting of senior officers, Rumsfeld used these revised processes to strengthen his control over every aspect of Pentagon activity and to enforce his vision of a transformed military. Not surprisingly, the Rumsfeld generals and admirals accepted it. As JCS Chairman General Richard Myers said, "There is not a DOD process of any sort that we haven't turned on its ear in the past four years."[64]

Congress has also been largely supportive of the transformation efforts. Despite pressures from employee unions and uncertainty over how the system would work in practice, it repealed existing Civil Service rules for DOD civilians and enacted a new National Security Personnel System which gave senior management great flexibility in assigning people to jobs and rewarding them with merit pay rather than time-in-grade pay hikes. Congress voted for another base reduction round in 2005 and accepted the relatively minor closings and realignments.

The clearest indicator of congressional support, of course, is approval of huge spending requests. After approving the requested 5 percent increase for defense for fiscal year 2002, Congress responded to the 9/11 attacks with an immediate $14 billion supplemental appropriations for defense and then boosted 2003 fiscal year spending by nearly 23 percent. Additional defense supplementals of $14 billion for the 2002 fiscal year, $62 billion for the 2003 fiscal year and $65 billion for the 2004 fiscal year were approved with only token cuts of less than $1 billion overall. By the 2005 fiscal year, regular defense spending, not counting supplementals for Iraq, was 25 percent above the pre-9/11 level. Not only did Congress approve most of the funds requested for war and transformation, but it also loosened the historically tight purse strings by allowing greater flexibility for emergency spending and transfers between accounts.[65]

Where Congress pushed back, however, is on issues that aroused public interest and concern. When troops in Iraq told loved ones back home that they lacked body armor, or that their vulnerable vehicles could use armor protection, congressional committees responded with sharp questions and extra money. When searing pictures of abuse of prisoners in the Abu Ghraib prison were publicized, the Armed Services Committees held hearings and demanded accountability. And when army officers complained of the problems caused by repeated deployments to the war zones, Congress forced Rumsfeld to accept, at least "temporarily", an increase in army end strength of 30,000.

Bush–Rumsfeld legacy

When George W. Bush was reelected in 2004, many expected his defense secretary to leave office after a few months, perhaps after completing the 2005 QDR. But Bush wanted him to stay on, and Don Rumsfeld gave many indications that he believed he had just begun to succeed at the difficult job of Pentagon transformation. "Change takes time", he told a writer. "Any CEO in a corporation, you ask him what the rough amount of time to do it, and it's eight or ten years."[66]

The most important historical judgment on both men, of course, will be the outcome in Iraq and the level of US security over the next several years. What is more certain is the evaluation of their handling of the Defense Department and the US military. Bush and Rumsfeld set out to change the way America made war, and they succeeded in many aspects. They accelerated jointness and expanded experimentation and backed their new ideas with hard dollars.

They promoted a new generation of warriors, trained both to push back in argument and then to acquiesce in decisions quietly. The president restored civil–military respect while his defense secretary enforced a tighter degree of civilian control. The civilian leaders found a general to fight two major wars the way they wanted, and without the complaints that historically accompanied combat. But they remained stymied when a different enemy emerged from the rubble of their expected victory.

12 Conclusions

US civil–military relations under stress

Regardless of how superior the military view of a situation may be, the civilian view trumps it. Civilians should get what they ask for, even if it is not what they really want. In other words, civilians have a right to be wrong.

Prof. Peter Feaver[1]

In wartime the politicians have to do *something* important every year.

General George Marshall[2]

This is the Way to have things go right: for Officers to correspond constantly with Congress and communicate their Sentiments freely.

John Adams, 1776[3]

It is one of the greatest sources of frustration for soldiers that their political masters find it difficult (or what is worse from their point of view, merely inconvenient) to fully elaborate in advance the purposes for which they have invoked military action, or the conditions under which they intend to limit or terminate it.

Prof. Eliot Cohen[4]

Warriors and politicians have different roles to perform in defending a nation. Democracies believe in civilian control of the military because they believe that the people are sovereign. The armed forces in democracies give at least lip service to the principle of civilian control, but each side may understand it differently. And those differences give rise to disagreements, sometimes even sharp conflicts.

Many commentators have argued that American civil–military relations have been under stress in recent years – in a "crisis" or even "out of control."[5] While some writers were quick to attribute the tensions to the particular character of Bill Clinton and his military policies, the evidence of civil–military disagreements under George W. Bush suggests deeper causes.

This book seeks to demonstrate that there are enduring and recurring patterns in US civil–military relations, patterns of conflict and tension for predictable reasons. They are not unique to the post-Cold War world, or even to the rise of large standing forces beginning with the Second World War. On the contrary, these tensions were visible in the earliest days of the Republic and have been evident throughout American history, albeit to varying degrees.

The simplest explanation for the conflict is the political scientist's notion that politics is a struggle over who gets what, when, and how – and that the institutions of government, including the military, are inevitably caught up in that struggle. It is true that the armed forces have a unique role, for they alone in theory have a monopoly of legitimate violence and must be strong enough to defend the state but not willing or capable of overthrowing it. One concern is that the US military may be becoming an "interest group" with parochial concerns that may be in tension with its role as guardian.

Nature of civilian control

Civil–military relations, as analyzed here, deal with the interactions among the top civilian leadership – legislative and executive in the case of the United States – and the senior military leadership, including both the members of the Joint Chiefs of Staff (JCS) and the major combatant commanders. These relationships encompass both the formal structures and the rules and procedures, as well as the comparative power and influence of the various entities.

Civilian control is both descriptive and prescriptive, a measurable condition and a norm. The degree of influence can be calculated, for example, by noting who prevails when preferences diverge. As a principle for resolving disputes, civilian control offers a simple rule: the civilians are supposed to set ends, the military is limited to decisions about means, but the civilians get to draw the line between ends and means.[6]

The tests for civilian control which I find most persuasive and useful were devised by Allan Millett. He says

> civilian control requires that:
> a. the armed forces do not dominate government or impose their unique (however functional) values upon civilian institutions and organizations.
> b. the armed forces have no independent access to resources of military unity.
> c. the armed forces' policies on the recruitment, pay, education, training, treatment, promotion, and use of personnel are not inconsistent with basic civil liberties and individual rights – with some compromises for military discipline and combat effectiveness.
> d. the use of military force is not determined by the values of the military establishment itself, either *for* or *against* military action, either in the conduct of foreign or domestic policies. Conversely, civilian decisions on the use of forced should not disregard the

relationship of policy ends and military institutional characteristics in terms of personnel, doctrine, training, equipment and morale.[7]

By these measures, I believe most would conclude that the United States has a system of civilian control that has worked historically and currently. But these conditions also make clear that the legislative branch has a major role in providing the civilian control.

Using Millett's criteria, one can see Congress as a major guarantor of civilian control. The armed forces do not dominate the US government, nor impose their values. They may ally with others who share their values, as they did when President Clinton tried to repeal the ban on gays in uniform. Large segments of the Congress would have blocked any change if the President had not retreated to the "don't ask, don't tell" policy.

The US armed forces do not have independent access to resources of military unity – except through the Congress, and only in accordance with close oversight. Even secret funding for military and intelligence activities is known to key congressional figures.

There may be more dispute on Millett's third point – whether there is a balance between military needs for discipline and the individual's basic civil liberties – but this is less an issue of civilian control than of civilianization, that is, the infusion of civilian values into military behaviors. On this question, key members of Congress have often allied with military leaders to slow or deflect pressures to change military practices to reflect civilian attitudes, for example, on gender issues. There is political support for military traditionalism, just as there is also support for changes designed to comport with civilian views. Here again, Congress is the venue for balancing the competing claims.

On the use of force, military values do not determine the choices, and civilian leaders have regularly considered military views. While I contend that the US military has a veto on the use of force, the practical effects are primarily to ensure consideration of the very issues Millett specifies. Congress is involved only as a sounding board, if necessary, for military concerns.

By these tests, then, the United States has civilian control, and that control is exercised both by the President and Congress, though in differing ways and in differing circumstances. The most stressful situations are those that occur when troops are in combat.

Civil–military relations in wartime

Not surprisingly, civilian control is strong when the armed forces are engaged in major military operations. In war time, political leaders understand that the stakes are high and they will be held accountable. The warriors accept their role and hope to be given clear and reasonable orders. Presidents have usually shown strong leadership, though their decisions have been greatly influenced by domestic political calculations. Congress has tended to defer to the Executive once major combat begins, while still conducting at least limited oversight. Tensions have arisen between the politicians and the warriors, however, over strategy and over the degree of military autonomy in planning and executing operations.

After the problems with command and control by committee during the Revolutionary War, described in Chapter 2, the Framers of the Constitution created a strong chief executive to conduct war after it had been declared by Congress. Presidents have taken seriously their mandated role as commander-in-chief. George Washington led troops sent to quell the Whiskey Rebellion in 1794. James Madison briefly paraded in uniform with the troops but then let his several secretaries of war plan battles directly with field commanders. James K. Polk gave strong strategic direction to the war with Mexico, and he clashed repeatedly with his military commanders in the field. As Chapter 3 indicates, Abraham Lincoln and his Secretary of War practiced close oversight and involvement in the conduct of the Civil War. William McKinley ran the Spanish–American War from the White House with his cabinet making key decisions.[8]

The only anomaly in this historical record of active presidential control was Woodrow Wilson during the First World War. He and his War Secretary gave supreme authority for the conduct of US forces in France to General Pershing – although the President did insist on deciding all matters related to conditions for ending the war.[9]

Franklin Roosevelt was an undisputed commander-in-chief in the Second World War and Harry Truman, as Chapter 7 shows, asserted strong civilian control in the Korean War when his theater commander proved insubordinate. While these men were seen as effective leaders, Lyndon Johnson and Robert McNamara have been roundly condemned for their intrusive management of the Vietnam War. Richard Nixon used a lighter touch and was more responsive to military views during his phase of that war, but he frequently ordered military actions to bolster his peacemaking diplomacy.[10]

The presidents during the remainder of the twentieth century ordered numerous military operations but tried to adhere to the military's preference for maximum flexibility and minimal interference. George W. Bush and Donald Rumsfeld, however, restored the prior practice of intrusive civilian control, and even circumvented the Joint Chiefs of Staff and dealt directly with the regional combatant commander, as Chapter 11 describes.

Political considerations have, of course, often influenced presidential decisions in wartime. James K. Polk was concerned that his two senior generals, both from the opposition party, might use their victories to run for President – as in fact both of them later did. Lincoln feared that General McClellan might defeat him in 1864, but first he had to overcome rivals in his own party. Harry Truman worried that firing MacArthur might undermine his presidency, as in fact it did.

Franklin Roosevelt used wartime secrecy to help conceal his deteriorating health in 1944, and he had desperately wanted the North African invasion

Figure 12.1   Defense Secretary Donald Rumsfeld and Chairman of the Joint Chiefs of Staff, General Richard Myers (Defense Department photo)

– the first US attack on Hitler's forces – to occur before rather than just after the midterm congressional elections in 1942.

Lyndon Johnson got the Tonkin Gulf Resolution authorizing war in Southeast Asia just before he began a presidential campaign pledging peace. As Chapter 4 shows, he told his generals they would have to wait until after the election to begin their war. His conduct during 1968 was also shaped by his political goals – of vindicating his policies and helping his Vice President succeed him. Richard Nixon and Melvin Laird took office intending to have the war over by the 1972 elections, and they went far enough in that direction – with troop withdrawals, publicized peace talks, and an end to the draft – that he won overwhelmingly.

More recently, Ronald Reagan withdrew troops from Lebanon before the failures there interfered with his 1984 reelection campaign. George Bush the elder resisted intervention in Somalia until after his defeat in 1992. Bill Clinton promised that US peacekeeping troops would be in Bosnia only one year, thus trying to remove that conflict from the 1996 campaign. And George W. Bush used the pending midterm congressional elections in 2002 as leverage to get Congress to approve military operations against Iraq. He then accelerated the transfer of sovereignty to an interim Iraqi government in June 2004, so that he could demonstrate progress as his own reelection campaign approached.

Congress declared war in response to presidential messages on five occasions and consented to fund other major military operations, at least after the fact. The votes were overwhelming on almost all occasions, although in 1812 they came entirely from the Democratic Republicans, Madison's party, while New England Whigs were strongly opposed. The Democratic-controlled twenty-ninth Congress voted for war with Mexico in 1846, but two years later, the Whig-controlled House of Representatives approved, 82–81, a measure denouncing that war as "unnecessarily and unconstitutionally begun by the President of the United States."[11]

On only four occasions have presidents sought congressional support for combat operations when their party did not control both houses of Congress – in 1983 when Ronald Reagan sought and received war powers authorization for 18 months for troops in Lebanon; in January 1991 when George Bush the elder asked for a vote supporting the ouster of Iraq from Kuwait; and after September 11, 2001 when George W. Bush sought and received congressional authorization for operations against terrorists and later Iraq. Despite some partisan disagreement, the presidents prevailed in each case.

The curious anomaly here is Congress' indifference on the issue of declaring war in Korea. Truman's advisors argued that it was not necessary, particularly since the UN Security Council had passed a binding resolution calling for armed forces for Korea's defense. Truman met with congressional leaders, but only a couple of argumentative Republicans pressed for legislative action. With public opinion supporting the president at the time, the Senate Majority Leader decided not to recall his chamber from a July 4 recess. Later on, of course, Congress voted the necessary supplemental spending bills, but without ever legislating on the war itself.

Assertive congressional oversight – or "interference", from the executive branch point of view – has been sporadic and inconsistent. Congress caused problems during the War of 1812 by lengthy disputes over the funding of the war and the acquisition of military supplies. The Joint Committee during the Civil War, as Chapter 3 describes, investigated widely, subjected combat generals to grueling and detailed hearings, proffered its own strategic advice, and had a marked impact on the war. Congressional committees used hearings to expose contracting and supply problems in the Spanish–American War, the First World War, and the Second World War – when Senator Harry Truman (D-Mo) earned a favorable reputation that propelled him into the Vice Presidency with his committee's investigation of contracting abuses.

Only in more recent times have congressional committees tried to inquire into or to influence grand strategy. A joint Senate committee took several weeks of testimony from General MacArthur and others following his ouster during the Korean War, giving vent to MacArthur's views as well as those of Truman Administration civilians and military leaders. As Chapter 4 relates, Senators Fulbright and Stennis used their committees to promote opposing strategic views on the Vietnam War. While Congress never succeeded in blocking military operations until after US ground troops had been withdrawn from Vietnam, the repeated battles over antiwar amendments constrained the conduct of the war in the Nixon administration. Congress was also supportive of the Afghan and Iraq Wars, devoting its investigative hearings to such issues as armor equipment for troops and the prisoner abuse scandal.

Despite congressional enactment of the war powers resolution in 1973 over Richard Nixon's veto, lawmakers have tended to be satisfied with the limited compliance shown by subsequent presidents. While none acknowledged the legitimacy of the measure, all have been willing to provide official notification of troop deployments. War powers arguments have been used by policy critics, but never pushed to the point of halting unpopular military operations. The basic rule remains: Americans support short and successful wars and tend to oppose long or unsuccessful ones, and Congress reflects those opinions.

With Congress rarely interjecting itself into the chain of command during wartime, military leaders have accepted presidential civilian control without complaint. On those occasions when the warriors have become unhappy, however, they have regularly gone to the Hill – usually quietly and to their patrons – to complain. MacArthur did that during Korea; the Chiefs did during Vietnam. The practice is much more common in peacetime, including rearmament periods, when the different services fight for budget dollars.

On strategy, there has been a notable recurring difference between the warriors and politicians. Time and again – from the Revolutionary War through the Civil War to the Second World War and even into the Iraq Wars – the civilians have pressed for "attack, attack, attack", while the generals have preferred defensive maneuvers and careful preparation for battle. As Chairman of the JCS, Colin Powell even acknowledged that he was a reluctant warrior because he wanted to be sure that America did not sacrifice its blood and treasure needlessly nor ineffectively.

Civil–military relations during rearmament

Preparations for war tend to exacerbate a different set of civil–military tensions. The warriors are usually pleased to be getting additional resources, though they may compete with their rivals for the lion's share. The politicians may clash, however, over which forces to acquire, or over the best strategy to pursue against the supposed threat. Various civil–military alliances maybe formed, and the resolution is usually similar to the outcomes of other political issues.

Political considerations tend to dominate rearmament fights for both warriors and politicians. The very first rearmament effort, described in Chapter 5, exposed deep political divisions over US relations with Britain and France. John Adams succeeded in winning even opposition support for a much larger standing army and more ships for the fledgling navy by stirring nationalist outrage over the treatment of US envoys in the XYZ affair. To his everlasting discredit, however, he used his favorable political momentum to enact the Alien and Sedition Acts, which were used chiefly against his political enemies. Adams then sought a diplomatic settlement with France when he feared that he was in danger of losing control of the army to his Federalist rival, Alexander Hamilton. Peace in the quasi-war with France was not enough, however, to prevent his defeat a few months later by Thomas Jefferson.

To endorse rearmament, presidents have to determine, and then persuade the Congress, that there is an emerging enemy and that the nation must prepare for war at least to try to preserve peace and if necessary to fight and win the conflict. George Washington avoided choosing between France and Britain in 1793, when he made his Neutrality Proclamation, but Adams had good reason to fear France more than Britain in 1797.

For the next 140 years, until the late 1930s, America rearmed only after war broke out. It had the luxury of time and the protection of distance to deal with its foes. And Congress proved willing, once the conflict began, to fund the increases in personnel and equipment to fight the battles which followed.

Chapter 6 tells of Franklin Roosevelt's astute political maneuvering to win support for a massive US military buildup and measures short of war, but just barely, in the years leading to US involvement in the Second World War. FDR made a political alliance with interventionist forces of both parties and had to fight isolationists even in his own cabinet. The two camps fought to win public opinion, and Roosevelt limited his requests and actions to measures which, step by step, the public was willing to endorse. His secret orders, however, were of questionable constitutionality and unrepeatable in an age of policy debates by press leaks. Military leaders supported Roosevelt's policies for professional reasons and they often provided political cover, as when General Marshall took the lead in asking for conscription in the presidential election year of 1940.

Harry Truman, by contrast, was slow to embrace full-scale rearmament until after the Korean War broke out. But his subordinates prepared the ground and helped build the support that made Truman begin to reverse course a few months before North Korea attacked the South. Both parties supported rearmament, although lawmakers differed on how best to defend against the communists. Airpower advocates stressed nuclear weapons as the most cost-effective way. At first, the navy fought the air force on this issue, then decided to embrace naval aviation to carry nuclear weapons. Former marines in Congress also fought Truman's efforts to cut back the Marine Corps.

Rearmament struggles, in short, stimulate inter-service rivalries, which are often cloaked in terms of strategic debates. The warriors court their patrons and supporters in Congress and in the Executive Branch, and the politicians in turn echo the military's logic, even when disputed. The result is varying cycles of buildup, driven by anticipated threats and patriotic fervor and then reduction, when budgetary concerns and examples of waste become prominent.

Since the Korean War, there have been several oscillating periods in defense spending. Dwight Eisenhower slashed the army in order to save money and concentrate on the nuclear deterrent forces. John F. Kennedy was elected in 1960 in part because he promised to close the missile gap – which turned out to be nonexistent, since US missiles actually outnumbered Soviet missiles. Robert McNamara then used defense increases to suppress military resistance to his transformation efforts, described in Chapter 9. Spending then fell as the Vietnam War ended, only to begin rising in the Carter Administration in response to concerns about Soviet military power. Ronald Reagan accelerated the buildup, only to have it cut short after 1985 by bipartisan congressional interest in reducing the soaring budget deficits. Budget politics forced George Bush the elder to agree to new taxes and defense cuts in his administration. And Bill Clinton continued reductions until forced by readiness problems to allow some increases in the late 1990s. George W. Bush promised smaller defense increases than his opponent in the 2000 elections, but then responded to the 9/11 attacks with a huge buildup both of military forces and homeland security activities.

Military leaders seem to have accommodated these disputes by adherence to the compact described below. They have ostensibly supported the Executive Branch while providing the necessary ammunition to their friends on the Hill who want to help them.

Civil–military relations during transformation

When political leaders seek radical change in the armed forces, they tend to meet with strong resistance from the warriors, who are conservative and evolutionary by nature and who resent outsiders presuming expertise in their profession. Here, as during rearmament, cross-cutting alliances may be formed, including factions in the Congress. Successful transformation requires either military acceptance of the changes or the creation of a self-sustaining element within the military.

By transformation, I mean more than ordinary reorganization and restructured management techniques. I mean the fundamental wrenching changes made by strong leaders to embrace new strategies or technologies. Most significant changes have taken place during the twentieth century, but one such change occurred during and just after the Civil War. America's armed forces had remained small until the Civil War, then suddenly encountered the challenges of fighting with the newly available technologies of rifles, railroads, and the telegraph. The Union acquitted itself quite well, and the postwar army, though once again very small, fashioned a new professionalism that allowed it successfully to expand to fulfill its new imperial role after 1898. The navy also became more professional and gradually more accepting of the new technologies of steam, steel, and even submarines.

The Spanish–American War exposed poor planning and coordination, both within and between the armed services, as described in Chapter 8. In response, a new team of reformers, led by Theodore Roosevelt and Elihu Root imposed a top-down transformation on the army. The navy was also expanded and modernized. Congress was supportive, but the greatest resistance came from army leaders – a typical reaction from an institution which, by its nature, emphasizes predictability and reliability of performance.

Most nations transform their military establishments after suffering major defeats. The US military, by contrast, has been largely successful in combat, though not always in the broader goals of war. Its most serious defeat, in Vietnam, was political more than military. On the other hand, the US military has often been forced by outsiders to embrace new technologies and new forms of organization. Reformers from within have often been discredited mavericks like airpower advocate Billy Mitchell, who have succeeded only by making strategic alliances with patrons in Congress or the Executive Branch who could direct resources to their fledgling efforts.

The US military in the twentieth century was eager to adopt new technology, and American science and industry provided numerous opportunities. Far-reaching transformation was more difficult, however, because that required changes in doctrine and organization that would take full advantage of new technology. Such a transformation usually required pressure from outside the military.

The usual pattern in the United States is for the innovation advocate – sometimes within the system, sometimes an outsider – to build a community of supporters who ultimately attract a patron who can nurture the idea as it gains more adherents. Resistance is natural from those who feel criticized by the proposed change, or who fear a loss of power or resources if the innovators should prevail. Those who resist do so usually with questions and delays rather than outright opposition, but those tactics may outlast the interest or terms of service of the patrons. Often the only way to create a lasting, successful innovation is to create a new and separate organization to implement it – special forces for counterinsurgency or an air force for strategic bombing.[12]

This was an important lesson which Congress recognized in imposing the Goldwater–Nichols Act and the related legislation putting Special Operations Forces in their own budget category, as told in Chapter 10. Congress agreed to give innovative organizations their own personnel systems to reward and promote their members.

Robert McNamara, whose managerial revolution is described in Chapter 9, exemplified the most successful application of the American penchant for trying to impose private business practices on the Pentagon. He succeeded through persistence and longevity in office, and because many in Congress welcomed either his effectiveness or the bigger budgets he initially secured for the military. Donald Rumsfeld's imitation of many of McNamara's techniques suggests that civilian leaders see these techniques as the best way to achieve transformation.

Before and since 1961, prestigious commissions periodically have discovered the same old problems which somehow have not been satisfactorily addressed by earlier reforms. Civilians, especially those with business experience, find it hard to tolerate the non-capitalist nature of the Pentagon. The warriors, drawing on their own professional experience and remembering the fickle public, tend to resist wrenching change.

The differences between civilians proposing change and warriors resisting it raise a moral issue: How can one put a price tag on death or defeat? There is no reliable measure in peacetime of how successful a particular set and number of military units will be in combat. Branches and sequels can be anticipated; simulations can be performed; troops can be trained, again and again, as they are supposed to fight. But there is still the chaos and friction of combat, the fog of war, and a reacting enemy which cannot be calculated. No leader can be sure that a decision to reduce forces, or to adopt a new technology, or to reorganize units used to a different arrangement will tip the balance between victory and defeat. Commanders view their people as their most precious asset. Thus, they do not wish to risk lives needlessly, or when other actions would greatly reduce those risks. That is why military professionals are usually slow to innovate, and why such wrenching changes often need to be imposed from outside. Even when the innovation advocates promise revolutionary advances – nuclear-powered submarines, aircraft invisible to radar, unmanned aerial weapons, precision-guided weapons, special counterinsurgency teams – their comrades may be suspicious, for they have heard hollow promises before.

Politicians tend to favor efficiency criteria, which are measurable, to effectiveness ones, which are not, except in the crucible of war. Members of Congress will support new organizations and technologies especially when they promise jobs and contracts back home. Civilian executives will push for change both to achieve better results and to assert their leadership. The end result is conflict and the outcomes sometimes depend on luck.

Cultural differences pervade civil–military relations. Warriors and politicians thrive in different organizational cultures. Officers are used to established hierarchies and formal procedures. Civilian officials live in a fluid world of shifting relations, where today's adversary is often tomorrow's key ally, and vice versa. Military officers demand decisiveness and clarity, while politicians tolerate ambiguity and often prefer incremental steps and hedging strategies. Military planners are taught to anticipate future contingencies and begin preparing for them. People in politics, who often say that 24 hours is an eternity, learn to wait until the last possible moment to commit themselves. These differences make it harder for warriors and politicians to understand, empathize, and work closely with each other.

Shortcomings of existing theories

Many scholars have broadened and deepened our understanding of US civil–military relations, but most have tended to ignore the special significance and impact of the dual nature of civilian control under the US Constitution. The "great books" of Samuel Huntington and Morris Janowitz stimulated years of exciting scholarship by their students, but they are inadequate for addressing the changed world and new problems of the twenty-first century. Huntington wrote in a tense, Cold War era of inter-service rivalry and prescribed an apolitical professionalism which had lasted for only a short period in US history. He also used loaded terms – "business pacifism", "objective control" – to buttress an essentially political argument. Janowitz, as James Burk laments, has no answers for the era of the small volunteer army. Sociologists have since concentrated on practical issues of recruitment and training in the United States, and on civil–military issues facing emerging democracies.[13]

Political scientists – most with conscious emphasis on the "science" of their discipline – have followed in Huntington's broad wake. Most interesting and prominent are: Eliot Cohen, Michael Desch, Peter Feaver, Deborah Avant, and Amy Zegart.

Eliot Cohen, in his fascinating and provocative book, *Supreme Command: Soldiers, Statesmen, and Leadership in Wartime* attributes the "normal" theory of civilian control to Huntington and then modifies it to argue for a much more interventionist civilian leadership in wartime, with military commanders subject to a necessary but "unequal dialogue" with their civilian superiors. Cohen draws upon historical cases to prescribe a particular form of civilian control for normative and practical reasons. I find Cohen's work quite persuasive, but limited to the special cases of wartime command and control.

Michael Desch applies a structural, realist approach in his book, *Civilian Control of the Military: the changing security environment*. He argues that the structure of the international system, and in particular the degree of external threats in relation to internal threats, determines the degree of civilian control. While his analysis is interesting with regard to other nations and other times, and his catalogue of "Major US Civil–Military Conflicts, 1938–1997" most helpful, his predictions are indeterminate for the current era of low internal and external threats in the United States. He says the best indicator of civilian control is who prevails when military and civilian preferences diverge. While this is a sensible definition, his deterministic analytical approach offers no guidance for preferable ways of obtaining civilian control.

Peter Feaver is a prolific and provocative scholar, a rigorous theory-builder who draws upon principal–agent analysis. Similarly, Deborah Avant and Amy Zegart have offered insights into civil–military relations based upon agency theory as part of their analyses of particular American cases.[14]

While I find much of their writings interesting and helpful, I have the nagging feeling that they are stretching the concepts to cover the peculiarities of US civil–military relations and that they do not adequately deal with the dual-principal nature of the American political system. Nor do they address why military advice is or is not accepted by civilian superiors.

Principal–agent theory, as elaborated by Feaver, Avant and Zegart, tries to explain how institutions like the armed forces are established and managed over time. This analytical approach highlights matters of delegation and incentives for compliance, along with problems of "shirking" and "moral hazard." If one's key question is how to maintain control over an institution, and especially how to impose innovation or other major change, this approach has valuable insights. But it tends to presume a single principal acting with only one or a very few goals in a linear action–reaction way. When there are multiple principals and numerous goals and a complex matrix of interactions, this approach is far less helpful.

Feaver calls civil–military relations as "a game of strategic interaction." But his model is linear, with branches limited to the binary choice of "working" or "shirking." According to Feaver, "Working is doing things the way the civilians want, and shirking is doing things the way the military want." But he also calls shirking "part of a broader range of deviant behavior in which a soldier might engage." He admits that the terms have colloquial meanings that are "unhelpful", but even their specified definitions create confusion. He says that end runs by the military to Congress "can reach the level of shirking", whereas I would list that as an example of "working" for the alternate source of civilian control.[15]

The model seems to be limited to the implementation of orders, when the key tension in civil–military relations is often over the consideration of military advice prior to decisions and orders. Military resistance more often has been and is the result of disagreements over preferred courses of action. The principal–agent approach does not cover the complexities of the policy process, whereby ideas are advocated, debated, sometimes compromised, decided, and then re-decided perhaps numerous times during implementation. Compliance may be in degrees, rather than binary.

The principal–agent theorists also have difficulty handling the role of Congress as a second, competing principal over the military. Feaver, in trying to articulate hypotheses for testing, suggests, for example, that "The less unified the civilian political leadership, the less the civilian delegation" and "Countries with divided civilian governments will have more inter-service rivalry than will countries with unified civilian governments."[16] But his model "assumes only two players, a civilian principal and a military agent."[17]

Avant acknowledges congressional activity as a major component of US civil–military relations,[18] but her focus has been on promoting doctrinal change, an area where the Congress has been less directly or regularly involved. Applying agency theory, she says that when there are multiple principals three consequences follow: there are compromises that make policy less efficient; the agent tends to act strategically and "play the principals off one another in order to gain support for its own preferences"; and the principals tend to require increasingly confining procedures to ensure control. These are significant observations, but Avant found that her theory did not explain or predict US military interventions in the first Clinton Administration. There, she concluded, "military advice has not driven policy." But "Principal–agent theory would *expect* military advice to have the most impact on policy when civilians disagree."[19] I think we need to revise our thinking and theories to deal with the special role of Congress in US civil–military relations.

Zegart also deals explicitly with the role of Congress but reaches some conclusions which I find unpersuasive. She argues that national security institutions and issues operate differently from the domestic ones to which the "new institutionalism" first applied principal–agent theory. Her "strict new institutionalist model" hypothesizes that: Congress drives agency design and evolution and strongly oversees the bureaucracy. But for national security agencies, she argues, the executive branch is the driver, and "Congress exercises only sporadic and ineffectual oversight; legislators have weak incentives and blunt tools." I believe that proposition is not confirmed by the history of congressional activity in recent decades.[20]

A descriptive model of US civil–military relations

History shows variation and some evolution toward a new and stable relationship between warriors and politicians, especially in the decades since the Second World War. Instead of the incomplete model offered by the principal–agent theory, I think we need a revised model closer to the bureaucratic politics tradition. There are some testable propositions to support such a model, but few predictions, because most outcomes depend upon personality factors and changing power relationships:

1 The president and secretary of defense control the US military on the use of force, including strategy and rules of engagement.
2 The Congress controls the US military directly on matters of force size, equipment, and organization, and indirectly on doctrine and personnel.
3 The US military accepts both forms of civilian control in principle, but insists on offering advice that represents and tries to protect its institutional and professional autonomy.
4 On use of force decisions, the US military is treated by the president as having a veto.
5 Instead of exercising that veto, however, the US military insists on and is usually granted terms and conditions for the planned use of force.
6 By not resigning in protest, the US military leadership implicitly agrees to support presidential decisions on the budget and use of force, but it

    also recognizes an obligation to provide alternative personal views in response to congressional inquiries.

7   Congress exerts its controls with less regard to military preferences than to political considerations of individual members and committees.

8   When the president and Congress are in agreement, the military complies; when the two branches are in disagreement, the military tends to side with the branch that favors its own views, but never to the point of direct disobedience to orders of the commander-in-chief.

I think that the evidence for these propositions is clear and compelling.

For Constitutional and political reasons, there are two competing sources of civilian control of the US military – the president and secretary of defense for the executive branch and the numerous defense committees for the legislative branch. In practice, there is mutual recognition of each branch's roles and little interference. The chain of command from the president controls the commitment and ordering of forces. The chain of command from the Congress controls spending but is otherwise less clear and direct.

Congress' command is less direct because the legislative branch issues its orders in the form of authority to spend money and of basic laws. The civilian leaders in the executive branch have some leeway in carrying out those laws and appropriations. Congressional command is less clear also because subunits in Congress – committees and individual members – give guidance in forms short of formal laws which may conflict with other guidance from either Congress or the president.

From the standpoint of the members of the armed forces, Congress is an escape valve, a locus for venting disagreements with the executive branch leadership, and a potential ally when warriors wish to challenge or change policy.

The existence of a strong legislature, and its functioning as an alternative source of civilian control, explain why the United States has been mercifully free from the threat of excessive military influence in government or anything approaching a coup – which are genuine concerns in many other nations. Is this "inefficient", as Avant complains? Yes, if your standard is unilinear control and consistency. Do the agents – the military – play the principals off against one another? Sometimes, but not necessarily with bad consequences.

Despite ritual congressional protests regarding the Constitutional right to declare war, presidents have exercised broad freedom of action throughout US history. The only time Congress terminated a conflict which the president wished to continue was the 1973 cutoff of funds to fight in Southeast Asia – an action which proved that the power of the purse, even when exercised over a veto, trumped the power of the sword in the hands of the president. Civilian leaders also delegated more or less control over the setting of strategy and rules of engagement, as they wished. As Eliot Cohen notes, it is not unusual, and is indeed usually preferable, for presidents to question military plans closely and impose their own judgments.[21]

Congress exercises its civilian control by approving budgets and establishing basic laws governing the armed forces. While it tends to approve Executive Branch proposals, it frequently modifies them to reflect parochial and political concerns of influential Members. Congress also frequently allies with military leaders whose recommendations are disregarded by the president while coinciding with the interests of key legislators. In order to assert its controls, Congress uses a broad array of tools – from formal laws to committee reports and earmarks, to intimidating hearings and investigations, to delays or denials of military promotions.

The US military, like most governmental organizations, seek to maximize their autonomy and the resources they control. They have developed standards of professionalism which make it difficult for either source of civilian control to interfere. Unlike virtually all other departments of government, there is no mid-career lateral entry into the officer corps.

This is not, however, the "objective control" favored by Huntington. He accurately described but deeply lamented the role of Congress. "The separation of powers is a perpetual invitation, if not an irresistible force, drawing military leaders into political conflicts. Consequently, it has been a major hindrance to the development of military professionalism and civilian control in the United States."[22] Huntington could not accept – although the officer corps has accepted – the competing sources of legitimate civilian control. He wants a greater consistency of purpose and action than the American political system can ever guarantee.

On use of force issues, there is strong evidence that US presidents, at least in the last half of the twentieth century, treated the US military as having a veto over action. Dick Betts found only one instance where military operations were launched when more than one of the members of the Joint Chiefs of Staff were strongly opposed. That case was the peacekeeping mission to Lebanon in 1983.[23] That exception may prove the rule, however, since it is also the only case where Congress formally approved the troop deployment, under the War Powers Act, for an 18-month period. Despite some doubts about the mission, the legislative branch sided with the executive, and the US military was forced to comply.

Peter Feaver also found evidence supporting the military veto hypothesis. He says that during the Cold War civilian preferences on use of force issues prevailed in 23 of 29 cases – and that the six contrary cases were when the US military successfully opposed combat action. He also supports the notion that the military prevailed on the terms and conditions of how force was to be used except in four cases, two of which involved General MacArthur, a highly exceptional circumstance.[24]

I believe that miltary veto power exists because presidents recognize the prestige of the military and foresee high political risks if they disregard military advice. While good management calls for vetting ideas with those who would implement the decisions, the US military has added power because it can go to the Congress when its views are disregarded.

Instead of resignations in protest or insubordination, US military leaders have insisted upon terms and conditions for the use of force which have generally been accepted by post-Vietnam presidents. Vietnam was the turning point because, until then, the US military had been generally successful in its conflicts. But the war in Southeast Asia seared a generation of officers who were angry at the lack of political support from civilian leaders. They resented the restrictive rules of engagement, the antagonistic reporting of the press, and the failure to provide the desired combat resources. In response, they came to espouse notions best articulated by former Defense Secretary Caspar Weinberger, whose six tests before using force included concepts of vital interests, clear missions, and an intent to win. Drawing upon German and Soviet military literature, the US Army in particular also developed doctrine for what was called the operational level of war – between grand strategy and local tactics – where military professionalism was supposed to dominate.

Those terms and conditions often followed what came to be known as the Powell Doctrine: overwhelming force, clear and achievable missions, predetermined exit strategies in case of success or failure, and robust rules of engagement. As will be shown later, recent presidents have tended to grant those terms and conditions as a means of securing military support for planned operations.

Military support for Executive Branch policies also extends to the budget. Although US defense budgets since the Second World War have been set top-down for politico–economic reasons, rather than bottom-up for strategic reasons, and although they have consistently been viewed by military leaders as insufficient to achieve declared goals, the Joint Chiefs of Staff with few exceptions have ritually defended the annual budget requests. Sometimes the Chiefs' support has been obviously faint-hearted, and congressmen have obtained suggestions for additions to the official requests. These behaviors may strike some as a minuet or kabuki dance – a ritual to imply disagreement without actually saying so. I see them differently – as the fulfillment of an implicit compact to respond to both sources of civilian control with loyalty and deference.[25]

By not resigning even if they view the sums as insufficient, the Chiefs are obligated to defend the numbers in Hill testimony. In return, however, they may express discomfort with the level of risk involved in the proposed budget and they may respond with specificity to congressional questions as to how they would spend additional funds, if approved. This practice serves the interests of all three participants: it protects the president from political criticism for ignoring military advice; it protects the military leaders from having to disappoint either source of civilian control; and it enables some members of Congress to get grudging acknowledgement of some of their own arguments.

The power to investigate – and therefore embarrass – the services or the president, also gives Congress influence. Vigorous criticism of the Tailhook sexual harassment scandal prompted the navy to impose tougher discipline than it might have preferred and may even have modified the culture of naval aviation. Congressional views on other gender issues may also have imposed more civilian attitudes on a reluctant military.

Congressional preferences usually support vocal advocates within the services who feel ignored by their civilian superiors. The legislative branch functions well as an arbiter of conflicting views – unlike the executive branch, which thrives on hierarchical uniformity and is uncomfortable with dissent. Congress is also less concerned with – or able to practice – consistency of action, while consistency is prized in the executive branch.

Congress is far from a unitary institution. On military issues, majorities sometimes side with the President, sometimes with the military leaders. Sometimes members of the president's party will join to support his policies, sometimes they will side with military opponents. Members of the opposition party may also switch sides, sometimes supporting the president on a bipartisan basis and other times embarrassing him by exposing disagreements by the military. The majorities line up on an issue-specific basis, and key members often push themes and policies that they have long favored, regardless of the changing political balance

In the three-way tug of war, the US military will accede to the views of civilians when unified, as in Lebanon in 1983, despite their own professional misgivings. I think the same pattern was followed in Bosnia in 1995, when both the president and majorities in Congress favored some kind of intervention. The same logic applied to Iraq in 2003, where Congress voted for a war sought by the president, despite some dissenting views among the military.

When the president and Congress disagree, military leaders are freer to voice concerns to reinforce the views of the side with which they agree. Such agreement, however, is most vocal before final decisions are made, and is rarely continued afterwards. The president can make final decisions by issuing deployment orders, or Congress can make them by passing laws and budgets. Whether military views prevail or not depends upon the normal operation of the policy process and attendant politics. If military views are not fully accepted, the actual outcomes will be modified in part to accommodate military concerns.

While these principles have been reflected throughout US history, recent history has shown at least a temporary reversion to military quiescence and congressional acquiescence in strong executive branch control. Defense Secretary Rumsfeld has groomed and selected a new generation of military leaders who confine their dissent, if any, to internal debates. The Congress, concerned about public support for difficult military operations and controlled by the same party as the president, has confined its oversight to the most egregious examples of poor planning. Although these developments have reduced evidence of civil–military tensions, they have also furthered ominous trends toward partisanship in US civil–military relations.

The danger of politicization

In the early years of the Republic, partisanship was the rule, and officer commissions were a form of patronage. John Adams and Alexander Hamilton saw to it that Federalists dominated the expanded army in 1798, and Jefferson used his appointments to make the army a Republican bastion after he took office. Thereafter, officers did not hesitate to use political means to pursue what they viewed as professional goals – such as career advancement and the interests of their particular branch of service – but they steered clear of domestic political controversies. In 1833 the Secretary of War tried to prohibit officers from visiting Washington except on official business, but he had to cancel his order. An officer in 1855 explained the siren call of the capital: "I must get to Washington & try to get promotion …. There is nothing like being on the spot."[26]

Despite these pressures and practices, the officer corps did not become a force in American politics. As a leading historian concluded, "Although they resorted to political channels in seeking support for professional goals, most regulars avoided involvement in civilian controversies, viewed political parties and partisanship as divisive and potentially dangerous, and saw the army as a neutral instrument of government."[27]

After the Civil War, and until quite recently, many officers followed the tradition of George Marshall and Dwight Eisenhower and did not even vote. In recent years, however, US military officers have increasingly been willing to identify with only one political party, the Republican Party (GOP). As late as 1976, the largest segment of military officers described themselves as "Independents" – 46 percent, compared to 12 percent Democratic and 33 percent Republican. By 1996, however, two-thirds of the officers surveyed called themselves "Republican", surveyed called themselves "Republican", with only 7 percent Democratic and 22 percent independent.[28]

There are, of course, many explanations for these trends. Officers are overwhelmingly conservative and disproportionately from the South, while the Democratic Party is more liberal and less strong is the South.[29] But officers can be conservative and still nonpartisan, especially if they view their service as to the nation, regardless of which party controls the branches of government.

Younger officers also have more partisan role models. Bill Clinton sought out retired officers to endorse his candidacy in 1992, in part to offset doubts about his leadership, because of his avoidance of the draft and critical comments about the US military. Both major party candidates recruited retirees in the 2000 and 2004 elections, and the trend is likely to continue unless senior officers practice self-restraint.

This trend toward overt partisan identification encourages politicians to treat the military as just another interest group, one to be courted at election time as just one of many parts of a potential coalition. If Democrats view the officer corps as Republican, they are likely to be distrustful of its advice and insistent upon close supervision and perhaps even tests of loyalty. That could ultimately lead to the identification of "Democratic" and "Republican" generals and the politicization of their protégés. By the same logic, Republican civilian leaders might also treat the officer corps as a political special interest, to be appeased occasionally but often ignored because "they have nowhere else to go."

Either outcome would be corrosive of trust and dangerous to continued civilian control. Only an ethic of nonpartisanship protects military professionalism as a branch of public service. That ethic cannot be imposed from outside, but needs to be adopted and inculcated from within the officer corps. Until and unless that happens, the normal stresses in US civil–military relations will be in danger of an even greater fracture.

Notes

1 Introduction: The peculiar nature of US civil-military relations

1 Quoted in Richard H. Kohn, *Eagle and Sword: The Federalists and the Creation of the Military Establishment, 1783–1802*, New York, NY: Free Press, 1975, p. 2.
2 Kohn, *Eagle and Sword*, p. 2.
3 Articles of Confederation, articles IX, VI, and VIII. One of many sources for the text of the Articles is Appendix A of Christopher Collier and James Lincoln Collier, *Decision in Philadelphia: The Constitutional Convention of 1787*, New York, NY: Ballantine Books, 1986.
4 Kohn, *Eagle and Sword*, pp. 17–39.
5 Richard H. Kohn (ed.), *The U.S. Military under the Constitution, 1789–1989*, New York, NY: New York University Press, 1991, p. 71. Many of these concerns were reiterated in the ratification debates, particularly in Federalist papers 3, 4, 11, 15, 23 and 24.
6 Collier and Collier, p. 104.
7 Quoted in Kohn, *Eagle and Sword*, pp. 76 and 77.
8 Quoted in Collier and Collier, p. 316.
9 Collier and Collier, p. 323.
10 Collier and Collier, p. 330.
11 Kohn, *Eagle and Sword*, pp. 81 and 83.
12 Kohn, *Eagle and Sword*, pp. 85–6.
13 Article I, section 8.
14 Article I, section 9.
15 Article II, sections 2 and 4.
16 For a discussion of some of these matters, see David Halberstam, *War in a Time of Peace: Bush, Clinton, and the Generals*, New York, NY: Scribner, 2001; Peter D. Feaver, *Armed Servants: Agency, Oversight, and Civil–Military Relations*, Cambridge, MA: Harvard University Press, 2003; Charles A. Stevenson, *SecDef: The Nearly Impossible Job of Secretary of Defense*, Washington, DC: Potomac Books, 2006.
17 For example, see: Eric Larrabee, *Commander in Chief*, New York, NY: Harper & Row, 1987; Warren Zimmerman, *The First Great Triumph*, New York, NY: Farrar, Straus and Giroux, 2002; Ernest R. May, *Imperial Democracy*, New York, NY: Harper, 1973; Ernest R. May (ed.), *The Ultimate Decision: The President as Commander in Chief*, New York, NY: George Braziller, 1960.
18 For the latter two cases, see Stevenson chapters on McNamara and Weinberger.
19 See Stephen Peter Rosen, *Winning the Next War*, Ithaca, NY: Cornell University Press, 1991; Williamson Murray and Allan R. Millett, *Military Innovation in the Interwar Period*, Cambridge: Cambridge University Press, 1996.

20 For this, see A.J. Bacevich, "The paradox of professionalism: Eisenhower, Ridgway, and the Challenge to Civilian Control, 1952–1955", *The Journal of Military History*, April 1997.

21 See, for example, the stimulating works of: Amy B. Zegart, *Flawed by Design: The Evolution of the CIA, JCS, and NSC*, Stanford, CA: Stanford University Press, 1999; Michael C. Desch, *Civilian Control of the Military: The Changing Security Environment*, Baltimore, MD: Johns Hopkins University Press, 1999; Peter D. Feaver, *Armed Servants: Agency, Oversight, and Civil-Military Relations*, Cambridge, MA: Harvard University Press, 2003; Dale R. Herspring. *The Pentagon and the Presidency: Civil–Military Relations from FDR to George W. Bush*, Lawrence, KS: The University Press of Kansas, 2005.

2 Revolutionary war by committee

1 Quoted in E. Wayne Carp, *To Starve the Army at Pleasure*, Chapel Hill, NC: University of North Carolina Press, 1984, p. 181.

2 Lynn Montcross, *The Reluctant Rebels: The Story of the Continental Congress, 1774–1789*, New York, NY: Harper & Brothers, 1950, p. 147.

3 Quoted in Douglas Southall Freeman, *George Washington, Volume Three: Planter and Patriot*, New York, NY: Scribner's, 1951, p. 453.

4 Montcross, pp. 50 and 57.

5 Montcross, pp. 70–1; Russell F. Weigley, *History of the United States Army*, Bloomington, IN: Indiana University Press, 1984, pp. 28 and 31.

6 Quoted in Don Higginbotham, *The War of American Independence*, New York, NY: Macmillan, 1971, pp. 84–5.

7 James Kirby Martin and Mark Edward Lender, *A Respectable Army: The Military Origins of the Republic, 1763–1789*, Arlington Heights, IL: Harlans Davidson, 1982, p. 75.

8 Quoted in Higginbotham, *War*, p. 206.

9 *Journals of the Continental Congress*, volume 2, June 17, 1775, p. 96.

10 *Journals*, volume 2, June 20, 1775, pp. 100–1.

11 Higginbotham, *War*, p. 211.

12 Feeman, volume 3, p. 446.

13 *Journals*, volume 2, June 30, 1775, pp. 111–22

14 Martin and Lender, p. 76

15 Montcross, p. 89.

16 *Journals*, volume 2, pp. 100 and 112.

17 Proclamation of Rebellion, August 23, 1775, at http://www.britannia.com/history/docs/procreb.html.

18 Montcross, pp. 140–2.

19 Montcross, p. 144.

20 Montcross, pp. 131 and 191.

21 Montcross, p. 82.

22 See text at Yale Law School's Avalon Project: http://www.yale.edu/lawweb/avalon/arms.htm.

23 Montcross, pp. 77, 79, 83 and 85.

24 Russell F. Weigley, *The American War of War*, Bloomington, IN: Indiana University Press, 1973, pp. 5, 10 and 11; Montcross, p. 94.

25 Weigley, *Way of War*, p. 5.

26 Quoted in Weigley, *Way of War*, p. 4.

27 Weigley, *Way of War*, p. 13.

28 Jack N. Rakove, *The Beginnings of National Politics: An Interpretive History of the Continental Congress*, Baltimore, MD: Johns Hopkins University Press, 1979, pp. 195 and 199.

29 Quoted in Carp, p. 37; Louis Clinton Hatch, *The Administration of the American Revolutionary Army*, New York, NY: Burt Franklin, 1904, p. 20.
30 Montcross, p. 205.
31 Higginbotham, *War*, p. 92.
32 Montcross, p. 72.
33 Quoted in Martin and Lender, p. 43
34 Mark V. Kwasny, *Washington's Partisan War, 1775–1783*, Kent, OH: Kent State University Press, 1996, pp. 58 and 136.
35 Washington had to rely on regulars for the attack; no militia were willing to join the operation. Kwasny, p. 136.
36 T. Harry Williams, *The History of American Wars From 1745 to 1918*, New York, NY: Knopf, 1981, p. 46.
37 Don Higginbotham, *War and Society in Revolutionary America,* Columbia, SC: University of South Carolina Press, 1988, p. 91.
38 Williams, pp. 44–5; Larry H. Addington, *The Patterns of War since the Eighteenth Century,* Bloomington, IN: Indiana University Press, Second Edition, 1994, p. 12; Higginbotham, *War and Society*, p. 99.
39 Martin and Lender, p. 143.
40 Lucille E. Horgan, *Forged in War: The Continental Congress and the Origin of Military Supply and Acquisition Policy*, Westport, CT: Greenwood Press, 2002, p. 109; Addington, p. 14.
41 Quoted in Weigley, *Army*, p. 46.
42 This story is told in impressive detail in Horgan. See ch. 1, pp. 1–22.
43 R. Arthur Bowler, "Logistics and Operations in the American Revolution", in Don Higginbotham (ed.), *Reconsiderations on the Revolutionary War*, Westport, CT: Greenwood Press, 1978, p. 59.
44 Horgan, p. 101.
45 Horgan, pp. 11 and 13.
46 Montcross, p. 266.
47 Montcross, p. 194.
48 Montcross, p. 194.
49 Montcross, p. 227.
50 Montcross, p. 301.
51 Montcross, p. 323.
52 Martin and Lender, p. 187.
53 Martin and Lender, pp. 191–3; Montcross, pp. 349–50.
54 Weigley, *Army*, p. 77.
55 Weigley, *Army*, p. 81.
56 Richard H. Kohn, "American Generals of the Revolution: Subordination and Restraint", in Don Higginbotham (ed.), *Reconsiderations on the Revolutionary War*, Westport, CT: 1978, pp. 117 and 109.

3   Lincoln, Congress and the generals

1 Eliot A. Cohen, *Supreme Command*, New York, NY: Free Press, 2002, p.15.
2 Quoted in Benjamin P. Thomas and Harold M. Hyman, *Stanton: The Life and Times of Lincoln's Secretary of War,* New York, NY: Knopf, 1962, p.128.
3 Bruce Tap, *Over Lincoln's Shoulder: The Committee on the Conduct of the War*, Lawrence, KS: University Press of Kansas, 1998, p. 200.
4 Thomas and Hyman, p. 262.
5 Tap, p. 200.
6 Elisabeth Joan Doyle, "The Conduct of the War, 1861", in Arthur M. Schlesinger, Jr. and Roger Bruns (eds), *Congress Investigates, 1792–1974,* New York, NY: Chelsea House Publishers, 1975, p. 73.

7 David Herbert Donald, *Lincoln*, New York, NY: Simon & Schuster, 1995, p. 285.
8 Burton J. Hendrick, *Lincoln's War Cabinet*, Boston, MA: Little, Brown, 1946, p. 172.
9 Cohen, p. 19.
10 C. Percy Powell, *Lincoln Day by Day: A Chronology, 1809–1865, Volume III: 1861–1865*, Washington, DC: Lincoln Sesquicentennial Commission, 1960, April 1, 1861, p. 32.
11 Donald, p. 291; James M. McPherson, *Battle Cry of Freedom: The Civil War Era*, New York, NY: Oxford University Press, 1988, pp. 267–8.
12 McPherson, p. 260; Hendrick, p. 4.
13 Donald, p. 256; Hendrick, p. 4; Inaugural address, available at http: whitehousehistory.org/04/subs/activities_03/c02_01.html.
14 April 15, 1861, Presidential Proclamation, available at http:whitehousehistory. org/04/subs/activities_03/c02_02.html.
15 Geoffrey R. Stone, *Perilous Times: Free Speech in Wartime*, New York, NY: W.W. Norton, 2004, pp. 84–5, 120 and 124.
16 Stone, pp. 85, 87 and 124.
17 McPherson, pp. 352–3 and 355–6.
18 McPherson, p. 322.
19 McPherson, pp. 333–4.
20 McPherson, p. 336.
21 McPherson, pp. 362–3.
22 Hendrick, p. 52; Donald, p. 266.
23 Harry J. Carman, and Reinhard H. Luthin, *Lincoln and the Patronage*, Gloucester, MA: Peter Smith, 1964, p. 148.
24 Hendrick, p. 222.
25 Quoted in Donald, p. 325.
26 Hendrick, pp. 230–1.
27 Quoted in Thomas and Hyman, p. 135.
28 Quoted in Thomas and Hyman, p. 128.
29 Hendrick, p. 289.
30 Donald, pp. 319–20.
31 Thomas and Hyman, pp. 63–6; Hendrick, pp. 257 and 259.
32 Hendrick, pp. 260 and 261.
33 Quoted in T. Harry Williams, *Lincoln and the Radicals*, Madison, WI: University of Wisconsin Press, 1965, p. 110.
34 Thomas and Hyman, p. 155; Cohen, p. 27.
35 Thomas and Hyman, pp. 152–4, 223 and 287.
36 Thomas and Hyman, pp. 185 and 186.
37 Thomas and Hyman, pp. 147 and 148.
38 Thomas and Hyman, p. 386.
39 Donald, p. 334.
40 Thomas and Hyman, p. 390.
41 Cohen, p. 31; Michael D. Pearlman, *Warmaking and American Democracy*. Lawrence, KS: University Press of Kansas, 1999, p. 128; Russell F. Weigley, *The American Way of War*, Bloomington, IN: Indiana University Press, 1977, p. 134.
42 Thomas and Hyman, p. 412.
43 Hendrick, p. 282; William Whatley Pierson, Jr., "The Committee on the Conduct of the Civil War", *American Historical Review*, vol. 23, no. 3, April 1918, pp. 556–7; Marcus Cunliffe, *Soldiers & Civilians: The Martial Spirit in America, 1775–1865*, Boston, MA: Little, Brown, 1968, p. 329.
44 *The Congressional Globe*, January 15, 1863, p. 324.
45 Cunliffe, p. 330.
46 Pearlman, p. 134.

47 Tap, p. 99.
48 Thomas and Hyman, p. 262.
49 Quoted in Cohen, pp. 19–20.
50 Cohen, pp. 15, 47 and 41.
51 Cohen, p. 43.
52 Cohen, pp. 39 and 40.
53 Williams, p. 83; *Day by Day*, January 8, 1862, p. 88.
54 Quoted in *Day by Day*, January 10, 1862, p. 89.
55 *Day by Day*, January 13, 1862, p. 89; Williams, p. 110.
56 Russell F. Weigley, *A Great Civil War*, Bloomington, IN: Indiana University Press, 2000, p. 119; Thomas and Hyman, p. 170.
57 Thomas and Hyman, p. 171.
58 Quoted in Tap, pp. 112–3.
59 Tap, p. 113.
60 Pierson, p. 568; *Day by Day*, March 11, 1862, pp. 99–100.
61 Quoted in Thomas and Hyman, p. 189.
62 Weigley, *American Way*, p. 248; Pendleton Herring, *The Impact of War*, New York, NY: Farrar & Rinehart, Inc., 1941, pp. 151–2.
63 Quoted in Thomas and Hyman, pp. 205–6.
64 Tap, p. 127.
65 Thomas and Hyman, pp. 217–8.
66 Cohen, p. 20.
67 Cohen, p. 41.
68 Pearlman, p. 129.
69 Thomas and Hyman, p. 299.
70 Thomas and Hyman, p. 299.
71 Cunliffe, p. 328; Donald, p. 491.
72 Richard B. Morris, *Encyclopedia of American History*, New York, NY: Harper & Brothers, 1953, p. 406.
73 Doyle, p. 72.
74 Carman and Luthin, p. 151. The Secretary of War tried to prohibit officers from visiting Washington except on official business in 1833 but had to cancel his order. An officer in 1855 explained the siren call of the capital: "I must get to Washington & try to get promotion .... There is nothing like being on the spot", Willliam B. Skelton, "Officers & Politicians", reprinted in Peter Karsten (ed.), *The Military in America*, New York, NY: Free Press, rev. ed., 1986, p. 91.
75 Williams, pp. 26 and 27; Richard H. Abbott, *Cobbles in Congress: The Life of Henry Wilson, 1812–1875*, Lexington, KY: University Press of Kentucky, 1972, pp. 122–3.
76 Abbott, pp. 126–7.
77 Donald, p. 325; Abbott, p. 123.
78 H. L. Trefousse, *Benjamin Franklin Wade: Radical Republican from Ohio*, New York, NY: Twayne Publishers Inc., 1963, p. 154.
79 Tap, pp. 22–4 and 32; Pierson, pp. 555 and 558.
80 T. Harry Williams, for example, says (p. 71): the JCCW "represented a full-throated attempt on the part of Congress to control the executive's prosecution of the war."
81 Doyle, pp. 67 and 74.
82 Pierson, pp. 561–3.
83 Pierson, p. 569.
84 Pierson, p. 573.
85 Tap, pp. 200 and 34; Doyle, p. 73.
86 Russell F. Weigley, *History of the United States Army*, Bloomington, IN: Indiana University Press, Enlarged Edition, 1984, pp. 208 and 209.

87 Allan G. Bogue, *The Earnest Men: Republicans of the Civil War Senate,* Ithaca, NY: Cornell University Press, 1981. pp. 160–6.
88 Abbott, pp. 132, 133, 135 and 138.
89 Stone, p. 92.
90 Weigley, *Army,* p. 210.
91 Morris, p. 406.
92 Thomas and Hyman, pp. 294–5.
93 Thomas and Hyman, pp. 332–3; Pearlman, p. 140.
94 Donald, p. 510; Thomas and Hyman, p. 310.
95 Cohen, p. 45.
96 Thomas and Hyman, pp. 525, 527, 549, 569, 573, 585, 592–3 and 608.

4 Managing the Vietnam war

 1 Leslie H. Gelb and Richard K. Betts. *The Irony of Vietnam: The System Worked,* Washington, DC: Brookings, 1979, p. 121.
 2 Dale R. Herspring, *The Pentagon and the Presidency: Civil–Military Relations from FDR to George W. Bush,* Lawrence, KS: University of Kansas Press, 2005, p. 150.
 3 US Senate, Committee on Armed Services, ninetieth Congress, first session, "Air War Against North Vietnam", Summary Report by Preparedness Investigating Subcommittee, August 31, 1967, p. 10.
 4 Richard Nixon, *RN: The Memoirs of Richard Nixon,* New York, NY: Grosset & Dunlap, 1978, p. 734.
 5 David Halberstam, *The Best and the Brightest,* New York, NY: Ballantine, 1993, p. 135.
 6 Halberstam, pp. 298 and 342.
 7 *New York Times,* October 8, 1964.
 8 *New York Times,* October 4 and 2, 1964.
 9 Randall Bennett Woods, *Fulbright: A Biography,* New York, NY: Cambridge University Press, 1995, p. 347.
10 Robert S. McNamara, *In Retrospect: The Tragedy and Lessons of Vietnam,* New York, NY: Random House/Times Books, 1995, p. 135.
11 Public Law, pp. 88–408.
12 William Conrad Gibbons, *The US Government and the Vietnam War: Executive and Legislative Roles and Relationships,* part IV: July 1965–January 1968, Princeton, NJ: Princeton University Press, 1995, pp. 812–17.
13 The new Congress had 36 more Democratic House members, giving them a 295–140 majority over the Republicans. In the Senate, the ratio was 68 D to 32 R.
14 Stanley Karnow, *Vietnam: A History,* New York, NY: Penguin Books, 1983, p. 363.
15 Arthur M. Schlesinger, Jr., *A Thousand Days: John F. Kennedy in the White House,* Boston, MA: Houghton Mifflin, 1965, p. 992.
16 *Pentagon Papers: The Senator Gravel Edition,* Boston, MA: Beacon Press, 1975, 3:687. Emphasis in original.
17 *Pentagon Papers,* 3:690.
18 *Pentagon Papers,* 3:496.
19 *Pentagon Papers,* 3:498.
20 *Pentagon Papers,* 3:126 and 3:550.
21 *Pentagon Papers,* 3:628.
22 Gelb and Betts, p. 373.
23 Gelb and Betts, p. 121.
24 Quoted in Gelb and Betts, p. 120.

25 *Congress and the Nation*, vol. III, 1969–1972, Washington, DC: CQ Press, 1973, (henceforth CQ III), p. 901; R. Ernest Dupuy and Trevor N. Dupuy, *The Harper Encyclopedia of Military History*, New York, NY: HarperCollins, 1993, p. 1333.
26 CQ III, p. 937.
27 US Senate, Committee on Armed Services, ninetieth Congress, first session, "Air War Against North Vietnam", Hearings before the Preparedness Investigating Subcommittee, August 1967, p. 277.
28 *Pentagon papers*, 4:29; Richard K. Betts. *Soldiers, Statesmen, and Cold War Crises*, New York, NY: Columbia University Press, Morningside Edition, 1991, pp. 25–8.
29 *Pentagon Papers*, 4:180.
30 Quoted in Deborah Shapley, *Promise and Power: The Life and Times of Robert McNamara*, Boston, MA: Little, Brown, 1993, pp. 418–19.
31 H.R. McMaster, *Dereliction of Duty,* New York, NY: HarperCollins, 1997, pp. 309–12.
32 Air War hearings, pp. 278 and 334.
33 Air War hearings, pp. 320 and 330.
34 Gibbons, p. 746. And that is what McNamara was able to tell the Stennis subcommittee – 85 percent of the requested targets had been approved.
35 Senate Armed Services Subcommittee Report, pp. 2, 8 and 10.
36 Mark Perry, *Four Stars,* Boston, MA: Houghton Mifflin, 1989, pp.163–5.
37 Herspring, p. 150.
38 McMaster, p. 328.
39 Fredrik Logevall, "The Vietnam War", in Julian E. Zelizer (ed.), *The American Congress*, Boston, MA: Houghton Mifflin, 2004, pp. 594 and 585.
40 Quoted in Gibbons, p. 253.
41 Quoted in Gelb and Betts, p. 216.
42 Gibbons, pp. 32 and 213; Logevall, p. 592.
43 CQ III, p. 944.
44 *Congress and the Nation*, vol. II, 1965–1968, Washington, DC: CQ Press, 1969, (henceforth CQ II), p. 81.
45 Gibbons, pp. 306 and 448.
46 Gibbons, pp. 413 and 422–3.
47 Quoted in Gibbons, pp. 672 and 685.
48 CQ II, pp. 83–4.
49 Gibbons pp. 834, 891, 896 and 940.
50 Gibbons, pp. 925–8.
51 Betts, p. 161.
52 Clark Clifford, *Counsel to the President: A Memoir,* New York, NY: Random House, 1991, pp. 516 and 518.
53 Clifford, pp. 493–4.
54 Herspring, pp. 178–80.
55 William Safire, *Before the Fall*, Garden City, NY: Doubleday, 1975, p. 48.
56 Henry Kissinger, *Ending the Vietnam War*, New York, NY: Simon & Schuster, 2003, p. 57.
57 Quoted in Jeffrey Kimball, *The Vietnam War Files,* Lawrence, KS: University Press of Kansas, 2004, p. 55.
58 Perry, p. 222.
59 Perry, pp. 217n and 218.
60 Willard J. Webb, *The Joint Chiefs of Staff and the War in Vietnam, 1969–1970,* Washington, DC: Office of Joint History, Office of the Chairman of the Joint Chiefs of Staff, 2002, pp. 38–40 and 231.
61 Lewis Sorley, *Vietnam Chronicles: The Abrams Tapes, 1968–1972,* Lubbock, TX: Texas Tech University Press, 2004, p. 141.

62 *Congress and the Nation*, vol. IV, 1973–1976, Washington, DC: CQ Press, 1977, (henceforth CQ IV), p. 946. The charge was considered but not included in the final impeachment resolution by the House Judiciary Committee.
63 Kimball, pp. 77 and 79.
64 Webb, pp. 56, 60 and 90.
65 Sorley, p. 269. Emphasis in original.
66 Special National Intelligence Estimate, July 17, 1969, reprinted in National Intelligence Council, *Estimative Products on Vietnam, 1948–1975*, Washington, DC: GPO, 2005, p. 475.
67 Dupuy and Dupuy, pp. 1329–33.
68 Kissinger, pp. 92–3.
69 Herspring, p. 200.
70 Herspring, p. 196; Perry pp. 232–4.
71 Perry, pp. 234–6.
72 The quotations are from the Nixon tapes, reported in James Rosen, "Nixon and the Chiefs", *Atlantic Monthly*, April 2002, p. 55.
73 Perry, p. 241. The author was also involved in the investigation of these matters for members of the Senate Armed Services Committee.
74 Kissinger, p. 69.
75 Kissinger, pp. 156 and 198.
76 Don Oberdorfer, *Senator Mansfield*, Washington, DC: Smithsonian Books, 2003, pp. 372–4.
77 Oberdorfer, pp. 372, 377–8, 413–4 and 408–9.
78 Logevall, p. 598; Gelb and Betts, p. 159.
79 Sorley, p. 274.
80 CQ III, p. 944.
81 CQ III, p. 226–9.
82 Kimball, pp. 169 and 168.
83 Perry, p. 237.
84 Kissinger, pp. 385 and 392.
85 Kimball, pp. 270–1.
86 Kimball, p. 325n; Nixon, p. 734.
87 CQ III, p. 933.
88 CQ IV, p. 907.
89 See the appendix to Eliot A. Cohen, *Supreme Command*, New York, NY: Free ress, 2002.
90 The text is in the appendix to Caspar W. Weinberger, *Fighting for Peace: Seven Critical Years in the Pentagon*, New York, NY: Warner Books, 1990.

5   John Adams and the politics of rearmament, 1798

1 Stanley Elkins and Eric McKitrick, *The Age of Federalism*, New York, NY: Oxford University Press, 1993, pp. 616–7.
2 See Charles A. Stevenson, "The Neutrality Proclamation of 1793", Case study for Institute for the Study of Diplomacy, Georgetown University, 2002.
3 Elkins and McKitrick, pp. 418–9.
4 Elkins and McKitrick, p. 415.
5 John Ferling, "'Father and Protector' President Johns Adams and Congress in the Quasi-War Crisis", in Kenneth R. Bowling and Donald R. Kennon (eds), *Neither Separate Nor Equal: Congress in the 1790s*, Athens, OH: Ohio University Press, 2000, pp. 296–7 and 299.
6 Ferling, pp. 306–7; Richard H. Kohn, *Eagle and Sword: The Beginnings of the Military Establishment in America*, New York, NY: Free Press, 1975, p. 203.
7 See his inaugural address online at http://www.bartleby.com/124/pres15.html.

8 Alexander DeConde, *The Quasi-War*, New York, NY: Scribner's, 1966, p. 341; Message to Congress at http://www.yale.edu/lawweb/avalon/presiden/messages/ja97-03.html

9 Elkins and McKitrick, p. 596; Ferling, p. 309.

10 Elkins and McKitrick, p. 596.

11 Presidential message at http://www.yale.edu/lawweb/avalon/president/messages/ja97-03.html.

12 James Roger Sharp, *American Politics in the Early Republic*, New Haven, CT: Yale University Press, 1993, p. 315 n 2; Ferling, p. 308; DeConde, p. 341.

13 Ferling, pp. 309–10.

14 Rudolph M. Bell, *Party and Faction In American Politics: The House of Representatives, 1789–1801*, Westport, CT: Greenwood Press, 1973, pp. 150, 151, 160, 166, 172 and 180; William T. Bianco and Jamie Markham, "Vanishing Veterans: The Decline of Military Experience in the US Congress", ch. 7 in Peter D. Feaver and Richard H. Kohn (eds), *Soldiers and Civilians: The Civil–Military Gap and American National Security*, Cambridge, MA: MIT Press, 2001, p. 278; Abraham, D. Sofaer, *War, Foreign Affairs and Constitutional Power: The Origins*, Cambridge, MA: Ballinger, 1976, p. 150.

15 Ron Chernow, *Alexander Hamilton*, New York, NY: Penguin Press, 2004, p. 553; *Historical Statistics of the United States, Colonial Times to 1970*, Washington, DC: Department of Commerce, 1975, p. 1115.

16 Elkins and McKitrick, pp. 594–5.

17 Kohn, pp. 220, 183, 185 and 186.

18 Adams regularly spent several months a year in Quincy when Congress was not in session, thereby making it difficult for his cabinet to consult with him. He returned home both for his own health and to be with his wife Abigail. He spent several months in Massachusetts in the fall of 1798 because Abigail was quite ill. Ferling, pp. 310 and 311.

19 Presidential message at http://www.yale.edu/lawweb/avalon/president/sou/adamsme1.htm.

20 Elkins and McKitrick, p. 582; DeConde, p. 342.

21 That is about $2.6 million in current dollars. Chernow, p. 549; DeConde, p. 47; Ferling, p. 314.

22 Elkins and McKitrick, p. 582.

23 Ferling, p. 314; Chernow, p. 550; Elkins and McKitrick, p. 584.

24 Presidential message at http://www.yale.edu/lawweb/avalon/president/messages/ja98-01.htm; Sharp, p. 173; Elkins and McKitrick, pp. 585–6; Ferling, p. 314.

25 Elkins and McKitrick, p. 587; Sharp, p. 174.

26 Elkins and McKitrick, p. 587.

27 Elkins and McKitrick, p. 588; DeConde, p. 343.

28 Ferling, p. 318; DeConde, p. 343; Kohn, pp. 224–5.

29 Quoted in Sharp, p. 173.

30 Quoted in Ferling, pp. 317 and 315.

31 Kohn, pp. 216, 212–3 and 218; DeConde, p. 51; James Morton Smith. *Freedom's Fetters*, Ithaca, NY: Cornell University Press, 1956, p. 14.

32 Kohn, pp. 212 and 215; Elkins and McKitrick, p. 598.

33 Quoted in Kohn, pp. 194 and 193.

34 Quoted in Sharp, p. 175; Kohn, p. 213.

35 Quoted in Chernow, p. 552.

36 Ferling, p. 319; Elkins and McKitrick, pp. 595 and 596.

37 DeConde, p. 102. For an approximate current value, multiply by 10. Thus, the tax on slaves would be the equivalent of $5 per person today.

38 David P. Currie, *The Constitution in Congress: The Federalist Period, 1789–1801*, Chicago, IL: University of Chicago Press, 1997, pp. 185, 226 and 227.

39 Kohn, p. 226; Ferling, p. 318; Elkins and McKitrick, p. 598.

40 Leonard D. White, *The Federalists*, New York, NY: Free Press, 1948, pp. 160 and 159; DeConde, p. 343.
41 Smith, p. 21.
42 Elkins and McKitrick, p. 590.
43 Elkins and McKitrick, p. 591.
44 Elkins and McKitrick, p. 591.
45 Elkins and McKitrick, p. 592.
46 Public Statutes at Large, fifth Congress, II session, ch. LXXIV, July 14, 1798.
47 For comparison, look at the section of the Uniform Code of Military Justice forbidding contemptuous words about many officials: Article 88: "Any commissioned officer who uses contemptuous words against the President, the Vice President, Congress, the Secretary of Defense, the Secretary of a military department, the Secretary of Transportation, or the Governor or legislature of any State, Territory, Commonwealth, or possession in which he is on duty or present shall be punished as a court-martial may direct."
48 Quotes from Sharp, pp. 176 and 177.
49 Kohn, pp. 231–2.
50 Quoted in Chernow, p. 559.
51 White, p. 240; Ferling, p. 299.
52 Elkins and McKitrick, p. 593.
53 Quoted in Elkins and McKitrick, p. 603.
54 Kohn, pp. 232–7; Elkins and McKitrick, p. 603.
55 Ferling, p. 324.
56 As Richard Kohn points out (p. 229n) there were five American "armies" at this point – four regiments of the old or western army; 12 regiments of New Army; Volunteer companies taken into federal service under the May, 1798 Provisional Army Law; the 10,000 man "Provisional Army" authorized by that law; and the Eventual Army of 28 regiments authorized in March 1799, but for which the president had only a year to appoint only officers. Only the New Army enlisted soldiers; the others never really organized.
57 DeConde, p. 112; Chernow, p. 564.
58 Kohn, pp. 239 and 240; Ferling, p. 324.
59 Quoted in Kohn, p. 257.
60 Ferling, p. 321.
61 June presidential message at http://www.yale.edu/lawweb/avalon/president/messages/ja98-04; Elkins and McKitrick, pp. 605, 610 and 612.
62 Presidential message at http://www.yale.edu/lawweb/avalon/president/sou/adamsme2.htm#france; Kohn, p. 258.
63 http://www.yale.edu/lawweb/avalon/president/sou/adamsme2.htm#france.
64 Kohn, p. 247; Elkins and McKitrick, p. 616.
65 Elkins and McKitrick, p. 617.
66 Elkins and McKitrick, pp. 616–7.
67 Ferling, pp. 327 and 328.
68 Elkins and McKitrick, p. 615; Kohn, pp. 248 and 249. It is noteworthy that Jefferson, in one of his first official acts as president, pardoned all those convicted under the Sedition Act and freed those still in jail. And 40 years later, Congress voted to repay with interest, all the fines imposed on those convicted under the act. Geoffrey R. Stone, *Perilous Times: Free Speech in Wartime*, New York, NY: W.W. Norton & Company, 2004, p. 73.

6 Franklin Roosevelt and the politics of rearmament

1 Robert Dallek, *Franklin D. Roosevelt and American Foreign Policy, 1932–1945*, New York, NY: Oxford University Press, 1995, p. 154.

2 Forrest C. Pogue, *George C. Marshall: Ordeal and Hope, 1939–1942*, New York, NY: Viking, 1966, p. 58.
3 Mark Skinner Watson, *Chief of Staff: Prewar Plans and Preparations*, Washington, DC: Historical Division, Department of the Army, 1950, p. 166.
4 Richard M. Ketchum, *The Borrowed Years, 1938–1941: America on the Way to War*, New York, NY: Random House, 1989, pp. 542 and 543; James F. Cook, *Carl Vinson: Patriarch of the Armed Forces*, Macon, GA: Mercer University Press, 2004, p. 74; US Department of Commerce, *Historical Statistics of the United States: Colonial Times to 1970*, Washington, DC: Bureau of the Census, 1975, p. 1115.
5 Samuel I. Rosenman, *Working with Roosevelt*, New York, NY: Harper & Brothers, 1952, pp. 165 and 166.
6 Robert Shogan, *Hard Bargain*, New York, NY: Scribner, 1995, p. 267; Hadley Cantril, *Public Opinion, 1936–1946*, Princeton, NJ: Princeton University Press, 1951, pp. 966, 780, 940 and 458.
7 Ketchum, pp. 129–31.
8 US Department of State, *Peace and War: United States Foreign Policy, 1931–1941*, Washington, DC: Government Printing office, 1943, pp. 23 and 25, document 49.
9 *Peace and War*, pp. 35 and 37, documents 68 and 83.
10 Ketchum, p. 225.
11 Historical Statistics, p. 1115; Elias Huzar, *The Purse and the Sword; Control of the Army by Congress through Military Appropriations, 1933–1950*, Ithaca, NY: Cornell University Press, 1950, pp. 142n; Table III, p. 141.
12 Kenneth J. Hagan, *This People's Navy*, New York, NY: Free Press, 1991, pp. 284 and 286.
13 Hagan, p. 283; Watson, p. 34.
14 Pogue, p. 22.
15 Cantril, pp. 939 and 941.
16 Pendleton Herring, *The Impact of War*, New York, NY: Farrar & Rinehart, 1941, pp. 125–6; Huzar, pp. 137–8 and 141.
17 Eric Larrabee, *Commander in Chief*, New York, NY: Harper & Row, 1987, p. 108.
18 Pogue, p. 34; Watson, p. 7.
19 Larrabee, pp. 101–2; Pogue, pp. 98 and 100.
20 Ketchum, p. 536.
21 Larrabee, p. 109; Pogue, pp. 22 and 23.
22 Ketchum, pp. 556–7.
23 Herring, p. 209.
24 Pogue, p. 21.
25 Ketchum, p. 538.
26 Rosenman, p. 169.
27 *Peace and War*, document 104; Russell F. Weigley, *History of the United States Army: Enlarged Edition*, Bloomington, IN: Indiana University Press, 1984, p. 417; Hagan, p. 286; Cook, pp. 129, 131 and 138.
28 Cantril, pp. 949 and 941.
29 *Roosevelt's Foreign Policy, 1933–1941, Franklin D. Roosevelt's Unedited Speeches and Messages*, New York, NY: Wilfred Funk, Inc., 1942, p. 15; Henry Kissinger, *Diplomacy*, New York, NY: Simon & Schuster, 1994, p. 382; Hagan, p. 287.
30 Dallek, pp. 172 and 173; Weigley, p. 418.
31 Watson, p. 5; Kent Roberts Greenfield, *American Strategy in World War II: A Reconsideration*, Malabar, FL: Robert E. Krieger Publishing Co., 1982, p. 52.
32 Dallek, p. 181.
33 Dallek, p. 185.
34 Cantril, pp. 781 and 458.
35 Larrabee, p. 21.

36 *Peace and War*, document 142.
37 Weigley, p. 424; *Peace and War*, document 143.
38 Cantril, p. 967; Dallek, p. 204.
39 Cook, p. 143; Watson, pp. 161 and 162.
40 Watson, pp. 164 and 165; *Peace and War*, document 146, p. 509.
41 Pogue, p. 28; Watson, p. 166.
42 Cantril, pp. 458, 942 and 1127.
43 Pogue, p. 30.
44 Pogue, p. 31.
45 Pogue, p. 32.
46 *Peace and War*, document 156; Watson, pp. 167–8.
47 Watson, p. 168; Cook, p. 148.
48 Franklin D. Roosevelt, *The Public Papers and Addresses of Franklin D. Roosevelt, 1940*, New York, NY: Macmillan, 1941, May 26, 1940 address, document 52.
49 Weigley, p. 425; Hagan, pp. 289–90.
50 Cantril, pp. 942, 458 and 1127.
51 Watson, p. 169; Pogue, pp. 57–8.
52 Pogue, p. 58.
53 Robert E. Sherwood, *Roosevelt & Hopkins: Revised Edition*, New York, NY: Universal Library, 1950, p. 190.
54 Cantril, p. 458.
55 Greenfield, pp. 53 and 81.
56 Shogan, pp. 87–92; Cook, pp. 155–6.
57 Robert H. Jackson, *That Man: An Insider's Portrait of Franklin D. Roosevelt*, New York, NY: Oxford University Press, 2003, pp. 87–99; Cook, pp. 156 and 158.
58 Rosenman, p. 242.
59 Ketchum, p. 558.
60 Henry L. Stimson and McGeorge Bundy, *On Active Service in Peace and War*, New York, NY: Harper & Brothers, 1948, p. 367.
61 Ketchum, p. 578.
62 Rosenman, p. 260.
63 *The Public Papers and Addresses of Franklin D. Roosevelt, 1940*, documents 151 and 152.
64 Cantril, pp. 409 and 410.
65 D. B. Hardeman and Donald C. Bacon, *Rayburn: A Biography*, Austin, TX: Texas Monthly Press, 1987, pp. 258–9; Kenneth S. Davis, *FDR: The War President, 1940–43: A History*, New York, NY: Random House, 2000, pp. 93 and 134–5; Ketchum, p. 581; Franklin D. Roosevelt, *The Public Papers and Addresses of Franklin D. Roosevelt, 1941*, New York, NY: Harper & Brothers, 1950, p. 677.
66 Pogue, pp. 146–7.
67 Pogue, p. 148; Hardeman, p. 261.
68 Maney, Patrick, "The Forgotten New Deal Congress", in Julian E. Zelizer (ed.), *The American Congress*, Boston, MA: Houghton Mifflin, 2004, p. 465; Watson, p. 223; Pogue, p. 149.
69 Cantril, p. 463; Watson, p. 223.
70 Pogue, pp. 150 and 153.
71 Stimson, p. 378; Watson, p. 229.
72 Hardeman, pp. 264–8; Watson, p. 231; Rosenman, p. 290.
73 Larrabee, p. 49.
74 Ketchum, pp. 553–4, 590; Hagan, p. 288.
75 Ketchum, p. 590; Kissinger, pp. 389–90; Hagan, p. 294.
76 Greenfield, pp. 53–4; Rosenman, p. 294.
77 Cantril, pp. 975, 1128 and 983.
78 *Peace and War*, document 212; Rosenman, p. 288.
79 May 27 address, *Peace and War*, document 210.

80 Larrabee, p. 60; Doris Kearns Goodwin, *No Ordinary Time*, New York, NY: Simon & Schuster, 1994, p. 137.
81 Watson, pp. 362–6.
82 Ketchum, p. 602; September 11 address in *The Public Papers and Addresses of Franklin D. Roosevelt, 1941*, document 88; Rosenman, p. 292.
83 Sherwood, pp. 410–5.
84 October 9 message in *The Public Papers and Addresses of Franklin D. Roosevelt, 1941*, p. 409; Sherwood, p. 382.
85 Sherwood, p. 382; *The Public Papers and Addresses of Franklin D. Roosevelt, 1941*, pp. 438–44; Ketchum, p. 606.
86 Watson, pp. 506–7; Ketchum, p. 697.

7 Harry Truman and the politics of rearmament

1 Walter S. Poole, *The Joint Chiefs of Staff and National Policy, vol. IV, 1950–1952*, Washington, DC: Office of Joint History, Office of the Chairman of the Joint Chiefs of Staff, 1998, p. 9.
2 Public Papers, October 29, 1949, accessible via Truman Presidential Museum & Library, at www.trumanlibrary.org.
3 Paul Y. Hammond, "Super Carriers and B-36 Bombers: Appropriations, Strategy and Politics", in Harold Stein (ed.), *American Civil–Military Decisions: A Book of Case Studies*, Birmingham, AL: University of Alabama Press, 1963, p. 551.
4 Walter Millis (ed.), *The Forrestal Diaries*, New York, NY: Viking, 1951, pp. 437–8.
5 Douglas Kinnard, *The Secretary of Defense*, Lexington, KY: University Press of Kentucky, 1980, p. 36.
6 Thomas D. Boettcher, *First Call: The Making of the Modern US Military, 1945–1953*, Boston, MA: Little, Brown, 1992, p. 250; Margaret Truman, *Harry S. Truman*, New York, NY: William Morrow, 1973, p. 407.
7 The total figure was 347, but over half were "secretaries, clerks, mess attendants and chauffeurs", Townsend Hoopes and Douglas Brinkley, *Driven Patriot: The Life and Times of James Forrestal*, New York, NY: Knopf, 1992, p. 359.
8 Michael J. Hogan, *A Cross of Iron: Harry S. Truman and the Origins of the National Security State, 1945–1954*, New York, NY: Cambridge University Press, 1998, p. 267; Mark Perry, *Four Stars*, Boston, MA: Houghton Mifflin, 1989, pp. 14–5; Omar N. Bradley and Clay Blair, *A General's Life*, New York, NY: Simon & Schuster, 1983, pp. 498 and 499.
9 Bradley, pp. 497–8; Hogan, p. 273.
10 Office of Management and Budget, Historical Tables; Department of Defense, Selected Manpower Statistics.
11 Hammond, "Super Carriers and B-36 Bombers", pp. 517 and 524.
12 Hammond, "Super Carriers and B-36 Bombers", p. 491.
13 Hammond, "Super Carriers and B-36 Bombers", pp. 493 and 536.
14 Bradley, pp. 503–4.
15 Statement by Navy Secretary Matthews, Truman Library, Public Papers, October 29, 1949.
16 Perry, p. 19.
17 OMB, Budget Historical Tables.
18 Steven Kull and I. M. Destler, *Misreading the Public: The Myth of a New Isolationism*, Washington, DC: Brookings, 1999, pp. 123–4.
19 Bradley, pp. 490–1.
20 Francis H. Heller (ed.), *The Truman White House: The Administration of the Presidency, 1945–1953*, Lawrence, KS: Regents Press of Kansas, 1980, p. 229.
21 Warner R. Schilling, "The Politics of National Defense: Fiscal 1950", in Warner R. Schilling, Paul Y. Hammond, Glenn H. Snyder, *Strategy, Politics, and Defense*

Budgets, New York, NY: Columbia University Press, 1962, p. 63; James F. Cook, *Carl Vinson: Patriarch of the Armed Forces*, Macon, GA: Mercer University Press, 2004, p. 230.
22 Schilling, p. 89; Heller, p. 231.
23 Boettcher, pp. 174–81.
24 Hammond, "Super Carriers and B-36 Bombers", pp. 496–7; Cook, pp. 229–30.
25 Cook, p. 226; National Security Act of 1949, PL 81-216, sec 202 (b)(6).
26 NSC 34/2, A Report to the National Security Council by the Secretary of State on US Policy toward China, February 28, 1949, pp. 3–4.
27 CIA, "Probable Developments in China", ORE 45-49, June 16, 1949, p. 1.
28 NSC 48, A Report to the National Security Council by the Secretary of Defense on United States Policy Toward Asia, June 10, 1949.
29 Bradley, p. 518.
30 NSC37/7, A Report to the National Security Council by the Secretary of Defense on the Position of the United States with Respect to Formosa, August 22, 1949, p. 1.
31 Doris M. Condit, *History of the Office of the Secretary of Defense, Volume II, The Test of War, 1950–1953*, Washington, DC: Historical Office, Office of the Secretary of Defense, 1988, p. 279.
32 Condit, pp. 280–1.
33 CIA, "The Possibility of Direct Soviet Military Action during 1949", ORE 46-49, May 3, 1949, p.1.
34 Schilling, p. 38.
35 NSC 52/3, A Report to the President by the National Security Council on Governmental Programs in National Security and International Affairs for the fiscal year 1951, September 22, 1949, p. 3.
36 Bradley, pp. 515–6.
37 Foreign Relations of the United States, 1950, Volume I: National Security Affairs, Foreign Economic Policy (FRUS 1950), Washington, DC: GPO, 1977, p. 142.
38 Paul Y. Hammond, "NSC-68: Prologue to Rearmament", in Warner R. Schilling, Paul Y. Hammond, Glenn H. Snyder, *Strategy, Politics, and Defense Budgets*, New York, NY: Columbia University Press, 1962, pp. 288–9.
39 Hammond, NSC-68, pp. 292 and 296.
40 FRUS 1950, pp. 261, 266–7, 277, 282 and 285.
41 Hammond, NSC-68, p. 319.
42 Dean Acheson, *Present at the Creation: My Years in the State Department*, New York, NY: W.W. Norton, 1969, p. 373.
43 Hammond, NSC-68, pp. 324–6.
44 Hammond, NSC-68, pp. 328–30.
45 Poole, p. 9.
46 Truman Library, Public Papers.
47 FRUS 1950, p. 311.
48 Hammond, NSC-68, pp. 340–1 and 344.
49 Truman Library, Public Papers.
50 Joseph Lawton Collins, *War in Peacetime: The History and Lessons of Korea*, Boston, MA: Houghton Mifflin, 1969, pp. 42–3; Glenn D. Paige, *The Korean Decision: June 24–30, 1950*, New York, NY: Free Press, 1968, p. 71.
51 Boettcher, p. 194.
52 Paige, pp. 93 and 116–7.
53 Boettcher, p. 206; John W. Spanier, *The Truman–MacArthur Controversy and the Korean War*, New York, NY: Norton, 1965, p. 20.
54 Bradley, p. 235.
55 Notes, dated June 27, 1950 by George M. Elsey, Truman Library, Korean War documents, 4.
56 Bradley, pp. 536 and 538–9.

57 Paige, pp. 187–91.
58 Paige, p. 262; Draft by George Elsey summarizing a June 30,1950 meeting, Truman Library, Korean War documents, pp. 7–8.
59 Memorandum of Conversation, dated July 3, 1950, by Philip C. Jessup, Truman Library, Korean War documents.
60 Presidential Message, Truman Library, Public Papers.
61 Hogan, pp. 307 and 308.
62 NSC 68/2, September 30, 1950, Note by the Executive Secretary to the National Security Council on United States Objectives and Programs for National Security.
63 Hogan, p. 310.
64 Congressional Quarterly. *Congress and the Nation, 1945–1964,* Washington: Congressional Quarterly, 1965, pp. 260 and 357.
65 Paige, pp. 122, 151, 154, 196, 217 and 265.
66 CQ, pp. 1650 and 1655.
67 Paige, p. 43.
68 Heller, pp. 221 and 155.
69 Wilber W. Hoare, Jr., "Truman (1945–1953)", in Ernest R. May (ed.), *The Ultimate Decision: The President as Commander in Chief*, New York, NY: George Braziller, 1960, p. 193.
70 Collins, p. 120.
71 Hoare, p. 186.
72 Bradley, p. 599n.
73 Paul Y. Hammond, *Organizing for Defense*, Princeton, NJ: Princeton University Press, 1961, pp. 248 and 251.
74 Bradley, pp. 552–3 and 539.
75 Bradley, p. 585.
76 Collins, p. 211.
77 Bradley, p. 536.
78 David McCullough, *Truman*, New York, NY: Simon & Schuster, 1992, p. 801.
79 Bradley, p. 575.
80 Bradley, p. 598.
81 Margaret Truman, *Harry S. Truman*, New York, NY: William Morrow, 1973, p. 492.
82 McCullough, p. 817.
83 Bradley, p. 599.
84 Truman Library, Public Papers.
85 "Personal for MacArthur from JCS, 31 JUL 50" at www.trumanlibrary.org/whistlestop/study_collections/korea/large/sec3/kw133_1.htm.
86 Message to Congress, Truman Library, Public Papers.
87 CQ, p. 260.
88 Address to the nation, Truman Library, Public Papers.
89 FRUS 1950, p. 469.
90 NSC 73/4, A Report to the National Security Council by the Executive Secretary on the Position and Actions of the United States with respect to possible Soviet moves in the light of the Korean Situation, August 25, 1950, pp. 5 and 16.
91 FRUS 1950, pp. 463–4.
92 Bradley, p. 609.
93 Bradley, p. 557; Collins, p. 198.

8   Theodore Roosevelt and military modernization

1 Edmund Morris, *Theodore Rex*, New York, NY: Random House, 2001, p. 79.
2 Mario R. DiNunzio, *Theodore Roosevelt: An American Mind: A Selection from his Writings,* New York, NY: St. Martin's Press, 1994, p. 187.

3 Howard K. Beale, *Theodore Roosevelt and the Rise of America to World Power*, Baltimore, MD: Johns Hopkins Press, 1956, pp. 36–7; Edmund Morris, *The Rise of Theodore Roosevelt*, New York, NY: Ballantine Books, 1979, pp. 38–9.

4 DiNunzio, p. 173.

5 DiNunzio, p. 178.

6 June 2, 1897 speech, quoted in DiNunzio, p. 176.

7 DiNunzio, p. 177.

8 DiNunzio, pp. 176–7.

9 DiNunzio, p. 177.

10 Speech February, 1899 as NY Governor to the Lincoln Club dinner, quoted in DiNunzio, pp. 180–3.

11 Beale, p. 22.

12 DiNunzio, pp. 189 and 187.

13 DiNunzio, p. 187.

14 John Morton Blum, *The Republican Roosevelt*, Cambridge, MA: Harvard University Press, Second edition, 1978, p. 107.

15 Alvin M. Josephy, Jr., *On the Hill,* New York, NY: Simon & Schuster, 1979, p. 283.

16 Robert C. Byrd, *The Senate: 1789–1989, Addresses on the History of the United States Senate*, Washington, DC: GPO, 1988, p. 37.

17 Quoted in Stephen Skowronek, *The Politics Presidents Make: Leadership from John Adams to George Bush*, Cambridge, MA: Harvard University Press, 1993, p. 239.

18 Edward Ranson, "Nelson A. Miles as Commanding General, 1985–1903", *Military Affairs* 29, no. 4, Winter, 1965–6, p. 194.

19 Ranson, p. 182.

20 Ranson, p. 184.

21 Ranson, pp. 187–8.

22 Ranson, p. 190; Philip C. Jessup, *Elihu Root*, Vol. I, 1845–1909, New York, NY: Dodd, Mead, 1938, pp. 244 and 245.

23 Jessup, pp. 244–5.

24 Morris, *Theodore Rex*, p. 79.

25 Russell F. Weigley, *History of the United States Army*, New York, NY: Macmillan, 1967, p. 319.

26 Jessup, pp. 245–6.

27 Philip L. Semsch. "Elihu Root and the General Staff", *Military Affairs*, 27, no. 1, Spring, 1963, p. 21.

28 Ranson, p. 194.

29 Otto L. Nelson, Jr., *National Security and the General Staff,* Washington, DC: Infantry Journal Press, 1946, p. 54.

30 Warren Zimmerman, *First Great Triumph: How Five Americans Made Their Country a World Power*, New York, NY: Farrar, Straus and Giroux, 2002, p. 124.

31 Nelson, p. 54; Morris, *Theodore Rex,* p. 97.

32 Ranson, pp. 195 and 195n.

33 Ranson, p. 197.

34 Semsch, p. 20; Jessup, p. 261.

35 Oyos, 2000, p. 317.

36 Nelson, pp. 47–52.

37 Kenneth J. Hagan, *This People's Navy: The Making of American Sea Power,* New York, NY: Free Press, 1991, p. 232.

38 Henry P. Beers, "The Development of the Office of the Chief of Naval Operations", *Military Affairs* 10, no. 1, Spring 1946, pp. 58 and 54.

39 Quoted in Matthew M. Oyos, "Theodore Roosevelt, Congress, and the Military: U.S. Civil–Military Relations in the Early Twentieth Century", *Presidential Studies Quarterly* 30, no. 2, June 2000, p. 316.

40 Oyos, 2000, p. 317.
41 Arthur P. Wade, "Roads to the Top: An Analysis of General-Officer Selection in the United States Army, 1789–1898", *Military Affairs* 40, no. 4, December 1976, p. 162.
42 DiNunzio, p. 175.
43 DiNunzio, p. 189.
44 Quoted in Oyos, 2000, p. 322.
45 Elting E. Morison, *Men, Machines, and Modern Times,* Cambridge, MA: MIT Press, 1974, pp. 28–31.
46 Mathew M. Oyos, "Theodore Roosevelt and the Implements of War", *Journal of Military History* 60, October 1996, p. 636; Oyos, 2000, pp. 322–3.
47 Zimmerman, p. 275; Oyos, 2000, pp. 323 and 324.
48 Oyos, 2000, p. 313; Oyos 1996, pp. 635–7.
49 Oyos 1996, pp. 63–9.
50 Oyos, 1996, pp. 640–1.
51 Morison, pp. 114, 98–9 and 116–7.
52 Oyos 1996, pp. 642–4.
53 Oyos 1996, pp. 645–9.
54 Walter Millis, *Arms and Men,* New York, NY: New American Library, 1956, p. 172n; Hagan, p. 240.
55 Harold and Margaret Sprout, *The Rise of American Naval Power, 1776–1918,* Princeton, NJ: Princeton University Press, 1944, p. 267n.
56 Historical Statistics of the United States, Colonial Times to 1970, Washington, DC: Department of Commerce, 1975, p. 1141.

9 The McNamara revolution

1 Robert S. McNamara, *In Retrospect: The Tragedy and Lessons of Vietnam,* New York, NY: Random House/Times Books, 1995, p. 6.
2 Quoted in H. R. McMaster, *Dereliction of Duty,* New York, NY: HarperCollins, 1997, p. 20.
3 Public Law 85-599.
4 Alain Enthoven and K. Wayne Smith, *How Much is Enough? Shaping the Defense Program, 1961–1969,* New York, NY: Harper & Row, 1971, p. 30.
5 Deborah Shapley, *Promise and Power: The Life and Times of Robert McNamara,* Boston, MA: Little, Brown, 1993, pp. 82 and 93; Clark A. Murdock, *Defense Policy Formulation: A Comparative Analysis of the McNamara Era,* Albany, NY: State University of New York Press, 1974, p. 51.
6 McNamara, p. 17.
7 Shapley, p. 99.
8 Fred Kaplan, *The Wizards of Armageddon,* New York, NY: Simon & Schuster, 1983, pp. 273 and 271; Shapley, pp. 97–8.
9 Kennedy message to Congress, March 28, 1961, Public Papers of the President at http://www.jfklink.com/speeches/jfk/publicpapaers/1961.jfk99_61.html.
10 JFK message, March 28, 1961.
11 JFK message, March 28, 1961.
12 Shapley, pp. 103 and 101.
13 McNamara, p. 23.
14 Kaplan, p. 257; Shapley, p. 359.
15 Enthoven and Smith, p. 24.
16 McNamara testimony to House Appropriations Committee, 1964, quoted in Edward A. Kolodziej, *The Uncommon Defense and Congress, 1945–1963,* Columbus, OH: Ohio State University Press, 1966, p. 363.
17 Quoted in Kaplan, p. 256.
18 Quoted in Kaplan, p. 254.

19 Enthoven and Smith, p. 34.
20 Enthoven and Smith, p. 33.
21 Enthoven and Smith, p. 66.
22 Arnold Kanter, *Defense Politics: A Budgetary Perspective*, Chicago, IL: University of Chicago Press, 1979, p. 79.
23 Charles J. Hitch, *Decision-Making for Defense*, Berkeley, CA: University of California Press, 1965, p. 25; Enthoven and Smith, p. 21.
24 Thomas D. White, "Strategy and the Defense Intellectuals", *Saturday Evening Post*, May 4, 1963. Even in the mid-1970s the author recalls hearing former JCS Chairman Adm. Thomas Moorer complain, "We never lost a war before they created the Department of Defense, and we haven't won one since."
25 Thomas M. Coffey, *Iron Eagle: The Turbulent Life of General Curtis LeMay*, New York, NY: Crown Publishers, 1986, p. 370.
26 John M. Taylor, *General Maxwell Taylor: The Sword and the Pen*, New York, NY: Doubleday, 1989, pp. 235–6 and 276.
27 Coffey, p. 358; Dale R. Herspring, *The Pentagon and the Presidency*, Lawrence, KS: University Press of Kansas, 2005, p. 139.
28 Shapley, pp. 201–2.
29 Kennedy message, March 28, 1961.
30 Kennedy message, March 28, 1961.
31 Enthoven and Smith, pp. 175 and 207.
32 Shapley, ch. 10.
33 Richard A. Stubbing with Richard A. Mendel, *The Defense Game*, New York, NY: Harper & Row, 1986, p. 271.
34 See National Security Action Memorandum 2 at http://www.jfklibrary.org/images/nsam2.jpg; Arthur M. Schlesinger, Jr., *A Thousand Days: John F. Kennedy in the White House*, Boston, MA: Houghton Mifflin, 1965, p. 341.
35 Stephen Peter Rosen, *Winning the Next War*, Ithaca, NY: Cornell University Press, 1991, p. 101.
36 Rosen, pp. 101 and 103.
37 Enthoven and Smith, pp. 100–4.
38 Rosen, pp. 87–91.
39 Enthoven and Smith, p. 41.
40 James F. Cook, *Carl Vinson: Patriarch of the Armed Forces*, Macon, GA: Mercer University Press, 2004, p. 293.
41 Cook, pp. 294 and 295.
42 Cook, pp. 295–6.
43 Cook, p. 297.
44 Cook, p. 297.

10 The Goldwater–Nichols revoluton fron above

1 Admiral William J. Crowe, Jr. with David Chanoff, *The Line of Fire: From Washington to the Gulf, the Politics and Battles of the New Military War*, New York, NY: Simon & Schuster, 1993, p. 159.
2 James R. Locher, III. *Victory on the Potomac: The Goldwater–Nichols Act Unifies the Pentagon*, College Station, TX: Texas A&M University Press, 2002, p. 11. This chapter draws heavily on Jim Locher's comprehensive and definitive account of the passage of Goldwater–Nichols and on the personal observations of the author, a Senate staffer during this period.
3 Quoted in Locher, p. 49.
4 Quoted in Locher, p. 47.
5 David C. Jones, "What's Wrong with our Defense Establishment", *New York Times Magazine*, November 7, 1982, p. 38ff.
6 Locher, p. 31.

7 Locher, pp. 48 and 50.
8 Quoted in Locher, p. 49.
9 Locher, pp. 54–5.
10 Locher, p. 34; David C. Jones, "Why the Joint Chiefs Must Change", *Armed Forces Journal International*, March 1982, pp. 65 and 66.
11 Edward C. Meyer, Edward C., "The JCS: How Much Reform is Needed?", *Armed Forces Journal International*, April 1982, p. 88.
12 Locher, p. 62.
13 Locher, pp. 67 and 71.
14 Locher, p. 75.
15 Locher, p. 78.
16 Quoted in Locher, p. 79.
17 *Congressional Quarterly, Congress and the Nation* vol. VI, 1981–1984, Washington, DC: Congressional Quarterly, 1985, p. 225.
18 Locher, pp. 100, 101, 109 and 111.
19 David C. Martin and John Walcott, *Best Laid Plans: The Inside Story of America's War Against Terrorism*, New York, NY: Touchstone Book by Simon & Schuster, 1988, p. 134.
20 Locher, pp. 135 and 311; Colin Powell with Joseph E. Persico, *My American Journey*, New York, NY: Random House, 1995, p. 292.
21 Locher, pp. 142 and 152–3.
22 Locher, p. 243.
23 Quoted in Locher, p. 119.
24 Powell, p. 298.
25 Locher, pp. 255 and 269.
26 Locher, pp. 189 and 270–2.
27 Locher, pp. 177 and 174–5.
28 Locher, pp. 113 and 83.
29 Locher, pp. 114–6 and 133.
30 Locher, pp. 186.
31 Locher, pp. 191–3.
32 Locher, pp. 168–71.
33 Locher, pp. 284 and 281.
34 *Congressional Quarterly, Congress and the Nation* vol. VII, 1985–1988, Washington, DC: Congressional Quarterly, 1990, p. 300.
35 Locher, p. 422.
36 Locher, pp. 318 and 299.
37 Quoted in Locher, pp. 324 and 326.
38 Locher, pp. 334 and 342.
39 Locher, pp. 329 and 330–1.
40 Locher, p. 352.
41 Locher, p. 386.
42 Crowe, pp. 148–9.
43 Crowe, pp. 152–3 and 155.
44 Locher, pp. 388, 3, 9 and 10.
45 Locher, p. 11.
46 Locher, pp. 387 and 404.
47 Locher, pp. 407, 408 and 410.
48 Locher, p. 403.
49 Locher, pp. 417 and 418.
50 Crowe, p. 159.
51 Locher, p. 424.
52 Locher, p. 433.

11 The Bush–Rumsfeld wars and transformation

1 Campaign speech at the Citadel, September 23, 1999.
2 Rowan Scarborough, *Rumsfeld's War*, Washington, DC: Regnery, 2004, p. 136.
3 David J. Rothkopf, *Running the World: The Inside Story of the National Security Council and the Architects of American Power*, New York, NY: Public Affairs, 2005, p. 407.
4 James Mann, *Rise of the Vulcans: The History of Bush's War Cabinet*, New York, NY: Viking, 2004, pp. 251–2.
5 Interview with person involved in Citadel speech preparation.
6 Interview.
7 Citadel speech, September 23, 1999.
8 Rothkopf, p. 422.
9 Mann, pp. 266–7; Midge Decter, *Rumsfeld*, New York, NY: Regan Books, 2003, p. 137.
10 *Transforming Defense: National Security in the 21st Century*. Report of the National Defense Panel. December 1997. Accessible at www.dtic.mil/ndp; Mann, p. 290.
11 Confirmation hearing before Senate Armed Services Committee, January 11, 2001, Lexis-Nexis transcript, pp. 11 and 17; Thomas E. Ricks, "Rumsfeld, Bush Agendas Overlap Little", *Washington Post,* January 11, 2001.
12 Pat Towell, "The Rumsfeld Mandate: Invent the Military's Future", *CQ Weekly*, May 12, 2001, p. 1054.
13 Rowan Scarborough, *Rumsfeld's War*, Washington, NY: Regnery, 2004, p. 137.
14 George C. Wilson, "Guns Aplenty, Butter be Damned", *National Journal*, January 27, 2001, pp. 252–3; "Washington Wire", *Wall Street Journal*, April 13, 2001.
15 Seymour M. Hersh, *Chain of Command*, New York, NY: HarperCollins, 2004, p. 271; Dana Priest, *The Mission*, New York, NY: W.W. Norton, 2003, p. 28.
16 Scarborough, pp. 113 and 127.
17 Thom Shanker and Eric Schmitt, "Rumsfeld Seeks Consensus through Jousting", *New York Times,* March 19, 2003.
18 Thomas E. Ricks, "Rumsfeld on High Wire of Defense Reform", *Washington Post,* May 20, 2001; Ricks, "Rumsfeld, Joint Chiefs Spar over roles in Retooling Military", *Washington Post,* May 25, 2001; Scarborough, pp. 121–2.
19 Nancy Soderber, *The Superpower Myth*, New York, NY: John Wiley & Sons, 2005, p. 120.
20 Robert Kagan and William Kristol, "No Defense", *Weekly Standard,* July 23, 2001; Greg Jaffe and John D. McKinnon, "Defense-Budget Increase of $18.5 Billion draws fire for being too much or little", *Wall Street Journal*, June 25, 2001.
21 White House News conference transcript, Crawford, Texas, August 24, 2001.
22 Thom Shanker, "Defense Chief may leave size of field forces up to services", *New York Times,* August 17, 2001.
23 Mann, pp. 290–1.
24 Remarks as delivered by Secretary of Defense, September 10, 2001. DOD transcript.
25 Bob Woodward, *Bush at War*, New York, NY: Simon & Schuster, 2002, pp. 15 and 19.
26 Woodward, *Bush at War,* pp. 38 and 145.
27 Woodward, *Bush at War,* p. 251.
28 Rothkopf, pp. 419 and 407.
29 Woodward, *Bush at War,* pp. 48–9, 83–5 and 107.
30 Woodward, *Bush at War,* pp. 79–80, 32 and 88.
31 Woodward, *Bush at War,* pp. 50–1, 76 and 97.
32 Peter J. Boyer, "The New War Machine", *The New Yorker,* June 30, 2003, p. 58.

33 General Tommy Franks, *American Soldier*, New York, NY: Regan Books, 2004, pp. 295 and 313.
34 Woodward, *Bush At War*, pp. 157–8.
35 Franks, pp. 269–72.
36 Richard Brookhiser, "The Mind of George W. Bush", *The Atlantic*, April 2003, p. 69.
37 Woodward, *Bush At War*, p. 300; Franks, p. 300.
38 Franks, p. 300.
39 Woodward, *Bush At War*, p. 245.
40 Franks, p. 315.
41 Hersh, pp. 249–50; Franks, pp. 333, 366, 410 and 433; Bob Woodward, *Plan of Attack*, New York, NY: Simon & Schuster, 2004, pp. 40, 96, 118, 121, 329 and 406.
42 Franks, pp. 362 and 440–1; Woodward, *Plan of Attack*, pp. 98 and 207–8.
43 Woodward, *Plan of Attack*, pp. 101 and 331; Franks, p. 372.
44 Woodward, *Plan of Attack*, pp. 137 and 232–3.
45 Thomas E. Ricks, "Military Sees Iraq Invasion Put on Hold", *Washington Post*, May 24, 2002; Dave Moniz and Jonathan Weisman, "Military Leaders Question Iraq Plan", *USA Today*, May 23, 2002; David A. Fulghum, "Military Wants Congressional OK before Iraq Offensive", *Aviation Week*, August 12, 2002, p. 31.
46 S.J. Res. 23, one hundred and seventh Congress, first session.
47 Woodward, *Bush At War*, pp. 198–9.
48 National Security Strategy Report, The White House, September 17, 2002.
49 Woodward, *Plan of Attack*, pp. 197–9 and 434.
50 *CQ Almanac, 2002*, vol. LVIII, Washington: Congressional Quarterly, 2003, pp. 9-3–9-5.
51 Public Law, pp. 107–243.
52 Public Law, pp. 107–296.
53 Amy Belasco and Daniel Else, "Military Construction in Support of Afghanistan and Iraq", Congressional Research Service Memorandum, April 11, 2005, p. 11.
54 Woodward, *Plan of Attack*, pp. 282–4; Jay Garner interview for Frontline, July 17, 2003, www.pbs.org/wgbh/pages/frontline/shows/truth/interviews/garner.html; James Fallows, "Blind into Baghdad", *The Atlantic*, January–February 2004, pp. 64–5.
55 Fallows, p. 65; Franks, p. 393.
56 Fallows, pp. 72–3.
57 Fallows, p. 73; Garner Frontline interview; Thomas E. Ricks interview for Frontline, January 28, 2004, at www.pbs.org/wgbh/pages/frontline/shows/truth/interviews/ricks.html.
58 Franks, p. 392.
59 See *Military Transformation: A Strategic Approach*, Director, Force Transformation, Office of the Secretary of Defense, Fall 2003.
60 Thomas P. M. Barnett, "Donald Rumsfeld: Old Man in a Hurry", *Esquire*, July 2005.
61 Barnett.
62 Barnett.
63 Barnett.
64 Thom Shanker and Eric Schmitt, "Rumsfeld Seeks Leaner Army, and a Full Term", *New York Times*, May 10, 2005.
65 Linwood B. Carter and Thomas Coipuram, Jr., "Defense Authorization and Appropriations Bills: A Chronology, FY1970–FY2006", CRS Report for Congress, May 23, 2005; Belasco, p. 11.
66 Barnett.

12 Conclusions: US civil-military relations under stress

1 Peter Feaver, *Armed Servants: Agency, Oversight, and Civil–Military Relations*, Cambridge, MA: Harvard University Press, 2003, p. 6.

2 William R. Emerson, "F.D.R.", in Ernest R. May, *The Ultimate Decision: The President as Command in Chief*, New York, NY: George Braziller, 1960, p. 157.

3 E. Wayne Carp, *To Starve the Army at Pleasure*, Chapel Hill, NC: University of North Carolina Press, 1984, p. 37.

4 Eliot A. Cohen, *Supreme Command: Soldiers, Statesmen, and Leadership in Wartime*, New York, NY: Free Press, 2002, pp. 241–2.

5 For example, see: Richard H. Kohn, "Out of Control: The Crisis in Civil–Military Relations", *The National Interest*, vol. 35, spring, 1994, pp. 3–17; John Hillen, "Must U.S. Military Culture Reform?", *Orbis*, vol. 43, winter 1999, pp. 43–57; Deborah Avant, "Conflicting Indicators of 'Crisis' in American Civil–Military Relations", *Armed Forces & Society*, vol. 24, Spring 1998, pp. 375–88; Michael C. Desch, "Explaining the Gap: Vietnam, the Republicanization of the South, and the End of the Mass Army", in Peter D. Feaver and Richard H. Kohn (eds), *Soldiers and Civilians: The Civil–Military Gap and American National Security*, Cambridge, MA: MIT Press, 2001.

6 Michael Desch, *Civilian Control of the Military: The Changing Security Environment*, Baltimore, MD: Johns Hopkins University Press, 1999; Kenneth W. Kemp and Charles Hudlin, "Civil Supremacy over the Military: Its Nature and Limits", *Armed Forces and Society*, 19, 1, Fall 1992, p. 8.

7 Allan R. Millett, "The American Political System and Civilian Control of the Military: A Historical Perspective", Mershon Center Position Papers in the Policy Sciences, Number 4, April 1979, p. 3.

8 For these historical cases, see: May, *Ultimate Decision*; John Seigenthaler, *James K. Polk*, New York, NY: Henry Holt/Times Books, 2003; Otis A. Singletary, *The Mexican War*, Chicago, IL: University of Chicago Press, 1960; Donald R. Hickey, *The War of 1812*, Urbana, IL: University of Illinois Press, 1990.

9 Donald Smythe, "'Your Authority in France Will be Supreme': The Baker-Pershing Relationship in World War I", in Lloyd J. Matthews and Dale E. Brown, *The Parameters of War*, Washington, DC: Pergamon-Brassey's, 1987, pp. 138–48.

10 See Dale R. Herspring, *The Pentagon and the Presidency: Civil–Military Relations from FDR to George W. Bush*, Lawrence, KS: University Press of Kansas, 2005.

11 Quoted in Seigenthaler, p. 146.

12 See Stephen Peter Rosen, *Winning the Next War*, Ithaca, NY: Cornell University Press, 1991.

13 Samuel Huntington, *The Soldier and the State*, Cambridge, MA: Harvard University Press, 1957; Morris Janowitz, *The Professional Soldier*, New York, NY: Free Press, 1960; James Burk, "Theories of Democratic Civil–Military Relations", *Armed Forces and Society*, 29, 1, Fall 2002, pp. 7–29.

14 See Deborah D. Avant, *Political Institutions and Military Change: Lessons from Peripheral Wars*, Ithaca, NY: Cornell University Press, 1994 and Amy B. Zegart, *Flawed by Design: The Evolution of the CIA, JCS, and NSC*, Stanford, CA: Stanford University Press, 1999.

15 Feaver, *Armed Servants*, pp. 58–60 and 131.

16 Peter D. Feaver, "Delegation, Monitoring, and Civilian Control of the Military: agency theory and American civil–military relations", Olin Institute for strategic studies, Harvard University, working paper no. 4, May 1996, pp. 23 and 37.

17 Feaver, *Armed Servants*, p. 98.

18 Avant, *Political Institutions and Military Change*.

19 Deborah D. Avant, "Are the Reluctant Warriors Out of Control?", *Security Studies* 6, no. 2, winter 1996/97, pp. 57–8, 87 and 88.

20 Amy B. Zegart, *Flawed by Design: The Evolution of the CIA, JCS, and NSC*, Stanford, CA: Stanford University Press, 1999: pp. 7 and 10.
21 Cohen, *Supreme Command.*
22 Huntington, *Soldier,* p. 177.
23 Richard K. Betts, *Soldiers, Statesmen, and Cold War Crises*, New York, NY: Columbia University Press, Morningside Edition, 1991, p. 218.
24 Feaver, *Armed Servants,* pp. 133–45.
25 For a description of this interplay, see George W. Wilson, *This War Really Matters: Inside the Fight for Defense Dollars*, Washington, DC: CQ Press, 2000.
26 William B. Skelton, "Officers and Politicians: The Origins of Army Politics in the United States before the Civil War", in Peter Karsten (ed.), *The Military in America,* rev. ed., New York, NY: The Free Press, 1986, pp. 91 and 97; William B. Skelton, *An American Profession of Arms: The Army Officer Corps, 1784–1861,* Lawrence, KS: University Press of Kansas, 1992, p. 283.
27 Skelton, *An American Profession of Arms,* p. xiii.
28 Ole R. Holsti, "A Widening Gap between the U.S. military and Civilian Society?", International Security, vol. 23, no. 2, winter 1998/99, pp. 5–42, cites from p 11.
29 Michael Desch, "Explaining the Gap: Vietnam, the Republicanization of the South, and the end of the Mass Army", ch. 8 in Peter D. Feaver and Richard H. Kohn (eds), *Soldiers and Civilians: The Civil–Military Gap and American National Security*, Cambridge, MA: MIT Press, 2001.

Bibliography

Abbott, Richard H., *Cobbles in Congress: The Life of Henry Wilson, 1812–1875*, Lexington, KY: University Press of Kentucky, 1972.

Acheson, Dean, *Present at the Creation: My Years in the State Department*, New York, NY: W.W. Norton, 1969.

Addington, Larry H., *The Patterns of War since the Eighteenth Century*, Bloomington, IN: Indiana University Press, Second Edition, 1994.

Adler, Selig, *The Isolationist Impulse*, New York, NY: Abelard-Schuman Ltd, 1957.

Avant, Deborah D., "Conflicting Indicators of 'Crisis' in American Civil–Military Relations", *Armed Forces and Society,* vol. 24, no. 3, Spring 1998, pp. 375–88.

Avant, Deborah D., "Are the Reluctant Warriors Out of Control?", *Security Studies* vol. 6, no. 2 (winter 1996/97): pp. 51–90.

Avant, Deborah D., *Political Institutions and Military Change: Lessons from Peripheral Wars*, Ithaca, NY: Cornell University Press, 1994.

Bacevich, A.J., "The paradox of professionalism: Eisenhower, Ridgway, and the Challenge to Civilian Control, 1952–1955", *The Journal of Military History*, April 1997.

Barnett, Thomas P. M., "Donald Rumsfeld: Old Man in a Hurry", *Esquire*, July 2005.

Beale, Howard K., *Theodore Roosevelt and the Rise of America to World Power,* Baltimore, MD: Johns Hopkins Press, 1956.

Beers, Henry P., "The Development of the Office of the Chief of Naval Operations", *Military Affairs* vol. 10, no. 1, Spring 1946, pp. 40–68.

Belasco, Amy and Daniel Else, "Military Construction in Support of Afghanistan and Iraq", Congressional Research Service Memorandum, April 11, 2005.

Bell, Rudolph M., *Party and Faction in American Politics: The House of Representatives, 1789–1801*, Westport, CT: Greenwood Press, 1973.

Betts, Richard K., *Soldiers, Statesmen, and Cold War Crises*, New York, NY: Columbia University Press, Morningside Edition, 1991.

Bianco, William T. and Jamie Markham, "Vanishing Veterans: The Decline of Military Experience in the U.S. Congress", in Peter D. Feaver and Richard H. Kohn (eds), *Soldiers and Civilians: The Civil–Military Gap and American National Security*, Cambridge, MA: MIT Press, 2001.

Binder, L. James, *Lemnitzer: A Soldier for His Time*, Washington, DC: Brassey's, 1997.

Blum, John Morton, *The Republican Roosevelt*, second edition, Cambridge, MA: Harvard University Press, 1977.

Boettcher, Thomas D., *First Call: The Making of the Modern U.S. Military, 1945–1953*, Boston, MA: Little, Brown, 1992.

Bogue, Allan G., *The Earnest Men: Republicans of the Civil War Senate*, Ithaca, NY: Cornell University Press, 1981.

Boot, Max, *The Savage Wars of Peace: Small Wars and the Rise of American Power*, New York, NY: Basic Books, 2002.

Bowler, R. Arthur, "Logistics and Operations in the American Revolution", in Don Higginbotham (ed.), *Reconsiderations on the Revolutionary War*, Westport, CT: Greenwood Press, 1978.

Boyer, Peter J., "The New War Machine", *The New Yorker*, June 30, 2003, pp. 55–71.

Bradley, Omar N. and Clay Blair, *A General's Life*, New York, NY: Simon & Schuster, 1983.

Brookhiser, Richard, "The Mind of George W. Bush", *The Atlantic*, April 2003, pp. 56–69.

Burk, James, "Theories of Democratic Civil–Military Relations", *Armed Forces and Society*, vol. 29. no. 1, Fall 2002, pp. 7–29.

Byrd, Robert C.,*The Senate: 1789–1989, Addresses on the History of the United States Senate*, Washington, DC: GPO, 1988.

Cantril, Hadley, *Public Opinion, 1936–1946*, Princeton, NJ: Princeton University Press, 1951.

Carman, Harry J. and Reinhard H. Luthin, *Lincoln and the Patronage*, Gloucester, MA: Peter Smith, 1964.

Carp, E. Wayne, *To Starve the Army at Pleasure*, Chapel Hill, NC: University of North Carolina Press, 1984.

Carter, Linwood B. and Thomas Coipuram, Jr., "Defense Authorization and Appropriations Bills: A Chronology, FY1970–FY2006", CRS Report for Congress, May 23, 2005.

Challener, Richard D., *Admirals, Generals, and American Foreign Policy, 1898–1914*, Princeton, NJ: Princeton University Press, 1973.

Chernow, Ron, *Alexander Hamilton*, New York, NY: Penguin Press, 2004.

Clifford, Clark, *Counsel to the President: A Memoir*, New York, NY: Random House, 1991.

Clodfelter, Mark, *The Limits of Air Power: The American Bombing of North Vietnam*, New York, NY: Free Press, 1989.

Coffey, Thomas M., *Iron Eagle: The Turbulent Life of General Curtis LeMay*, New York, NY: Crown Publishers, 1986.

Cohen, Eliot A., *Supreme Command: Soldiers, Statesmen, and Leadership in Wartime*, New York, NY: Free Press, 2002.

Collier, Christopher and James Lincoln Collier, *Decision in Philadelphia: The Constitutional Convention of 1787*, New York, NY: Ballantine Books, 1986.

Collins, Joseph Lawton, *War in Peacetime: The History and Lessons of Korea*, Boston, MA: Houghton Mifflin, 1969.

Condit, Doris M., *History of the Office of the Secretary of Defense. Volume II. The Test of War, 1950–1953*, Washington, DC: Historical Office, Office of the Secretary of Defense, 2001.

Congress and the Nation, 1945–1964. Washington, DC: Congressional Quarterly, 1965.

Congress and the Nation, vol. II, 1965–1968, Washington, DC: CQ Press, 1969.

Congress and the Nation, vol. III, 1969–1972, Washington, DC: CQ Press, 1973.

Congress and the Nation, vol. IV, 1973–1976, Washington, DC: CQ Press, 1977.

Congress and the Nation vol. VI, 1981–1984, Washington, DC: Congressional Quarterly, 1985.

Congress and the Nation vol. VII, 1985–1988, Washington, DC: Congressional Quarterly, 1990.

Cook, James F., *Carl Vinson: Patriarch of the Armed Forces,* Macon, GA: Mercer University Press, 2004.

CQ Almanac, 2002, vol. LVIII, Washington, DC: Congressional Quarterly, 2003.

Crowe, Admiral William J., Jr. with David Chanoff, *The Line of Fire: From Washington to the Gulf, the Politics and Battles of the New Military War,* New York, NY: Simon & Schuster, 1993.

Cunliffe, Marcus, *Soldiers & Civilians: The Martial Spirit in America, 1775–1865,* Boston, MA: Little, Brown, 1968.

Currie, David P., *The Constitution in Congress: The Federalist Period, 1789–1801,* Chicago, IL: University of Chicago Press, 1997.

Dallek, Robert, *Franklin D. Roosevelt and American Foreign Policy, 1932–1945,* New York, NY: Oxford University Press, 1995.

Davis, Kenneth S., *FDR: The War President, 1940–43: A History,* New York, NY: Random House, 2000.

DeConde, Alexander, *The Quasi-War,* New York, NY: Scribner's, 1966.

Decter, Midge, *Rumsfeld,* New York, NY: Regan Books, 2003.

Desch, Michael C. "Explaining the Gap: Vietnam, the Republicanization of the South, and the End of the Mass Army", in Peter D. Feaver and Richard H. Kohn, (eds), *Soldiers and Civilians: The Civil–Military Gap and American National Security,* Cambridge, MA: MIT Press, 2001.

Desch, Michael C., *Civilian Control of the Military: The Changing Security Environment,* Baltimore, MD: Johns Hopkins University Press, 1999.

DiNunzio, Mario R., *Theodore Roosevelt: An American Mind: A Selection from his Writings,* New York, NY: St. Martin's Press, 1994.

Donald, David Herbert, *Lincoln,* New York, NY: Simon & Schuster, 1995.

Doyle, Elisabeth Joan, "The Conduct of the War, 1861", in Arthur M. Schlesinger, Jr. and Roger Bruns (eds), *Congress Investigates, 1792–1974,* New York, NY: Chelsea House Publishers, 1975.

Dupuy, R. Ernest and Trevor N. Dupuy, *The Harper Encyclopedia of Military History,* New York, NY: HarperCollins, 1993.

Ehrlichman, John, *Witness to Power: The Nixon Years,* New York, NY: Simon & Schuster, 1982.

Elkins, Stanley and Eric McKitrick, *The Age of Federalism,* New York, NY: Oxford University Press, 1993.

Emerson, William R., "F.D.R.", in Ernest R. May (ed.), *The Ultimate Decision: The President as Command in Chief,* New York, NY: George Braziller, 1960.

Enthoven, Alain and K. Wane Smith, *How Much is Enough? Shaping the Defense Program, 1961–1969,* New York, NY: Harper & Row, 1971.

Fallows, James. "Blind into Baghdad", *The Atlantic,* January–February 2004, pp. 53–74.

Feaver, Peter D., *Armed Servants: Agency, Oversight, and Civil–Military Relations,* Cambridge, MA: Harvard University Press, 2003.

Feaver, Peter D., "Delegation, Monitoring, and Civilian Control of the Military: agency theory and American civil–military relations", Olin Institute for Strategic Studies, Harvard University, working paper no. 4, May 1996.

Feaver, Peter D. and Richard H. Kohn (eds), *Soldiers and Civilians: The Civil–Military Gap and American National Security*, Cambridge, MA: MIT Press, 2001.

Ferling, John, "'Father and Protector' President Johns Adams and Congress in the Quasi-War Crisis", in Kenneth R. Bowling and Donald R. Kennon (eds), *Neither Separate Nor Equal: Congress in the 1790s*, Athens, OH: Ohio University Press, 2000, pp. 294–332.

Foreign Relations of the United States, 1949, Volume I: National Security Affairs, Foreign Economic Policy (FRUS 1949), Washington, DC: GPO, 1976.

Foreign Relations of the United States, 1950, Volume I: National Security Affairs, Foreign Economic Policy (FRUS 1950), Washington, DC: GPO, 1977.

Franks, General Tommy, *American Soldier*, New York, NY: Regan Books, 2004.

Freeman, Douglas Southall, *George Washington. Volume Three: Planter and Patriot*, New York, NY: Scribner's, 1951.

"Frontline" interviews with Jay Garner and Thomas E. Ricks, available at www.pbs.org/wgbh/pages/frontline/shows/truth/interviews/.

Fulghum, David A., "Military Wants Congressional OK before Iraq Offensive", *Aviation Week*, August 12, 2002, p. 31.

Gelb, Leslie H. with Richard K. Betts, *The Irony of Vietnam: The System Worked*, Washington, DC: Brookings, 1979.

Gibbons, William Conrad, *The U.S. Government and the Vietnam War: Executive and Legislative Roles and Relationships, Part IV: July 1965–January 1968*, Princeton, NJ: Princeton University Press, 1995.

Goodwin, Doris Kearns, *No Ordinary Time*, New York, NY: Simon & Schuster, 1994.

Greenfield, Kent Roberts, *American Strategy in World War II: A Reconsideration*, Malabar, FL: Robert E. Krieger Publishing Co., 1982.

Hagan, Kenneth J., *This People's Navy: The Making of American Sea Power*, New York, NY: Free Press, 1991.

Halberstam, David. *War in a Time of Peace: Bush, Clinton, and the Generals*, New York, NY: Scribner, 2001.

Halberstam, David, *The Best and the Brightest*, New York, NY: Ballantine, 1993.

Haldeman, H.R., *The Haldeman Diaries*, New York, NY: Putnam, 1994.

Hammond, Paul Y. "Super Carriers and B-36 Bombers: Appropriations, Strategy and Politics", in Harold Stein (ed.), *American Civil–Military Decisions: A Book of Case Studies*, Birmingham, AL: University of Alabama Press, 1963.

Hammond, Paul Y., "NSC-68: Prologue to Rearmament", in Warner R. Schilling, Paul Y. Hammond, Glenn H. Snyder, *Strategy, Politics, and Defense Budgets*, New York, NY: Columbia University Press, 1962.

Hammond, Paul Y., *Organizing for Defense*, Princeton, NJ: Princeton University Press, 1961.

Hardeman, D. B. and Donald C. Bacon, *Rayburn: A Biography*, Austin, TX: Texas Monthly Press, 1987.

Hatch, Louis Clinton, *The Administration of the American Revolutionary Army*, New York, NY: Burt Franklin, 1904.

Heller, Francis H. (ed.), *The Truman White House: The Administration of the Presidency, 1945–1953*, Lawrence, KS: Regents Press of Kansas, 1980.

Hendrick, Burton J., *Lincoln's War Cabinet*, Boston, MA: Little, Brown, 1946.

Herring, Pendleton, *The Impact of War*, New York, NY: Farrar & Rinehart, Inc., 1941.

Hersh, Seymour M., *Chain of Command*, New York, NY: HarperCollins, 2004.

Hersh, Seymour M., *The Price of Power: Kissinger in the Nixon White House*, New York, NY: Summit, 1983.

Herspring, Dale R. *The Pentagon and the Presidency: Civil–Military Relations from FDR to George W. Bush*, Lawrence, KS: The University Press of Kansas, 2005.

Hickey, Donald R., *The War of 1812*, Urbana, IL: University of Illinois Press, 1990.

Higginbotham, Don, *War and Society in Revolutionary America*, Columbia, SC: University of South Carolina Press, 1988.

Higginbotham, Don, *The War of American Independence*, New York, NY: Macmillan, 1971.

Hillen, John, "Must U.S. Military Culture Reform?", *Orbis*, vol. 43, winter 1999, pp. 43–57.

Hilsman, Roger, *To Move a Nation*, Garden City, NY: Doubleday, 1967.

Historical Statistics of the United States, Colonial Times to 1970, Washington, DC: Department of Commerce, 1975.

Hitch, Charles J., *Decision-Making for Defense*, Berkeley, CA: University of California Press, 1965.

Hoare, Wilber W., Jr. "Truman (1945–1953)", in Ernest R. May (ed.),*The Ultimate Decision: The President as Commander in Chief*, New York, NY: George Braziller, 1960.

Hogan, Michael J., *A Cross of Iron: Harry S. Truman and the Origins of the National Security State, 1945–1954*, Cambridge: Cambridge University Press, 1998.

Hoopes, Townsend and Douglas Brinkley, *Driven Patriot: The Life and Times of James Forrestal*, New York, NY: Knopf, 1992.

Horgan, Lucille E., *Forged in War: The Continental Congress and the Origin of Military Supply and Acquisition Policy*, Westport, CT: Greenwood Press, 2002.

Huntington, Samuel P., *The Soldier and the State*, Cambridge, MA: Harvard University Press, 1957.

Huzar, Elias, *The Purse and the Sword; Control of the Army by Congress through Military Appropriations, 1933–1950*, Ithaca, NY: Cornell University Press, 1950.

Jackson, Robert H., *That Man: An Insider's Portrait of Franklin D. Roosevelt*, New York, NY: Oxford University Press, 2003.

Jaffe,Greg and John D. McKinnon, "Defense-Budget Increase of $18.5 Billion draws fire for being too much or little", *Wall Street Journal*, June 25, 2001.

Jessup, Philip C., *Elihu Root*, Vol. I, 1845–1909, New York, NY: Dodd, Mead, 1938.

Jones, David C., "What's Wrong with our Defense Establishment", *New York Times Magazine*, November 7, 1982, p. 38ff.

Jones, David C., "Why the Joint Chiefs Must Change", *Armed Forces Journal International* (March, 1982), pp. 62–70.

Josephy, Alvin M., Jr., *On the Hill*, New York, NY: Simon & Schuster, 1979.

Journals of the Continental Congress, available at http://memory.loc.gov/ammem/amlawlwjclink.html.

Kagan, Robert and William Kristol, "No Defense", *Weekly Standard*, July 23, 2001.

Kanter, Arnold, *Defense Politics: A Budgetary Perspective*, Chicago. IL: University of Chicago Press, 1979.

Kaplan, Fred, *The Wizards of Armageddon*, New York, NY: Simon & Schuster, 1983.

Karnow, Stanley, *Vietnam: A History*, New York, NY: Penguin Books, 1983.

Kemp, Kenneth W. and Charles Hudlin, "Civil Supremacy over the Military: Its Nature and Limits", *Armed Forces and Society* vol. 19, no. 1, Fall 1992, pp. 7–26.

Ketchum, Richard M., *The Borrowed Years, 1938–1941: America on the Way to War*, New York, NY: Random House, 1989.

Kimball, Jeffrey, *The Vietnam War Files*, Lawrence, KS: University Press of Kansas, 2004.

Kinnard, Douglas, *The Secretary of Defense*, Lexington, KY: The University Press of Kentucky, 1980.

Kissinger, Henry, *Ending the Vietnam War*, New York, NY: Simon & Schuster, 2003

Kissinger, Henry, *Diplomacy*, New York, NY: Simon & Schuster, 1994.

Klein, Maury, *Days of Defiance: Sumter, Secession, and the Coming of the Civil War*, New York, NY: Knopf, 1997.

Kohn, Richard H., "Out of Control: The Crisis in Civil–Military Relations", *The National Interest*, vol. 35, spring, 1994, pp. 3–17.

Kohn, Richard H. (ed.), *The U.S. Military under the Constitution, 1789–1989*, New York, NY: New York University Press, 1991.

Kohn, Richard H., "American Generals of the Revolution: Subordination and Restraint", in Don Higginbotham (ed.), *Reconsiderations on the Revolutionary War*, Westport, CT: 1978.

Kohn, Richard H., *Eagle and Sword: The Beginnings of the Military Establishment in America*, New York, NY: Free Press, 1975.

Kolodziej, Edward A., *The Uncommon Defense and Congress, 1945–1963*, Columbus, OH: Ohio State University Press, 1966.

Kull, Steven and I. M. Destler, *Misreading the Public: The Myth of a New Isolationism*, Washington, DC: Brookings, 1999.

Kwasny, Mark V., *Washington's Partisan War, 1775–1783*, Kent, OH: Kent State University Press, 1996.

Laird, Melvin R., Oral History Interviews, Historical Office of the Secretary of Defense, August 18, 1986; September 2, 1986; October 29, 1986.

Larrabee, Eric, *Commander in Chief*, New York, NY: Harper & Row, 1987.

Leahy, William D., *I Was There*, New York, NY: Arno Press, 1979.

Locher, James R., III, *Victory on the Potomac: The Goldwater–Nichols Act Unifies the Pentagon*, College Station, TX: Texas A&M University Press, 2002.

Logevall, Fredrik, "The Vietnam War", in Julian E. Zelizer (ed.), *The American Congress*, Boston, MA: Houghton Mifflin, 2004.

Maney, Patrick, "The Forgotten New Deal Congress", in Julian E. Zelizer (ed.), *The American Congress*, Boston, MA: Houghton Mifflin, 2004.

Mann, James, *Rise of the Vulcans: The History of Bush's War Cabinet*, New York, NY: Viking, 2004.

Martin, David C. and John Walcott, *Best Laid Plans: The Inside Story of America's War Against Terrorism*, New York, NY: Touchstone Book by Simon & Schuster, 1988.

Martin, James Kirby and Mark Edward Lender, *A Respectable Army: The Military Origins of the Republic, 1763–1789*, Arlington Heights, IL: Harlans Davidson, 1982.

Matloff, Maurice, *American Military History*, Washington, DC: Office of the Chief of Military History, United States Army, 1969.

May, Ernest R., *Imperial Democracy*, New York, NY: Harper, 1973.

May, Ernest R. (ed.), *The Ultimate Decision: The President as Commander in Chief*, New York, NY: George Braziller, 1960.

McCullough, David, *Truman*, New York, NY: Simon & Schuster, 1992.

McMaster, H.R., *Dereliction of Duty*, New York, NY: HarperCollins, 1997.

McNamara, Robert S., *In Retrospect: The Tragedy and Lessons of Vietnam*, New York, NY: Random House/Times Books, 1995.

McPherson, James M., *Battle Cry of Freedom: The Civil War Era*, New York, NY: Oxford University Press, 1988.

Meyer, Edward C., "The JCS: How Much Reform is Needed?", *Armed Forces Journal International* (April 1982), pp. 82–90.

Military Transformation: A Strategic Approach, Director, Force Transformation, Office of the Secretary of Defense, Fall 2003.

Millett, Allan R., "The American Political System and Civilian Control of the Military: A Historical Perspective", Mershon Center Position Papers in the Policy Sciences, Number 4, April 1979.

Millis, Walter, *Arms and Men*, New York, NY: New American Library, 1956.

Millis, Walter (ed.).*The Forrestal Diaries*, New York, NY: Viking, 1951.

Moniz, Dave and Jonathan Weisman, "Military Leaders Question Iraq Plan", *USA Today*, May 23, 2002

Montcross, Lynn, *The Reluctant Rebels: The Story of the Continental Congress, 1774–1789*, New York, NY: Harper & Brothers, 1950.

Morison, Elting E., *Men, Machines, and Modern Times*, Cambridge, MA: MIT Press, 1974.

Morris, Edmund, *Theodore Rex*, New York, NY: Random House, 2001.

Morris, Edmund, *The Rise of Theodore Roosevelt*, New York, NY: Ballantine Books, 1979.

Morris, Richard B., *Encyclopedia of American History*, New York, NY: Harper & Brothers, 1953.

Murdock, Clark A., *Defense Policy Formulation: A Comparative Analysis of the McNamara Era*, Albany, NY: State University of New York Press, 1974.

Murray, Williamson and Allan R. Millett, *Military Innovation in the Interwar Period*, Cambridge: Cambridge University Press, 1996.

National Intelligence Council, *Estimative Products on Vietnam, 1948–1975*, Washington, DC: GPO, 2005.

Nelson, Otto L., Jr,. *National Security and the General Staff*, Washington, DC: Infantry Journal Press, 1946.

Nixon, Richard, *RN: The Memoirs of Richard Nixon*, New York, NY: Grosset & Dunlap, 1978.

Oberdorfer, Don, *Senator Mansfield*, Washington, DC: Smithsonian Books, 2003.

Oyos, Matthew M., "Theodore Roosevelt, Congress, and the Military: U.S. Civil–Military Relations in the Early Twentieth Century", *Presidential Studies Quarterly* vol. 30, no. 2, June 2000, pp. 312–30.

Oyos, Matthew M., "Theodore Roosevelt and the Implements of War", *Journal of Military History* 60 (October 1996) pp. 631–56.

Paige, Glenn D., *The Korean Decision: June 24–30, 1950*, New York, NY: Free Press, 1968.

Pearlman, Michael D., *Warmaking and American Democracy*, Lawrence, KS: University Press of Kansas, 1999.

Pentagon Papers: The Senator Gravel Edition, Boston, MA: Beacon Press, 1975, 4 vols.

Perry, Mark, *Four Stars*, Boston, MA: Houghton Mifflin, 1989.

Petraeus, David H., "Military Influence and the Post-Vietnam Use of Force", *Armed Forces and Society*, vol. 15, no. 4, Summer 1989, pp. 489–505.

Pierpaoli, Paul G., Jr., *Truman and Korea*, Columbia, MO: University of Missouri Press, 1999.

Pierson, William Whatley, Jr., "The Committee on the Conduct of the Civil War", *American Historical Review*, vol. 23, no. 3, April 1918, pp. 550–76.

Pogue, Forrest C., *George C. Marshall: Ordeal and Hope, 1939–1942*, New York, NY: Viking, 1966.

Poole, Walter S., *The Joint Chiefs of Staff and National Policy, vol. IV, 1950–1952*, Washington, DC: Office of Joint History, Office of the Chairman of the Joint Chiefs of Staff, 1998.

Powell, C. Percy, *Lincoln Day by Day: A Chronology, 1809–1865, Volume III: 1861–1865*, Washington, DC: Lincoln Sesquicentennial Commission, 1960.

Powell, Colin with Joseph E. Persico, *My American Journey*, New York, NY: Random House, 1995.

Priest, Dana, *The Mission*, New York, NY: W.W. Norton, 2003.

Rakove, Jack N., *The Beginnings of National Politics: An Interpretive History of the Continental Congress*, Baltimore, MD: Johns Hopkins University Press, 1979.

Ranson, Edward, "Nelson A. Miles as Commanding General, 1985–1903", *Military Affairs* vol. 29, no. 4, Winter, 1965–1966, pp. 179–200.

Raymond, Jack, *Power at the Pentagon*, New York, NY: Harper & Row, 1964.

Reeves, Richard. *President Kenned*, New York, NY: Simon & Schuster, 1993.

Ricks, Thomas E., "Military Sees Iraq Invasion Put on Hold", *Washington Post,* May 24, 2002.

Ricks, Thomas E., "Rumsfeld, Joint Chiefs Spar over roles in Retooling Military", *Washington Post,* May 25, 2001.

Ricks, Thomas E., "Rumsfeld on High Wire of Defense Reform", *Washington Post,* May 20, 2001.

Roherty, James M., *Decisions of Robert S. McNamara: A Study of the Role of the Secretary of Defense*, Coral Gables, FL: University of Miami Press, 1970.

Roosevelt, Franklin D., *The Public Papers and Addresses of Franklin D. Roosevelt, 1939*, New York, NY: Macmillan, 1941.

Roosevelt, Franklin D., *The Public Papers and Addresses of Franklin D. Roosevelt, 1940*, New York, NY: Macmillan, 1941.

Roosevelt, Franklin D., *The Public Papers and Addresses of Franklin D. Roosevelt, 1941* , New York, NY: Harper & Brothers, 1950.

Roosevelt's Foreign Policy, 1933–1941, Franklin D. Roosevelt's Unedited Speeches and Messages, New York, NY: Wilfred Funk, Inc., 1942.

Rosen, James, "Nixon and the Chiefs", *Atlantic Monthly*, April 2002, pp. 53–9.

Rosen, Stephen Peter, *Winning the Next War*, Ithaca, NY: Cornell University Press, 1991.

Rosenman, Samuel I., *Working with Roosevelt*, New York, NY: Harper & Brothers, 1952.

Rothkopf, David J., *Running the World: The Inside Story of the National Security Council and the Architects of American Power*, New York, NY: Public Affairs, 2005.

Safire, William, *Before the Fall*, Garden City, NY: Doubleday, 1975.

Sanders, Ralph, *The Politics of Defense Analysis*, New York, NY: Dunellen, 1973.

Scarborough, Rowan, *Rumsfeld's War*, Washington, DC: Regnery, 2004.

Schilling, Warner R., "The Politics of National Defense: Fiscal 1950", in Warner R. Schilling, Paul Y. Hammond, Glenn H. Snyder (eds), *Strategy, Politics, and Defense Budgets*, New York, NY: Columbia University Press, 1962.

Schlesinger, Arthur M. Jr., *A Thousand Days: John F. Kennedy in the White House*, Boston, MA: Houghton Mifflin, 1965.

Schnabel, James F., *United States Army in the Korean War: Policy and Direction: The First Year*, Washington, DC: Office of the Chief of Military History, United States Army, 1972.

Seigenthaler, John, *James K. Polk*, New York, NY: Henry Holt/Times Books, 2003.

Semsch, Philip L., "Elihu Root and the General Staff", *Military Affairs*, vol. 27, no. 1, Spring, 1963, pp. 16–27.

Shanker, Thom and Eric Schmitt, "Rumsfeld Seeks Leaner Army, and a Full Term", *New York Times*, May 10, 2005.

Shanker, Thom and Eric Schmitt, "Rumsfeld Seeks Consensus through Jousting", *New York Times*, March 19, 2003.

Shapley, Deborah, *Promise and Power: The Life and Times of Robert McNamara*, Boston, MA: Little, Brown, 1993.

Sharp, James Roger, *American Politics in the Early Republic*, New Haven, CT: Yale University Press, 1993.

Sherwood, Robert E., *Roosevelt & Hopkins*, revised edition, New York, NY: Universal Library, 1950.

Shogan, Robert, *Hard Bargain*, New York, NY: Scribner, 1995.

Singletary, Otis A., *The Mexican War*, Chicago, IL: University of Chicago Press, 1960.

Skelton, William B., *An American Profession of Arms: The Army Officer Corps, 1784–1861*, Lawrence, KS: University Press of Kansas, 1992.

Skelton, William B., "Officers and Politicians: The Origins of Army Politics in the United States before the Civil War", in Peter Karsten (ed.), *The Military in America*, rev. ed., New York, NY: The Free Press, 1986.

Skowronek, Stephen, *The Politics Presidents Make: Leadership from John Adams to George Bush*, Cambridge, MA: Harvard University Press, 1993.

Smith, James Morton, *Freedom's Fetters*, Ithaca, NY: Cornell University Press, 1956.

Smythe, Donald, "'Your Authority in France Will be Supreme': The Baker–Pershing Relationship in World War I", in Lloyd J. Matthews and Dale E. Brown, *The Parameters of War*, Washington, DC: Pergamon-Brassey's, 1987.

Snider, Don M. and Gayle L. Watkins, *The Future of the Army Profession*, Boston, MA: McGraw-Hill, 2002.

Soderberg, Nancy, *The Superpower Myth*, New York, NY: John Wiley & Sons, 2005.

Sofaer, Abraham D., *War, Foreign Affairs and Constitutional Power: The Origins*, Cambridge, MA: Ballinger, 1976.

Sorley, Lewis, *Vietnam Chronicles: The Abrams Tapes, 1968–1972*, Lubbock, TX: Texas Tech University Press, 2004.

Spanier, John W., *The Truman–MacArthur Controversy and the Korean War*, New York, NY: Norton, 1965.

Sprout, Harold and Margaret, *The Rise of American Naval Power, 1776–1918*, Princeton, NJ: Princeton University Press, 1944.

Stevenson, Charles A. *SecDef: The Nearly Impossible Job of Secretary of Defense*, Washington, DC: Potomac Books, 2006.

Stevenson, Charles A., "The Joint Staff and the Policy Process", paper prepared for delivery at the 1997 annual meeting of the American Political Science Association.

Stimson, Henry L. and McGeorge Bundy, *On Active Service in Peace and War*, New York, NY: Harper & Brothers, 1948.

Stone, Geoffrey R., *Perilous Times: Free Speech in Wartime*, New York, NY: W.W. Norton, 2004.

Stubbing, Richard A. with Richard A. Mendel, *The Defense Game*, New York, NY: Harper & Row, 1986.

Tap, Bruce, *Over Lincoln's Shoulder: The Committee on the Conduct of the War*, Lawrence, KS: University Press of Kansas, 1998.

Taylor, John M., *General Maxwell Taylor: The Sword and the Pen*, New York, NY: Doubleday, 1989.

Taylor, Maxwell D., *Swords and Plowshares*, New York, NY: W.W. Norton, 1972.

Thomas, Benjamin P. and Harold M. Hyman, *Stanton: The Life and Times of Lincoln's Secretary of War*, New York, NY: Knopf, 1962.

Towell, Pat, "The Rumsfeld Mandate: Invent the Military's Future", *CQ Weekly*, May 12, 2001, p. 1054.

Transforming Defense: National Security in the 21st Century, Report of the National Defense Panel, December 1997. Accessible at www.dtic.mil/ndp.

Trefousse, H.L., *Benjamin Franklin Wade: Radical Republican from Ohio*, New York, NY: Twayne Publishers Inc., 1963.

Trewhitt, Henry L., *McNamara*, New York, NY: Harper & Row, 1971.

Truman Presidential Museum & Library, Public Papers and Korean War Documents, available at www.trumanlibrary.org.

Truman, Margaret, *Harry S. Truman*, New York, NY: William Morrow, 1973.

US Department of Commerce, *Historical Statistics of the United States: Colonial Times to 1970*, Washington, DC: Bureau of the Census, 1975.

US Department of State, *Peace and War: United States Foreign Policy, 1931–1941*, Washington, DC: Government Printing office, 1943.

US Senate, Committee on Armed Services, ninetieth Congress, first session, "Air War Against North Vietnam", Hearings before the Preparedness Investigating Subcommittee, August 1967, 5 parts.

US Senate, Committee on Armed Services, ninety-ninth Congress, first session, S.Prt. 99–86, "Defense Organization: The Need for Change", Staff Report to the Committee on Armed Services, October 16, 1985.

Wade, Arthur P., "Roads to the Top: An Analysis of General-Officer Selection in the United States Army, 1789–1898", *Military Affairs* vol. 40, no. 4, December 1976, pp. 157–63.

Watson, Mark Skinner, *Chief of Staff: Prewar Plans and Preparations*, Washington, DC: Historical Division, Department of the Army, 1950.

Webb, Willard J., *The Joint Chiefs of Staff and the War in Vietnam, 1969–1970*, Washington, DC: Office of Joint History, Office of the Chairman of the Joint Chiefs of Staff, 2002.

Weigley, Russell F., *A Great Civil War*, Bloomington, IN: Indiana University Press, 2000.

Weigley, Russell F., *History of the United States Army*, Bloomington, IN: Indiana University Press, Enlarged Edition, 1984.

Weigley, Russell F., *The American Way of War*, Bloomington, IN: Indiana University Press, 1977.

Weinberger, Caspar W., *Fighting for Peace: Seven Critical Years in the Pentagon*, New York, NY: Warner Books, 1990.

Westerfield, H. Bradford, *Foreign Policy and Party Politics: Pearl Harbor to Korea*, New Haven, CT: Yale University Press, 1955.

White, Leonard D., *The Federalists*, New York, NY: Free Press, 1948.

White, Thomas D., "Strategy and the Defense Intellectuals", *Saturday Evening Post*, May 4, 1963.

Williams, T. Harry, *The History of American Wars From 1745 to 1918*, New York, NY: Knopf, 1981.

Williams, T. Harry, *Lincoln and the Radicals*, Madison, WI: University of Wisconsin Press, 1965.

Wilson, George C., "Guns Aplenty, Butter be Damned", *National Journal*, January 27 2001, pp. 252–3.

Wilson, George W., *This War Really Matters: Inside the Fight for Defense Dollars*, Washington, DC: CQ Press, 2000.

Woods, Randall Bennett, *Fulbright: A Biography*, New York: NY: Cambridge University Press, 1995.

Woodward, Bob, *Plan of Attack*, New York, NY: Simon & Schuster, 2004.

Woodward, Bob, *Bush at War*, New York, NY: Simon & Schuster, 2002.

Zegart, Amy B., *Flawed by Design: The Evolution of the CIA, JCS, and NSC*, Stanford, CA: Stanford University Press, 1999.

Zimmerman, Warren, *First Great Triumph: How Five Americans Made Their Country a World Power*, New York, NY: Farrar, Straus and Giroux, 2002.

Zumwalt, Elmo R., Jr., *On Watch*, New York, NY: Quadrangle, 1976.

Index

Joint Chiefs of Staff, 116, 195; defense
reform opposition, 168, 175;
relations with McNamara, 58–61,
156–59; relations with Rumsfeld,
180–6, 192; spying scandal,
68; *see also* Vietnam war, JCS
recommendations.
Joint Committee on the Conduct of the
War 45–9
Jones, David, 165–7, 175

Kennedy, John F. 55, 152, 154–5, 158,
160–1, 163, 202
Key, John 40
Kissinger, Henry A. 65–8, 71–2
Kohn, Richard 3, 29
Korean War, 126–35, 199; Chinese
intervention, 133; consultation
with Congress, 127–8; JCS views,
126–7, 130–2; nuclear weapons
consideration, 133; political support,
128–30

Laird, Melvin 65–8, 198
Lavelle, John D. 68
Lee, Robert E. 42–4, 49–50
Lehman, John 169–70, 173, 175
LeMay, Curtis 152, 157–9
Lincoln, Abraham, 30–50, 197; and
cabinet, 31; and Congress, 32–3,
40–1, 46, 48, 50; and generals, 33,
39–45; military strategy, 40–3
Linebacker II 73
Locher, Jim 169, 172–3

MacArthur, Douglas 128, 130–35,
199–200
Madison, James 1, 8, 197
Mansfield, Mike 69–71
Marine Corps, U.S. 174; and Theodore
Roosevelt, 142, 146–7; 150; and
Truman, 116
Marshall, George C. 93, 96–9, 101,
103, 107–8, 110–13, 130, 194, 201,
212
Mason, George 4, 17
Matthews, Francis 113
McCarthy, Joseph 123
McClellan, George 30, 34–43, 47
McDonald, David 52, 160
McDowell, Irwin 34
McKinley, William 142–3, 145, 197
McNamara, Robert S. 152–64, 180,
202–3; budget reforms, 156–8; and

Congress, 162–3; "fashion show,"
159; legacy, 164; nuclear strategy,
159–61; relations with military,
158–9; and strategic weapons
programs, 155; and Vietnam War,
55–60
Meade, George 44
Mexican War 199
Meyer, Edward 167, 173
Miles, Nelson 142–5
military fitness tests 148
military innovation and modernization
9–10, 202–3
military partisanship 212–13
military strength, U.S: in 1890s, 142; in
1940s, 116–17
military veto on use of force 207–10
Millett, Allan 195–6
Moorer, Thomas 52, 68, 231n
Morgenthau, Henry 103
Morris, Gouverneur 4
Myers, Richard 182, 184, 192

National Defense Panel 179–80
Navy, U.S: creation, 88; fleet expansion
under Theodore Roosevelt, 150;
opposition to JCS reform 1980s,
169–70, 175
Neutrality Acts 95, 100–2, 110–13
Nichols, Bill 4. *See also* Goldwater-
Nichols.
Nixon, Richard, 52, 64–73, 197, 200
NSC 68, 124–6, 129,
nuclear weapons and strategy 117,
123–4, 155, 159–61
Nunn, Sam 168, 170–5

oaths, military 1
ORHA (Office of Reconstruction and
Humanitarian Affairs) 189–90
Oyos, Matthew 148–9

Paterson, William 4
Perle, Richard 177
Powell, Colin 169, 175–6, 178, 200,
210
presidential powers 7
Principal-Agent theory 206–7
public opinion, U.S.,1935–41, 99–102,
104, 107, 109

Quasi-War with France, 79–92;
congressional actions, 82–89;
cutbacks in 1800, 92; domestic